Revealing Antiquity

· 5 ·

G. W. Bowersock, General Editor

THE
ORIENTALIZING
REVOLUTION

Near Eastern Influence on
Greek Culture in
the Early Archaic Age

Walter Burkert

TRANSLATED BY
Margaret E. Pinder
and Walter Burkert

HARVARD UNIVERSITY PRESS
Cambridge, Massachusetts
London, England
1992

This book is printed on acid-free paper, and its binding
materials have been chosen for strength and durability.

Library of Congress Cataloging-in-Publication Data

Burkert, Walter, 1931-
The orientalizing revolution: Near Eastern influence on Greek
culture in the early archaic age / Walter Burkert; translated by
Margaret E. Pinder and Walter Burkert.
p.   cm. — (Revealing antiquity; 5)
Translation of: Die orientalisierende Epoche in der griechischen
Religion und Literatur.
Includes bibliographical references and index.
ISBN 0–674–64363–1 (acid-free paper)
1. Greece—Civilization—to 146 B.C. 2. Greece—Civiliza-
tion—Middle Eastern influences. I. Title. II. Series.
DF78.B85   1992   92–8923
938—dc20   CIP

CONTENTS

CONTENTS

ILLUSTRATIONS

PREFACE

The original version of this book was published in 1984 in *Sitzungsberichte der Heidelberger Akademie der Wissenschaften*. I am grateful to Glen Bowersock for promoting an English translation. With a view to a larger public and in order to reflect the current state of scholarship, I have revised the book throughout and in some places expanded the argument.

My thesis about the indebtedness of Greek civilization to eastern stimuli may appear less provocative today than it did eight years ago. This change may be partly an effect of the original publication, but mainly it reflects the fact that classics has been losing more and more its status of a solitary model in our modern world. Yet it still seems worthwhile to help bridge the gaps between related fields of scholarship and to make available materials often neglected by one or another. Such an exercise may convey the excitement of unexpected discoveries even when it necessitates a fair amount of annotation.

I owe special thanks to Peter Frei, Paul Hoskisson, Fritz Stolz, Rolf Stucky, and Markus Wäfler for their help on matters oriental, and to Peter Blome for detailed archaeological advice.

THE
ORIENTALIZING
REVOLUTION

INTRODUCTION

"God's is the Orient, God's is the Occident" says the Koran.[1] Classical scholars have found it difficult to maintain such a balanced perspective and have tended instead to transform "oriental" and "occidental" into a polarity, implying antithesis and conflict. The Greeks had become aware of their own identity as separate from that of the "Orient" when they succeeded in repelling the attacks of the Persian empire. But not until much later, during the crusades, did the concept and the term *Orient* actually enter the languages of the West.[2] This fact hardly explains why even today it should be difficult to undertake unprejudiced discussion of connections between classical Greece and the East. But whoever tries will encounter entrenched positions, uneasiness, apology if not resentment. What is foreign and unknown is held at a distance by an attitude of wary defensiveness.

To a large extent this is the result of an intellectual development which began more than two centuries ago and took root especially in Germany. Increasing specialization of scholarship converged with ideological protectionism, and both constructed an image of a pure, classical Greece in splendid isolation. Until well into the eighteenth century, as long as philology was closely connected with theology, the Hebrew Bible naturally stood next to the Greek classics, and the existence of cross-connections did not present any problems. Jephtha's daughter and Iphigenia were interchangeable models even in the realm of opera; Iapetos was traced to Japheth, the Kabeiroi to a Semitic designation for "great gods," and the "East" was found in the name of Kadmos the Phoenician, the "West" in the name of Europa.[3] In accordance with the *Odyssey* and Herodotus, "Phoenicians" were readily accepted as the link between East and West.

Then three new trends erected their own boundaries and collectively fractured the Orient–Greece axis. Philology broke free of theology—Friedrich August Wolf matriculated as *studiosus philologiae* at Göttingen in 1777[4]—and at the same time, with Johann Joachim Winckelmann, a new concept of classicism, one with rather pagan tendencies, asserted itself and came to attract high regard. Second, beginning with the work of Johann Gottfried Herder, the ideology of romantic nationalism developed, which held literature and spiritual culture to be intimately connected with an individual people, tribe, or race. Origins and organic development rather than reciprocal cultural influences became the key to understanding. In his reaction to Friedrich Creuzer's more universal model, Carl Otfried Müller gained considerable influence with his idea of "Greek tribal culture."[5] Precisely at the time when Jews were being granted full legal equality in Europe, national-romantic consciousness turned the trend against "orientalism" and thus gave anti-Semitism a chance. Third, linguistics scholars' discovery of "Indo-European"—the derivation of most European languages together with Persian and Sanskrit from a common archetype—at that time reinforced the alliance of Greek, Roman, and Germanic and thus banished the Semitic to another world.[6] It remained to defend the independence of the Greeks against the Indian relatives within the Indo-European family[7] in order to establish the concept of classical-national Greek identity as a self-contained and self-sufficient model of civilization which, at least in Germany, was to dominate the later nineteenth century.[8] Ulrich von Wilamowitz-Moellendorff's scornful assessment in 1884—"the peoples and states of the Semites and the Egyptians which had been decaying for centuries and which, in spite of the antiquity of their culture, were unable to contribute anything to the Hellenes other than a few manual skills, costumes, and implements of bad taste, antiquated ornaments, repulsive fetishes for even more repulsive fake divinities"—is not representative of his work; but even later he maintained that the spirit of late antiquity stemmed "from the Orient and is the deadly enemy of true Hellenism."[9]

Behind the irascibility a certain insecurity seems to lurk. In fact the image of pure, self-contained Hellenism which makes its miraculous appearance with Homer had been overtaken in the nineteenth century by three groups of new discoveries: the reemergence of the ancient Near East and Egypt through the decipherment of cuneiform and hieroglyphic writing, the unearthing of Mycenaean civilization, and the recognition of an orientalizing phase in the development of archaic Greek art.

Classical philology greeted these discoveries with hesitancy. The Mycenaean period was gradually accepted as Greek prehistory,[10] and the final decipherment of Linear B as Greek confirmed this as fact. The development of Assyriology with the initial difficulties of reading cuneiform—Gilgamesh made his entrance in the guise of Izdubar[11]—could be viewed from a distance and with some condescension by an established branch of scholarship. When a few unmethodical studies tried to promote the fundamental importance of Babylonian literature in relation to world history, it was left to the theologians to refute the "pan-Babylonianists."[12] Only outsiders wrote about "Homer and Babylon."[13] Historians, on the other hand, had less difficulty opening themselves to the new dimensions of world history. Eduard Meyer began to publish his monumental *History of Antiquity* in 1884, a fundamental and in fact unique achievement.[14] The pursuit of this universal aim was continued by the collective undertaking of *The Cambridge Ancient History.*

By contrast, the anti-oriental reflex was to prevail in the field which lay much closer to Hellenists, in the assessment of the Phoenicians, who had of old been regarded as the active intermediaries between the Orient and Hellas. Julius Beloch, a scholar of genius flawed by his idiosyncrasies and overt anti-Semitism, promulgated the theory that the significance of the Phoenicians in early Greece was close to zero, that the "Phoenician" Herakles of Thasos was no less of a fantasy than the mythical Phoenician Kadmos.[15] Instead, ancient Asia Minor was found to be of special importance, where soon Indo-Europeans were to appear, with the decipherment of the Hittite language. A barrier was erected against the Semitic.

Yet the marked impact of "the oriental" on Greek art between the geometric and the archaic periods—an impact made evident by imported objects as well as by new techniques and characteristic motifs of artistic imagery—could not be disregarded, at least after Fredrik Poulsen's book was published in 1912.[16] Even expert archaeologists, however, sometimes appear to feel uncomfortable about this fact and indeed advise against using the expression "the orientalizing period."[17] The foreign elements remain subject to a policy of containment: There is hardly a standard textbook that has oriental and Greek objects depicted side by side; many of the oriental finds in the great Greek sanctuaries have long remained—and some still remain—unpublished. The fact that Olympia is the most significant location for finds of eastern bronzes, richer in this respect than all the Middle Eastern sites, is seldom mentioned.

In Germany in the period between the two world wars a new hermeneutic approach promoted concentration on the individual, "internal" form and style in the interpretation of cultural achievements, to the detriment of outward influence. Archaeology thus achieved a deeper understanding of the archaic style and in fact discovered afresh the geometric style; historians such as Helmut Berve wished to renounce "universal" history in favor of Hellenism.[18] The joint work of Franz Boll and Carl Bezold in the arcane field of astrology remained a happy but isolated phenomenon. Another specialty which failed to attract general notice was the discovery by Otto Neugebauer that the "Pythagorean theorem" had been known and used in Babylonian mathematics a thousand years before Pythagoras.[19] Among German philologists only Franz Dornseiff took a close look at eastern culture from Israel to Anatolia, but in doing this he had the air of an outsider.

Dornseiff was one of the first to give credit to the new dimension of the impact of the Near East on classical Greece, which was discovered with the decipherment of Hittite mythological texts.[20] However, the first announcements and studies of "Illuyankas and Typhon" met with only a slight response. The breakthrough came with the text of *Kingship in Heaven,* published in 1946, the myth which has the castration of the god of heaven by Kumarbi, so similar to Hesiod's tale about Uranos and Kronos; since then the Kumarbi-Kronos parallel has been established and, largely as a result of the efforts of Albin Lesky, *Kumarbi* has become a standard reference text for classical philologists.[21] An important factor of acceptance, brought out by sympathetic Indo-Europeanists, was that with the Hittites an "Indo-European" people had emerged to represent the "Orient." But in the wake of Hittite epic and mythology similar texts of Semitic Ugarit came to the attention of classical scholars,[22] and the Greek fragments of Philon of Byblos dealing with Phoenician mythology attracted fresh interest.[23] In addition to mythological motifs the narrative techniques and the literary style of epic became the subject of comparative study, too. Since then, Homeric epic can no longer be held to have existed in a vacuum; it stands out against a background of comparable eastern literary forms.

However, a new line of defense quickly developed. It is generally and freely accepted that in the Bronze Age there were close contacts between Anatolia, the Semitic East, Egypt, and the Mycenaean world, that some "Aegean *koine*" can be found to characterize the thirteenth century B.C.[24] One can refer to Mycenaean imports in Ugarit; Alasia-Cyprus is mentioned as a nexus of East-West connections; Hesiod and Homer are also viewed from this perspective. What is much less in focus is the "orientalizing period" of the century between approximately 750 and 650 B.C.—that is, the Homeric epoch, when, as well as eastern skills and images, the Semitic art of writing was transmitted to Greece and made the recording of Greek literature possible for the first time. German scholars in particular had a strange tendency to lean toward an earlier dating of the Greek script,[25] thereby shielding Homeric Greece from the influence of the East which was so notable in material culture around 700. It should be clear anyhow that both possibilities, Bronze Age and later adoptions, are not mutually exclusive; the impossibility of always making clear-cut distinctions cannot be used to refute the hypothesis of borrowing in both areas to an equal degree.

In the meantime, archaeological research has rendered the "dark ages" increasingly legible and has cast the eighth century in particular in ever-sharper relief. What proved decisive were the discoveries of Greek settlements in Syria and on Ischia in connection with the excavations at Lefkandi and Eretria on Euboea. The Assyrian expansion to the Mediterranean together with the spread of trade in metal ores in the whole area provides a persuasive historical framework for the movement of eastern craftsmen to the West, as well as for the spread of the Phoenician-Greek alphabet.[26] We now seem within reach of a balanced picture of that decisive epoch in which, under the influence of the Semitic East, Greek culture began its unique flowering, soon to assume cultural hegemony in the Mediterranean.[27]

This volume pursues the hypothesis that, in the orientalizing period, the Greeks did not merely receive a few manual skills and fetishes along with new crafts and images from the Luwian-Aramaic-Phoenician sphere, but were influenced in their religion and literature by the eastern models to a significant degree.[28] It will be argued that migrating "craftsmen of the sacred," itinerant seers and priests of purification, transmitted not only their divinatory and purificatory skills but also elements of mythological "wisdom." Indeed Homer, in an often-quoted passage of the *Odyssey,* enumerates various kinds of migrant craftsmen "who are public workers": first, "a seer or a healer," only then the carpenter, and, in addition, the "godly singer."[29] While the second chapter tries to follow the tracks of "seers" and "healers," the third chapter turns to the realm of these singers, presenting correspondences between eastern and Greek literature which make it probable to assume connections, even direct literary influence of high eastern civilizations on the final phase of Homeric epic, that is, the beginning of Greek literacy, when writing took over from oral tradition.

The results which can be reached with any degree of certainty remain limited. The bridge that once provided the direct contact, the literary culture of ancient Syria, has irrevocably disappeared. On the other hand we have the unique opportunity to compare contemporaneous texts from both the Greek and the oriental sides. This task both enables and demands precision. By contrast, in the case of the more sensational connections between Kumarbi or Illuyankas and Hesiod a time gap of five or six centuries has to be bridged, in addition to the geographic distance between East and West. The Hesiodic problems, which have been the subject of much scholarly attention in recent decades, will not be discussed in detail here.[30] They complement the perspectives under consideration, especially in view of the clear link between Hesiod and Euboea.

The studies presented in this book may still run up against a final and perhaps insuperable line of defense, the tendency of modern cultural theories to approach culture as a system evolving through its own processes of internal economic and social dynamics, which reduces all outward influences to negligible parameters. There is no denying the intellectual acumen and achievement of such theories. But they may still represent just one side of the coin. It is equally valid to see culture as a complex of communication with continuing opportunities for learning afresh, with conventional yet penetrable frontiers, in a world open to change and expansion. The impact of written as opposed to oral culture is perhaps the most dramatic example of transformation wrought from the outside, through borrowing. It may still be true that the mere fact of borrowing should only provide a starting point for closer interpretation, that the form of selection and adaptation, of reworking and refitting to a new system is revealing and interesting in each case. But the "creative transformation" by the Greeks,[31] however important, should not obscure the sheer fact of borrowing; this would amount to yet another strategy of immunization designed to cloud what is foreign and disquieting.

The modest aim of this book is to serve as a messenger across boundaries,[32] to direct the attention of classicists to areas to which they have paid too little regard, and to make these fields of study more accessible even to nonspecialists. It may also encourage orientalists, hardly less prone to isolation, to keep or renew their contacts with neighboring fields.[33] My emphasis is deliberately on providing evidence for correspondences and for the likelihood of borrowings. If in certain cases the materials themselves do not provide incontrovertible evidence of cultural transfer, the establishment of similarities will still be of value, as it serves to free both the Greek and the oriental phenomena from their isolation and to create an arena of possible comparisons.

This is not to preclude more subtle interpretations of Greek achievements as a consequence. Yet in the period at about the middle of the eighth century, when direct contact had been established between the Assyrians and the Greeks, Greek culture must have been much less self-conscious and therefore much more malleable and open to foreign influence than it became in subsequent generations. It is the formative epoch of Greek civilization that experienced the orientalizing revolution.

CHAPTER ONE

"WHO ARE PUBLIC WORKERS"
The Migrant Craftsmen

Historical Background

After the upheaval and devastation which prevailed from Greece through Anatolia to Syria and Palestine about 1200 B.C. and which is generally attributed, on the basis of Egyptian texts, to "peoples of the sea"—among whom the Philistines are the most tangible—the kingdoms, palaces, artistic skills, and writing systems which had made the glory of the Bronze Age had largely disappeared.[1] In the eastern Mediterranean, outside Egypt, urban civilization and literacy survived only in the area of Cilicia-Syria-Palestine. A strong tradition of Hittite civilization continued to dominate Cilicia and extended as far as northern Syria. Hittite style is most distinctive in monumental sculpture and other art objects—important sites are Tell Halaf-Guzana, Carchemish, Malatya-Milid, Sam'al-Zincirli, Karatepe[2]—and particularly in the Hittite hieroglyphic script, which persisted at Karatepe until nearly the end of the eighth century; it was used for a language of the Hittite family which is now called Hieroglyphic Luwian. Conquering Aramaic tribes, speaking a Semitic language and using alphabetic writing, won supremacy in some places, founding princedoms such as Guzana and Sam'al. Southern Syria, including the cities of Byblos, Sidon, and Tyre, had long been affected by Egyptian style and influences. The

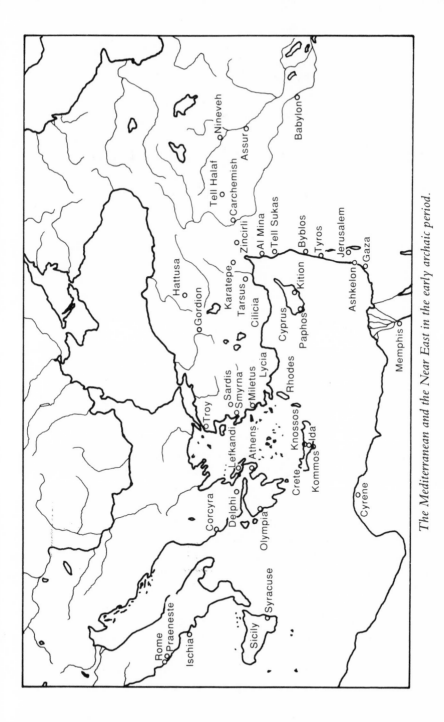

The Mediterranean and the Near East in the early archaic period.

western Semites based in this area, called *Phoinikes* by the
Greeks, were continuing to expand their sea trade. Early connections reached not only to Cyprus but also to Crete.[3] Increasingly important in these activities was the search for copper and
iron ores.[4]

The most portentous achievement in Syria-Palestine was the
development of the alphabetic script, which, through its inge-
nious simplification, made reading and writing more widely accessible for the first time. It was used equally by Hebrews,
Phoenicians, and Aramaeans.[5] The invention goes back to the
Bronze Age, but it gained its unique position only with the collapse of the Bronze Age, which made most of the other writing
systems disappear.

The expansion of Assyria into this heterogeneous assemblage
of cities, kingdoms, and tribal centers from the ninth century
onwards brought dynamic change of world-historical propor-
tions. For the Assyrians, too, the search for raw materials, particularly metals, seems to have been a driving force. In any event
Assur built up the strongest army of the time, employed it in
increasingly far-reaching raids with ruthless demands for sub-
mission and tribute, and thus founded the first world power.
Ashurnaṣirpal (884–858) and Shalmaneser III (858–824) led the
first successful advances to Syria; in 877 an Assyrian army stood
on the shores of the Mediterranean for the first time. In 841 Tyre
and Sidon were forced to pay tribute, and in 834 so was Tarsos
in Cilicia. The Hittite city-states were forced to follow suit or
were destroyed. The Greeks must have been aware of this eastern power, at least on Cyprus, because it was around this time—
about 850—that Phoenicians from Tyre were settling on Cyprus; Kition became a Phoenician city.[6] Phoenician colonization
was also reaching beyond to the far West: 814 is the traditional
date for the founding of Carthage.

After Shalmaneser, Assyrian forces did not appear on the
Mediterranean for a while. During this period Greek traders
first reached Syria. Greek merchants are present in Al Mina on
the Orontes estuary from the end of the ninth century;[7] from
there the connections reach to North Syria, to Urartu, and

along the shortest caravan route to Mesopotamia. In approximately the same period the Greeks are in evidence at Tarsos[8] and somewhat later at Tell Sukas.[9] There are also Greek finds from Rash-al-Basid (Poseidonia), Tell Tainat, Tyre, and Hama. Connections go to nearby Cyprus, but above all to Euboea, where excavations at Lefkandi have brought to light relics of a relatively affluent community in the tenth and ninth centuries which was open to trade with the East.[10] In the eighth century Eretria along with Chalkis reached its peak; but Athens was not negligible either. From Chalkis the Greeks reached the West even before the middle of the eighth century, as can be seen from the settlement of traders and craftsmen discovered at Pithekoussai-Ischia.[11] Here, too, the trade in ores was crucial, above all with the Etruscans; the Phoenician route via Cyprus to Carthage and then to Sardinia had to compete with that of the Greeks from Euboea via Ithaca to Pithekoussai. It is in connection with these routes that the first examples of Greek script appear, in Euboea, Naxos, Pithekoussai, and Athens.[12] Place-names like Soloi, "metal ingots"—attested both in Cilicia and on Cyprus—Chalkis, "bronze-home," and Tarshish, "foundry,"[13] mark the economic interests, as does that verse of the *Odyssey* which has the Taphian Mentes travelling overseas to trade for bronze with a cargo of iron.[14]

The renewed and strongest advance of the Assyrians began under Tiglath-pileser III (745–727), who crushed the power of Urartu, made vassals of Tyre and Byblos, and permanently anchored the Assyrian forces in the West. It was in his time—shortly after 738—that a report first mentions Ionians—that is, Greeks; an officer is reporting a counterattack on Syria: "The Ionians came. They attacked . . . the cities . . . [N.N. pursued them?] in his ships . . . in the middle of the sea."[15]

It has long been a matter of comment and discussion that the easterners came to call the Greeks Ionians[16]—*Jawan* in Hebrew, *Junan* in Arabic and Turkish. The Assyrian form is *Iawan(u)* or, with an internal change of consonants, *Iaman(u)*; in the text quoted above the designation is "(country) *Ia-u-na-a-a*"—that is, *Iaunaia*. It has been established that this is not the name of Cyprus, which the Assyrians in fact called *Iadnana*.[17] Greeks on Cyprus never called themselves Ionians. Nevertheless a reference around the middle of the eighth century can hardly be to Ionians from Asia Minor either, to Miletos or Ephesos. Those Ionians coming by sea who encountered the Assyrians must rather have been Greeks from Euboea, Athens, or both, as the archaeological evidence and the spread of writing suggest—not excluding islands such as Samos or Naxos. This conclusion is confirmed by the *Iliad:* In the one passage in which *Iaones* are referred to, they are fighting alongside the Opuntian Lokrians, and the Athenians are given prominence immediately after them. Clearly, neighboring tribes are referred to; it is appropriate that *Iaones* from Euboea should be placed between the Opuntians and the Athenians.[18]

Assyria reached the height of its power under Sargon II (722–705). Not only the small Hittite states of Carchemish and Zincirli, but also Cilicia became provinces of Assyria. In 708 the kings of Cyprus, including those of Greek cities such as Salamis and Paphos, paid homage to Sargon. In Kition Sargon left a stele attesting his deeds. But whether the usurper Iamani of Ashdod, who was driven out by Sargon in 711, was "the Ionian," as his name would suggest, has been disputed;[19] and the common view that Mita, king of the "Mushki," who paid homage to Sargon in 709, was king Midas of Phrygia, celebrated by the Greeks, and hence that the Assyrians were in contact with a great Phrygian kingdom in the eighth century, seems no longer tenable.[20]

Sennacherib (705–681) put down an uprising in Tarsos in 696. According to Greek accounts transmitted by Berossos the Greeks fought the Assyrians at sea and were defeated.[21] Even Al Mina was destroyed around 700, but was almost immediately rebuilt anew. On the whole the numerous violent incidents and catastrophes did not destroy East-West connections, but rather intensified them, perhaps because now streams of refugees were mingling with the traders. In any event oriental imports and domestic imitations of them appear more and more in Greece around 700, and a little later in Etruria. By then cuneiform writing is found in Tarsos alongside ceramics from Rhodes, Samos, and Corinth. On Cyprus the period of Assyrian domination is also a markedly "Homeric" epoch.

Essarhaddon (681–669) also treated the kings of Cyprus as his underlings.[22] His successor Ashurbanipal (669–629), the most splendid king of Nineveh, endured forever in the memory of the Greeks as "Sardanapallos."[23] Essarhaddon and Ashurbanipal fought the Cimmerians in Asia Minor, as did the Greeks. But the centers of gravity were shifting by then. Sidon, well known to the Greeks as a center of Phoenician trade, was totally destroyed by the Assyrians in 677.[24] By 663, however, King Psammetichus had been able to entrench his forces in Egypt and to shake off the Assyrian yoke at last. With the enrollment of Greek mercenaries into his service Egypt became more important from the Greeks' point of view than the ruined cities of Syria. At nearly the same time King Gyges, in his struggle against the Cimmerians, had founded the kingdom of the Lydians with its center in Sardis and established direct contact with Assyria by 665.[25] Thus the "Royal Road" was opened up which led from Sardis to the East.[26] It was this above all which brought Ionians into direct contact with the eastern trade, and thus ensured the rapid rise of the Ionians of Asia Minor. Meanwhile, on Euboea, Chalkis and Eretria lost their forces in the Lelantine war, having been outstripped in the western trade by the rise of Corinth, which colonized Kerkyra in the eighth century. In this network of changing interrelations Greek culture gained supremacy and eclipsed the orientalizing influence.

Oriental Products in Greece

It is not Greek texts, but rather archaeological finds which offer a solid foundation for tracing Eastern cultural influences in Greece in the eighth and early seventh centuries and for evaluating their significance. Objects of oriental provenience appear at Greek sites in increasing numbers, especially in the rapidly evolving Greek sanctuaries, and at the same time Greek representational style is undergoing basic modifications by taking up, imitating, and transforming the motifs of eastern art. This is not the place for a detailed study of sites and objects, contexts and proveniences. After Fredrik Poulsen and T. J. Dunbabin, John Boardman has provided a comprehensive treatment; a wealth of material has also been presented by Hans-Volkmar Herrmann and by Wolfgang Helck, and a rich survey has recently been added by Günter Kopcke.[1] The determination of local styles and hence the identification of the origin of individual pieces is still in progress. Many sites in the Near East remain unexplored or partially explored, and archaeologists are currently operating in the most unfavorable circumstances amidst incessant turmoil, warfare, and plundering. Nevertheless the outlines of cultural and economic development seem to be firmly established, while the central connecting role of Syria between the Late Hittite, Urartian, Assyrian, and Egyptian cultural influences has become increasingly clear.

As for Greece, trade with the East never completely stopped. There are individual imported pieces from the tenth and ninth centuries; their numbers increase significantly in the eighth century, and even more so in the first half of the seventh. The exotic origin is clear in the case of ivory carving—although this skill was subsequently adopted by the Greeks[2]—and even more so in the case of ostrich eggs or the tridacna shells from the Red Sea, which appear in the seventh century.[3] Jewelry is more frequently found, gold in many forms, faience beads, and also beads of glass—Hera's ear ornaments as described by Homer, "three-eyed and mulberry like," are identifiable as such a set.[4] The use and spread of gems and seals offer even more significant evidence of the connections with the East.[5] Nearly one hundred Syrian-Cilician seals have been found at Pithekoussai-Ischia;[6] amulet-type ornaments of Syrian and Egyptian style occur in the tombs of Lefkandi, and the prince who was interred in the Heroon at Eretria was carrying a Phoenician scarab in a gold setting.[7] Cylinder seals, the typical Mesopotamian form of seal, have been unearthed at Olympia as well as on Samos and Delos.[8]

The evidence in metalwork is more impressive. Phoenician

bronze and silver bowls were widely traded as special costly objects. As well as on Cyprus, they have been found in Athens, Olympia, and Delphi, in southern Italy, Praeneste, and Etruria. They have long been identified with the *krateres* from Sidon mentioned by Homer;[9] their technique and style also appear to present the closest analogy to the shield of Achilles as described in the *Iliad*. At least three of these bowls, found in Olympia, southern Italy, and Praeneste, carry Aramaic-Phoenician inscriptions; one, from Falerii, has an inscription in cuneiform.[10] At Olympia in about 670 B.C. bronze relief vessels from the Late Hittite city Tabal were reworked to form the drapery of large statues fabricated from bronze foil.[11] Other metal objects arrived in Greece from the same region, or from North Syria, or even from Urartu via North Syria: embossed stands and above all a new form of large tripod cauldrons, decorated with sirens or snakes. Greek craftsmen were quick to adopt the technique and to create their own masterpieces.[12] A unique set of orientalizing works of art is the bronze tympanon and the bronze shields from the Idaean cave on Crete; the tympanon in particular (Figure 1) has a plainly Assyrian look. Agreement on the dating of these objects has yet to be achieved, but it is hardly to be doubted that they served the cult of Zeus in the sacred cave of Ida.[13] Finally, there are pieces of horse harness skillfully worked in metal, prestige objects for the aristocracy like many other items.[14] Outstanding among these are the beautiful bronze plates identified by their inscriptions as given to King Hazael of Damascus but subsequently dedicated to Apollo of Eretria and to Hera of Samos, at whose sanctuaries they were found (Figure 2). King Hazael is known to have been active towards the end of the ninth century, and the dedication at Eretria can be dated archaeologically to the middle of the eighth—a rare case of precision as to the provenience and chronology of the oriental impact.

Cyprus and also Crete are in a special position; they have been "orientalizing" all the time. Rhodes becomes important in the eighth century as well. In contrast to Beloch's theses there is

Figure 1. Bronze tympanon from the Idaean cave, Crete, eighth century B.C.: "Master of Animals" holding up a lion, two demons: Zeus and kouretes?

now clear evidence that Phoenicians were manufacturing perfumes on Rhodes even before 700.[15] On Samos, too, the influx of oriental goods seems to begin before 700.[16] All the great sacred sites which came to flourish by the eighth century, Delos, Delphi, and above all Olympia, have produced substantial finds of oriental objects; and next to Eretria Athens deserves special notice.[17] Etruria started its own orientalizing period through independent contacts with Phoenician trade which spread to

Figure 2. North Syrian bronze plaque from horse harness, ninth century
B.C., found in the Hera sanctuary at Samos. Aramaic inscription:
"What (god) Hadad has given to Lord Hazael from Umqi in the year
when the Lord crossed the river."

neighboring Italy, including Latium;[18] it finds marvellous expression in the rich tombs of Praeneste excavated long ago.[19]

Domestic craftsmanship and production developed from these imports, in ivory carving as well as in metalwork.[20] Oriental pictorial motifs also appear in other forms of manufacture, above all in the most enduring and therefore the best preserved kind of products, ceramics.[21] Again a few references must suffice: The theme of the Mistress of the Animals and the Master of the Animals, which goes back to Bronze Age traditions, is given a new lease on life;[22] in addition there are characteristic representations of animal hunting and, in particular, the lion fight.[23] Few Greeks would ever have actually seen a live lion: It was from pictures that the lion became such a familiar concept to all (even if lions and panthers were occasionally confused in the images). An older, Hittite style of representing lions is superseded in the seventh century by an Assyrian model. The more exotic gallery of composite beasts—griffins, sphinxes, and sirens—likewise has Bronze Age ancestors, but was revived and adapted to the new fashion.[24] The chimaera can clearly be linked to Hittite representations,[25] while the Triton—a man with fish's tail—seems to come straight from Mesopotamia.[26] Finally the motif of the Tree of Life should be mentioned, and in general the animal friezes, the lotus and the palmette friezes.[27] But the *prothesis* scenes and the representations of the symposium with revellers reclining on couches also have an oriental pedigree, as the custom itself apparently evolved in the East.[28]

Religious iconography proper shows corresponding changes: The Mycenaean heritage gives way before the eastern examples. Thus individual bronze statuettes of the warrior god brandishing his weapon in his right hand, originating in the Syro-Hittite region, had appeared in Greece already in the Late Mycenaean period; more are found now, and they are copied in the eighth century.[29] Whether gods or human warriors are being represented in the Greek context is a matter of dispute; but there is no doubt that those later "typically Greek" images of Zeus and Poseidon, brandishing respectively thunderbolt or trident, are ultimately derived from these statuettes. The representation of the thunderbolt in the hand of the weather god, in particular, remains clearly dependent on the eastern model.[30] Quite different is the image of a naked goddess, standing, often touching her breasts, which had been common in Syria for a long time; it is presented to the Greeks both in the form of metal reliefs, especially of gold jewelry, and of simple clay tablets made from molds. She is usually called Astarte-Aphrodite, though on slight evidence.[31] Other types of divine images were occasionally imported, too.[32] In Greece the goddess was quickly provided with clothing, but the image of the standing goddess continued to proliferate; and the statues of goddesses—now often made of local wood to find their place in the newly erected temples— were clothed in robes that still imitated the luxury of the East, just as Hera's ear ornaments in the *Iliad* did. A signal example is Artemis of Ephesos, with the rectangular divisions of her robe, the fillet at the back of her headdress, and the woollen ribbons in her hands.[33] Even closer to cultic activities seem to be those curious masks which we find dedicated in Greek sanctuaries, on Samos and, above all, at Ortheia's precinct in Sparta. The grotesque form of some of them evidently imitates oriental Humbaba masks.[34] But even the form of the omphalos bowl which became universally employed for libation in Greek worship is of oriental type. Most of all, frankincense, generally introduced during this time into the worship of the gods, remained an oriental import, as its names, *libanos* and *myrrha*, continued to indicate.[35]

One area of more profound eastern influence on the practice of Greek religion at the time can only be touched upon: the construction of large altars for burnt offerings and above all the building of temples to serve as houses for divinities, represented by cult statues. There seems to be no Greek temple proper antedating the eighth century, the period of the impetus of eastern craftsmanship. A most peculiar intermingling of indigenous, Phoenician, and Greek cult is attested at Kommos, on the south coast of Crete.[36] This was evidently a place where passing ships used to anchor, to take on provisions and to do homage to local divinities. Use of the cult site is documented from the tenth century on, with various structures still identifiable, remains of ritual meals and votive figurines; but in the later ninth century there is a distinctively Phoenician shrine, with three pillars to represent the sacred center, between which offerings were crammed. It is integrated later with more Greek-looking structures. Kommos thus is one of the most remarkable meeting points of Phoenician and Greek religious practice.

The Phoenician merchants had always been regarded as the carriers of oriental culture, the suppliers of oriental imports to the Greeks, in accordance with the image presented by the *Odyssey:* Homer mentions *Phoinikes,* men of Sidon, as producers of costly metal vessels, trading by sea and occasionally indulging in piracy. Beloch tried to force the Phoenicians out of the Aegean picture, asserting a lack of clear archaeological proof of their presence, especially the lack of Phoenician ceramics. By now, however, Phoenicians are clearly attested even through their ceramics on Kos and Rhodes, and traces of their presence have been found at Ephesos, too.[37] But with the excavations at Al Mina, the spontaneous advance of the Greeks to the East has been widely recognized. The expansion of the Greeks and the Phoenicians in the Mediterranean appears from early on to develop in mutual competition. Both seem to start by establishing foreign trading facilities, following earlier Assyrian practice, but subsequently begin to found independent cities, colonies as we call them; for the Phoenicians these were primarily Kition on Cyprus and Carthage in Africa, while Greek cities came into being in southern Italy and Sicily; these developments led to new forms of competing power politics.

However, the trading connections set in motion, first by the Phoenicians and then by the Euboeans, were not the only channels for mutual contact. More intimate cultural contacts and exchanges took place on the level of skilled craftsmanship. It has long been suggested that, from the end of the ninth century, eastern craftsmen migrated to Greek cities and passed on their skills to the Greeks. In the hard times of the Assyrian conquests, migrations of refugees may readily be assumed. John Boardman has demonstrated this movement in detail, especially in the case of Crete. He points to three groups of evidence: A family of goldsmiths and gem cutters in Knossos began to reuse a Minoan Tholos tomb and consecrated it by a foundation deposit in oriental style, around 800 B.C.; a special workshop of bronzesmiths produced the tympanon with plainly Assyrian iconography and the bronze shields for the Idaean cave; finally, Syrian-style tombs comparable to those near Carchemish are found at Afrati, in central Crete, in the first half of the seventh century. These tombs as well as the half-finished goods in the Tomb of the Goldsmiths at Knossos are convincing indicators that immigration had taken place; and the two phases of immigration, before 800 and again around 700, correspond closely to the Assyrian campaigns.[38]

The actual proof that, connected with the appearance of eastern products, there was not just trade through various intermediate contractors but also learning and teaching through direct contact, lies in the adoption of new technical skills which do not arise from simply buying finished products. This applies to the art of goldsmiths and gem cutters[39] as well as to ivory carving and, in particular, to the various forms of bronzeworking, be it hammering (*sphyrelaton*) or casting with the "lost core" method; the replacement of the asphalt core of eastern technique with one of resin and bran shows just how craftsmen adapted creatively to new requirements.[40] Even the simple yet extremely productive technique of making clay figures in molds came from Mesopotamia and Syria; it appears at Gortyn and Corinth shortly after 700.[41] It would of course be possible to assume that some Greeks entered into apprenticeships under native craftsmen in the East, whether at Al Mina in Syria or at Tarsos; this would, in principle, lead to the same results. Neither case involves distant contacts, but rather intensive collaboration with detailed communication at least for the period of an apprenticeship. The Cretan finds tip the scale more towards the likelihood of immigrant craftsmen in the Greek sphere—which does not rule out the possibility of individual journeys in the opposite direction.

The presumption of the existence of migrant oriental crafts-men occasionally meets with criticism both from classical ar-chaeologists and from orientalists. Whereas the former, by rea-son of method, tend to be reluctant to consider opportunities for personal, almost anecdotal coincidence,[42] to the latter the image of free enterprise projected into the "dark ages" appears incompatible with the royal power and bureaucracy that char-acterized eastern civilizations.[43] Here indeed is a clear distinction between western and eastern traditions. That craftsmen are no-table for mobility, thanks to their skills, in contrast to resident peasants or landowning nobility, is clearly stated in that verse of Homer on the "public workers," *demioergoi* (*Od.* 17.383–385). Solon, according to Plutarch, realized this and encouraged the immigration of craftsmen to Athens: "to change residence for the sake of *techne*" is the term used here for such migration.[44] At the same time the tyrants of Corinth had sought after such craftsmen; later Themistokles attracted *technitai* with the offer of immunity from taxes "so that as many people as possible should take up residence."[45] To judge by their names—such as Amasis, Lydos, and Brygos—potters and vase painters of the sixth cen-tury seem to have immigrated from Egypt, Lydia, or Phrygia.[46] For Aristotle it is practically the rule that craftsmen are immi-grant noncitizens; he also speaks of slaves as craftsmen,[47] but it is certain that where highly qualified craft skills are concerned there can be no question of slavery. In Hellenistic times "migrant craftsmen" is a common term.[48] At least by this time they were taken for granted in the Semitic East, too. Jesus Sirach writes of craftsmen: "and even when they live in a foreign place, they do not need to starve."[49] A tentmaker from Tarsos became one of the historically most influential of these travellers: the apostle Paul.

To return to the archaic epoch: Assyrian craftsmen are pre-sumed to have been present in Urartu;[50] and in the same way metalwork spread to the Scythians and thence far on into Asia. Ancient tradition traces the encroachment of Greek craftsman-ship into Etruria to Demaratos of Corinth, the purported father of King Tarquinius Priscus; he was followed, it is said, by a host of craftsmen.[51] Even without the support of this anecdotal tradition it is certain that Greek potters and vase painters established themselves in various non-Greek areas in Italy. In the East, on the other hand, good craftsmen had long been much sought after and highly valued. It was precisely for this reason that the rulers attempted to keep control over them as far as was possible by bureaucratic means. Solomon had a whole troop of craftsmen, who were employed in the service of King Hiram of Tyre, sent to him for temple construction.[52] In a similar vein the *Ahiqar* novel recounts that the king of Egypt ordered an architect from the ruler of Nineveh.[53] When King Sargon built his palace in Khorsabad after the model of a "Hittite Hilani," as he states in his inscriptions,[54] he probably did not hesitate to requisition the appropriate craftsmen from North Syria. Documents from Mari show that craftsmen were organized by kings as mobile teams and kept ready for deployment as required.[55] In Mesopotamian myth, the hero of the flood did not fail to reserve a place for craftsmen in the ark.[56] A Hittite treaty expressly stipulates that fugitive craftsmen are to be extradited.[57] Yet even this clearly demonstrates the limits of the central organization: a craftsman who deserted would have calculated his chance of becoming independently employed in any new place. Letters from Mari speak of an architect or a smith simply "going away" apparently of his own free will and with the state taking no steps against him.[58] This is notable proof that, de facto, qualified specialists could not be denied a certain mobility already in the Bronze Age Orient. Not too different are the adventures of the physician Demokedes in the time of Darius, as related by Herodotus: he returned to his homeland against the will of the Great King, and the king was not able to get him back.[59] By that time other Greek specialists, craftsmen of all kinds as well as mercenaries, had long found their way to the oriental courts, to Nebuchadnezzar in Babylon[60] as well as to Darius in Persepolis.[61]

To sum up: For craftsmen in the East, at least the chance for free movement had existed for some time, since the influence of the despots was limited in extent. In the West this mobility was fully developed by the orientalizing period. It can be presumed that precisely this factor could act as a strong incentive for emigration to the freer West. We find the eastern craftsmen organized in the form of family guilds, as Sons of the Craftsmen (*marê ummani*) in Babylonia, as Sons of the Foundrymen (*bn nsk*) in Syria.[62] Such organizations guarantee forms of mutual support which must have operated very much to the benefit of émigrés. Even if free enterprise in craftsmanship was an invention of the early orientalizing period, the "orientals" were certainly involved too.

Another mobile element that should not be overlooked is the troops of mercenaries who could make a profitable life amidst the rise and fall of empires. We know of the Ionian and the Carian mercenaries of Psammetichus;[63] Antimenidas the brother of Alcaeus served as a mercenary for Babylon, as did Sappho's brother, Charaxos, for Egypt.[64] Whether *Krethi* and *Plethi* in David's bodyguard means Cretans serving together with Philistines is less certain.[65] It is more likely that the *Karim* attested in the ninth century at Jerusalem were in fact Carians from Asia Minor; at any rate Carian soldiers subsequently played an important role in seventh- and sixth-century Egypt.[66] Nor would there have been a shortage of Greeks trying their luck in the East at that time, even if the case of the Iamani of Ashdod remains uncertain.[67] The hoplite weaponry which came into use at the end of the eighth century in Greece is closely linked to Assyrian and Urartian arms. To illustrate a Gorgon shield such as is described in the *Iliad,* one can use an example from Olympia side by side with one from Carchemish on the Euphrates.[68]

Writing and Literature in the Eighth Century

For the general history of culture, by far the most important achievement of the orientalizing period is the adoption of the Phoenician script by the Greeks and its skillful adaptation to Greek phonetics.[1] It can almost stand as a model for cultural transmission at the time: As the borrowing from the Semitic is beyond all doubt, the creative development by Greek inventors is no less clear; and a date significantly after the collapse of Mycenaean culture, but no later than the middle of the eighth century, is now well established.

For us, the Greek script is the first perfect writing system, being the earliest alphabetic script to use signs for both vowels and consonants consistently, whereas Semitic writing was, and is, basically concerned with consonants. Its perfection is confirmed by its success in the West. Nevertheless the apparent invention, the notation of vowels, arose in fact from misunderstanding in a different phonological system: As the alphabetic sequence of the Semitic system was learned and the acrophonic principle understood by Greeks, they found a word such as *alpha* to begin with an *a* sound and not with a guttural glottal stop—denoted by Semitic *aleph*.[2] Just the deliberate creation of an additional letter for the fifth vowel, Y, which is not present in the Semitic model and thus was placed at the end of the series, is evidence of a conscious creation by some Greek "inventor." The letter Y appears in all Greek alphabets and all alphabets derived from them, including Phrygian[3] and Latin.

For the time and place of the adoption of the *Phoinikeïa,* as Herodotus says the letters were originally called,[4] there are many clues by now, but no fewer open questions; new finds could still alter the picture. The earliest Greek letters recognized to date originate in Naxos, Ischia, Athens, and Euboea and appear around or a little before 750.[5] This date fits perfectly the trading connections of the *Iawones* from Syria via Euboea to the West. On Ischia Greek graffiti are found in conjunction with Phoenician-Aramaic graffiti so that in one case even the linguistic identification is disputed; and finally a Greek graffito has been discovered on an eighth-century sherd from Al Mina.[6] Complication arises with the additional letters inserted in Greek alphabets after Y; it is precisely Chalkis/Euboea and Athens that differ in this respect—the letter X conveys the sound *kh* in Attic, but *x* at Chalkis and hence in the western colonies and finally in Latin; it seems natural that both the Chalcidian and the Attic alphabets should have been preceded by one of those "red" ones which have none of the additional letters, which is the case on Crete, Melos, and Thera; but there are no eighth-century documents of writing from these places so far, and the inference can be called into question.[7] There is much to substantiate the idea that Cyprus had a role to play as an intermediary station in the transmission of writing: The distinctive designation of the Greek letters as *Phoinikeïa* seems to presuppose that other "scribblings" (*grammata*) were known from which the Phoenician were different. This was the case only on Cyprus, where a linear script of Mycenaean type had been adapted to the Greek and persisted to Hellenistic times; the first document now known for its use in writing Greek dates from the eleventh century.[8] It is remarkable that the linear scripts had taken the direction from left to right, the direction that was to prevail in Greek and subsequent writing, in contrast to Semitic use; however, the change of direction from line to line, called *bustrophedon,* as often practiced in early Greek writing, is also found in some Phoenician documents and is common in Late Hittite hieroglyphs.[9] Of course the Greek script could also have been developed in Syria, although there is just one grafitto from Al Mina so far. We might still look to Crete, not so much because of the Phoenician inscription on a bowl that ended up in a tomb in Knossos around 900, but rather because of the particularly close connections with oriental craftsmanship and craftsmen from around 800; it was also on Crete that laws were recorded in writing earlier than elsewhere in Greece.[10] Nevertheless there is no evidence from Crete so far to rival the early graffiti from the sphere of the *Iaones*. In any case, the argument employed with great success at one time, that the great differences which appear from the start among local Greek alphabets presuppose a "long development" stretching over many decades, if not centuries, has been firmly refuted by Lilian Jeffery.[11] The so-called development, or rather the process of transmission, including some errors in copying, idiosyncrasies of "hands," and some intentional additions did happen extremely fast, within a few decades, if not years, reaching even the Phrygians in one direction and the Etruscans in the other nearly simultaneously.

Some Semitists still tend to plead that the Greek alphabet is significantly older, on the basis of certain details of the letter formations.[12] The finds of Phoenician-Aramaic inscriptions in Syria, however—and one should probably look to North Syria rather than to Palestine—are still too scanty to permit a definite sequence of letter forms to be established; every new find may change the picture.[13] From the Greek side, on the other hand, the *argumentum ex silentio* has become ever more overwhelming: In the increasing quantity of Greek geometric ceramics which can be classified and dated with a reasonable degree of precision, not a single scribbling has so far been discovered that looks like a Greek letter before, say, 770, while in the decades from 750 to about 700 there are now dozens and dozens of documents. A cultural explosion has happened here; there is nothing to suggest that the Greek alphabet had been in hiding for centuries before that date. Thus the existence of Greek script in the tenth and even in the ninth century appears, from the state of things, to be virtually impossible. The place of adoption currently remains open. The Greek reference to "Phoenicians" cannot be taken to mean that Phoenicians in the narrower sense—that is, the inhabitants of Byblos, Sidon, and Tyre—must have been the source. Phoenicians or Aramaeans from North Syria remain an equivalent option.

For the manner in which the transmission of writing occurred there is an invaluable clue, even if it is often overlooked: the Greek names of the letters (*alpha, beta, gamma,* and so on) with their unalterable order. These are Semitic words—bull, house, and so on—which have no sense at all in Greek. They were preserved for one particular reason: All teaching of reading and writing began with learning this sequence by heart. This explains also why much earlier the standardized sequence appears in two completely different Semitic alphabetic scripts, in the Ugaritic cuneiform alphabet attested in the thirteenth century and in the "Phoenician" alphabet, evidence of which has now been uncovered from as early as the twelfth century.[14] Even across language barriers, the same mnemonic sequence was learned by rote in the same way. With the alphabetic script, for the first time a system of writing had come into being which was so simple that it could be used by all people of normal intelligence even outside the circles of learned professional scribes; they need to be taught for only a short time and to get some practice in handwriting. We may form some picture of the teaching of writing in the Syro-Palestinian region.[15] When much later we read in Josephus that "of all those who dealt with the Greeks, the Phoenicians used writing the most, for private business as well as for their public affairs,"[16] he was referring to a school tradition going back a thousand years. The inference is that the "inventor" who first used these letters for the notation of the Greek language had participated in at least one school lesson, whether of the Aramaic or the Phoenician type, whether in Syria or on Cyprus, perhaps even somewhere else with some emigrant who had received an elementary education. This gives cause to reflect on the sheer coincidence that rules the evidence available to us: The Semitic letter names *alpha, beta,* and so on occur in Greek literature in the fifth century at the earliest,[17] but they must have been in current use ever since the eighth century, as they had been adopted along with the original alphabet; that those meaningless word patterns should have been introduced into Greek at any later time is quite impossible. The Latin alphabet can serve as a counterproof: Writers of Latin did not adopt the ancient Phoenician mnemonic sequence; rather, they let the vowels sound for themselves and added an *e*-vowel to the consonants, as the Greeks had already done with their additional letters $\Upsilon \ \Omega$ on the one hand and $\Phi \ X \ \Psi$, pronounced "phee," "khee," "psee," on the other; but even so the Latins and the Romans started school by learning their *a be ce*—as we still do today. It is remarkable that in this respect the Greek practice has remained closer to Phoenician-Aramaic school tradition than the Latin did to the Greek.

Thus it is clear that the adoption of the Phoenician script by the Greeks was more than the copying of letter forms; it included the transmission of the technique of teaching and learning how to read and write. This presupposes a certain intimacy of contacts, as is also indicated by those objects which almost never show up in the archaeological documentation and yet are much more significant for the tradition of writing than individual graffiti: writing tablets and leather scrolls together with the appropriate writing tools. These indeed must have accompanied the use of the Greek script from the start. The writing tablet, *deltos* in Greek, has even kept its Semitic name, *daltu—daleth* in Hebrew—together with the name of the special wax with which it is covered, *malthe*. *Daltu* originally means door but is used for a writing tablet already in thirteenth-century Ugarit, as it is in Hebrew later on.[18] Wooden writing tablets were in use in Mesopotamia as well as in Syria and Palestine; the find of one exemplar in the fourteenth-century wreck at Ulu Burun near Kaş, Turkey, is considered sensational, even if no trace of the writing for which it was used has been preserved; some writing tablets of ivory from Sargon's palace in Nimrud have been known for a long time.[19] In Greek the "folding tablet" on which to write makes its appearance with the Bellerophontes story in Homer, in the context of the "fatal letter" motif.[20] It is true that the oldest direct testimonies for the word *deltos* occur in Aeschylus, but the reference to "bronze *deltoi*" as a term for ancient sacral laws should point back to the seventh or sixth century.[21] What is remarkable is that the word *deltos* consistently carries the vowel *e* in normal Greek, as opposed to *a* in Semitic *daltu;* slight distortions of vowel coloring are not surprising with borrowed words, but the *e* is equally characteristic of the Greek letter name *delta,* which reproduces the same Semitic word. In contrast, in the Cypriot syllabic script, which remains unaware of the standard Greek alphabet, the expected form for the writing tablet is attested, *daltos,* closer to the Semitic, just as the Phoenicians were so close on Cyprus.[22] That the normal Greek term for the writing tablet and the letter name show exactly the same metamorphosis indicates that both belong together from the start—in other words, that the *deltos* in Greece is as old as the Greek alphabet.

Books were in general use in the Phoenician-Aramaic region in the form of leather scrolls; in the special case of the Israelite Torah, this form has remained mandatory. Aramaic "scroll scribes" made their way to Mesopotamia and became virtually indispensable to the Assyrian administration, even when the "tablet scribes" of the much less practical yet old and venerable cuneiform script insisted on their privileges and still enjoyed higher rank. Thus the administration of the Assyrian empire was based on two languages, or rather, two scripts.[23] Aramaic as an administrative language came definitely to the fore with the Achaemenids of Persia; by then it is called "imperial Aramaic" (*Reichsaramäisch*) by modern specialists. But even Darius deferred to the older tradition and deemed it necessary to have Persian cuneiform created. For practical purposes the Persians continued to use the scrolls; there was a library of leather scrolls in Persepolis, burnt down by Alexander.[24] In Greece the leather scroll, wrapped around a wooden stick, is already referred to in the seventh century by Archilochus, as he introduces his own poem with the curious term *skytale,* stick—admittedly this term was obscure even for Greek readers in later antiquity.[25] We have the word of Herodotus that the Ionians still called papyrus books *diphtherai,* skins, as this word had become established to designate books in the beginnings of literacy. For confirmation even more ancient evidence has come up: In sixth-century business letters from the Milesian colony Olbia, *diphtherion* as the "master book" is seen to contrast with single lead sheets used as letters, *molibdion.*[26] Thus it is hardly a coincidence that, in the fifth century, oracle books are referred to as *diphtherai,*[27] as these probably continue one of the earliest uses of writing. As contacts with Egypt became more frequent, papyrus, being so much cheaper and lighter, became the dominant writing material. It was called *byblos* from the Phoenician trading post Gubla/Byblos, or *chartes,* a foreign word of unknown origin. It seems that papyrus became available at the earliest in the era of Psammetichus, about 660, or more probably only when the Greeks settled at Naukratis around 600. The breakthrough to literacy precedes this date even in Ionia; this is reflected in the local dialect which adhered to the term for leather scroll, *diphthera.*

Akkadian cuneiform side by side with Aramaic, Phoenician, and Greek alphabetic script produces a continuum of written culture in the eighth century which stretches from the Euphrates to Italy. Cuneiform tablets are found not only as far as Syria but also on Cyprus and in Tarsos, where the Greeks were definitely present. A little farther east, at Guzana–Tell Halaf, a businessman would conduct his correspondence partly in cuneiform, partly in Aramaic, whereas an Aramaic-speaking community such as Huzirina-Sultantepe near Harran kept a library of cuneiform literature. The practice of written contracts can be followed from cuneiform through Aramaic and Hebrew down to the Greeks of the classical and Hellenistic periods.[28] Carl Wendel has drawn attention to connections that go beyond business documents: It is the practice of the *subscriptio* in particular that connects the layout of later Greek books with cuneiform practice, the indication of the name of the writer/author and the title of the book right at the end, after the last line of the text; this is a detailed and exclusive correspondence which proves that Greek literary practice is ultimately dependent upon Mesopotamia. It is necessary to postulate that Aramaic leather scrolls formed the connecting link.[29]

Here, however, we are confronted with the catastrophic state of preservation: The whole of Aramaic and Phoenician literature has been lost together with the perishable materials on which it was written, wood or leather, with the exception of that offshoot in Israel which was to develop into the Bible and thus remained preserved as a sacred text. There are, nevertheless, two pieces of evidence to show that cuneiform literary texts indeed exerted influence on Aramaic scroll-literature. The sole extant scraps of an early Aramaic literary text found so far are the *Ahiqar* fragments from Elephantine. The *Ahiqar* novel—long known in its later, Aramaic-Syrian form and in various versions in other languages—is set in Syria in the time of King Sennacherib and makes use of names that may be historical. The piece itself was, in all probability, written after the catastrophe of Nineveh, but the Assyrian period is felt to loom large in the picture. The transmission of this text is remarkable proof for a continuous tradition from Mesopotamia via Syria to Palestine and Egypt.[30] Another tale about Ashurbanipal is extant in Aramaic,[31] and Gilgamesh appears as a mythical giant among the remains of Aramaic leather scrolls from Qumran, in a fragment of the Aramaic Book of Henoch: The main character of the most brilliant work of cuneiform literature has left his echo in Aramaic writings of the third century B.C. By some route or other, the name Gilgamos even penetrated into Greek literature.[32]

Not all connections between Aramaic, Phoenician, or Hebrew book scrolls and Greek literature were necessarily made through *diphtherai* of the eighth century B.C. For a much later contact the Septuagint is a memorable piece of evidence, and even the Greek version of the *Ahiqar* novel which appears in the Life of Aesop was probably produced in Hellenistic times.[33] The merchants and craftsmen at Ischia were hardly much concerned with books in the literary sense—and yet the inscription on the Nestor cup evidently was made by someone who knew what a book of Greek verse looked like. In any event, the fashionable claim that the Greeks adopted only the alphabet from so-called Phoenicians and created all the further achievements of their written culture on their own[34] should be approached with caution. Writing tablets and leather scrolls at the very least came with the script and molded the techniques and the concept of the book. There was no *tabula rasa*. So much of Semitic written culture has been completely lost that general probability would suggest rather that there were far more numerous, richer, and denser connections than can be demonstrated by the meager remains available. In fact every new find this century, whether from Elephantine or Qumran, from Karatepe or Deir ʿAlla, has brought to light new and often unexpected connections.[35]

The Problem of Loan-Words

The clearest and most enduring evidence of cultural influences is embodied in language. What Christianity, Roman civilization, and Greek intellectual and artistic culture have meant for the West still speaks to us from our present language. The different picture presented by the Greek language—the impression of indigenous purity untroubled by external influences—is used, with some apparent justification, as an argument against

the existence of profound eastern influences: Close cultural contacts with the Semitic East, it is argued, would be betrayed in an
abundance of foreign and borrowed Semitic words.[1] The lack of
Semitic borrowings in Greek is offered as proof of the lack of
any such contact.

But the situation is not so clear-cut. There are at least some
recognized Semitic loan-words in pre-Hellenistic Greek, including such important ones as *mnea/mna,* mina, the basic unit of
weight and hence of currency; *kanon,* measuring rod, hence
ruler and standard in general; *deltos,* writing tablet, with its wax,
malthe. They provide the clearest evidence one could want for
the traffic of trade, craftsmen, and writing in the orientalizing
period.

Greek linguistics has been the domain of Indo-Europeanists
for nearly two centuries; yet its success threatens to distort reality. In all the standard lexicons, to give the etymology of a
Greek word means *per definitionem* to give an Indo-European etymology. Even the remotest references—say, to Armenian or
Lithuanian—are faithfully recorded; possible borrowings from
the Semitic, however, are judged uninteresting and either dis-
carded or mentioned only in passing, without adequate documentation. It is well known that a large part of the Greek vocabulary lacks any adequate Indo-European etymology; but it has
become a fashion to prefer connections with a putative Aegean
substratum or with Anatolian parallels, which involves dealing
with largely unknown spheres, instead of pursuing connections
to the well-known Semitic languages.[2] Beloch even wanted to
separate the Rhodian Zeus Atabyrios from Mount Atabyrion =
Tabor, the mountain in Palestine, in favor of vague Anatolian
resonances.[3] Anti-Semitism was manifest in this case; elsewhere
it was often operating on an unseen level. Even first-rank Indo-
Europeanists have made astonishing misjudgments: The number of Semitic loan-words in the Greek language is "quite insig-
nificantly small" (Debrunner); "indeed they don't even reach
double figures" (Meillet).[4] They seem to have forgotten even the
fifteen Semitic letter names. Emilie Masson, in her highly re-
strictive critical work (1967), has nevertheless established thirty-

seven definite and twelve possible Semitic words in the Greek language; using less rigid parameters Oswald Szemerényi was able to add another dozen; there is no shortage of further attempts.[5] Some of this material requires careful checking; but additional findings also are by no means to be excluded. This much is certain: There is a marked presence of Semitic loanwords in Greek.

It is true that dilettantes eager to make new discoveries have been guilty of carelessness and rash speculation in this field, while the negative statements of critics enjoy the advantage of seeming caution and strict methodology: Linguists can keep to well-established laws of phonetic evolution within a closed system, whereas borrowings are mostly inferred from similarities of sounds that may be fortuitous. But it is precisely methodology which is the problem. Greek language, at any rate the literary Greek that we know, absolutely rejects the use of unadapted foreign words; they are accepted only in perfectly assimilated form as to phonetics and inflexion. Thus there can be no method to discover borrowed words: They imitate and go into hiding, adapting themselves to the roots and suffixes of native Greek. In general, loan-words can be established definitively only on the basis of detailed documentation from both sides.[6] The word *hammock,* derived from some American Indian language, has become *Hängematte,* hanging mat, in German, which looks perfectly indigenous—until with a second or third look one may realize that there is not, in fact, a mat which is hanging. Popular etymology plays its role in metamorphosis; no rules of phonetic evolution can be established. Even the correspondence of meaning is seldom perfect; partial misunderstandings take place all the time. Thus the situation as far as the eighth century B.C. is concerned appears to be hopeless: Greek documentation is sparse, limited almost exclusively to the highly specialized sphere of Greek epic diction. The neighboring languages, Aramaic and Phoenician, are known mainly through casual inscriptions; the rest of the documentation is lost. For a conscientious judge, acquittal by lack of evidence will be the result again and again—and yet the outcome of minimalism, arrived at in this fashion, must be absolutely false, as a general consideration of probabilities will show. The underworld of loan-words is still there, camouflaged but influential.

We can attempt to penetrate beyond rhyming games with external assonances by taking into account necessary connections either between names and concrete objects and skills, or between groups of terms which belong together. In addition, very specific, particularly multisyllabic phonetic units and specific structures of meaning are indicative of cultural transfer, even if more context cannot be produced, because the probability of coincidental homonymy becomes exceedingly small.

If we look over the list of recognized Semitic loan-words in the Greek language, another stereotype makes its appearance: The Semitic origin of certain terms of trade and traded goods is gladly conceded,[7] following, it is to be suspected, that once-prevalent notion of "typically Jewish" activities; what remain obliterated are the areas of craftsmanship, warfare, and written culture, although, given historical circumstances, these are likely to have been no less important.

The list of traded goods with Semitic names is impressive indeed.[8] *Chrysos,* gold, and *chiton,* garment (related to the word *cotton*), are the two important borrowings which are already in evidence in the Mycenaean Linear B documents and which therefore offer proof of business traffic in the Bronze Age. Other kinds of fabric, such as *sindon, othone, bussos,* similarly penetrated into Greek as, naturally, did Arabian specialties such as *libanos* and *murra,* frankincense and myrrh, and other spices such as *nardos, kasia, kannabis, kinnamomon,* minerals such as *naphtha* and *nitron,* and plants such as *krokos* and *sasamon,* crocus and sesame. The expression *lipa aleiphesthai,* "to anoint oneself richly with oil," may easily go with *nitron.*[9] The Akkadian word for finely ground flour, *samidu,* became *semidalis* in Greek and is still current in modern Greek.[10] In addition there are the names of containers and vessels such as *kados, sipye,* and—quite a frequent word—*lekane,* corresponding to Aramaean *laqna;* here popular etymology has produced the mirage of a suffix in current use in Greek, *-ane.*[11] If *alabastron* belongs together with the

Akkadian *algameshu* and the Hebraic *älgabish,* there is only very partial correspondence; with *smaragdos,* smaragd, which is *barraqtu* in Akkadian, *pa-ra-ku* in Mycenaean, *bar'qa* in Aramaic, and *marakatam* in Sanskrit, it seems pointless to try to follow the path of the word through the oriental bazaars.[12] More clear seems to be *kalche* for a form of purple, which points to craftsmanship as well as to trading;[13] by contrast *kuanos,* a blue substance used for colouring, is traced to Hittite *kuwanna.*[14] How complex interrelations can be is shown in the case of *kaunakas,* woollen robe: the word is Persian and passed into Akkadian as well as into Greek in which the resonances of *nakos,* sheepskin, may well have played a part.[15]

From the activities of traders we find, next to the common word *gaulos,* ship, also the irreplaceable *sakkos,* sack; the market, *makellon;*[16] and above all the unit of weight already mentioned, the mina—Akkadian *mana,* Greek *mnea, mna;*[17] hardly less important is the term for down payment or deposit, *arrabon;* though not attested before the fourth century B.C., its use may be much older. The mina became one of the most commonly used Greek names for weight and currency without losing the stamp of its Mesopotamian origins: It is here and, for the archaic period, only here that the Babylonian sexagesimal system was adopted by the Greeks, as sixty minas make up one talent. This term for the higher unit, the talent (*talanton*), has an ancient Greek and in fact Indo-European name; at least indirectly it is attested in Mycenaean. Yet there is no trace of the mina and the sexagesimal system in the well-known Mycenaean system of weights and measures. Thus we may be confident that in this case we are dealing with post-Mycenaean borrowing on the trading route from Carchemish on the Euphrates to North Syria, reaching the Luwians and finally the Greeks.

Presumably the connections reach further than can strictly be proved. The mina was, above all, the unit of weight used for measuring silver. There are silver ingots originating from Zincirli, minas of apparently standardized weight which bear the incised name of King Barrakib of Sam'al-Zincirli (732–720);[18] these are noteworthy antecedents of minted money, which came into use about one century later. To scratch, to incise, is *haraṣu* in Akkadian, *charaxai* in Greek.[19] This then became the term for the minting of Greek coins, although in that case it was not actually the coin but rather the mold, now called *charakter,* which was incised directly. The term *scratcher* seems to point back to a practice which precedes the striking of coins, a practice which is shown most clearly in the talents of Zincirli. Borrowing or coincidence? Akkadian uses the same root to designate entrenchments fortified with palisades, *hariṣu,* while the palisade wall or even the individual palisades are called *charax* in Greek. That the same root is used twice in two not naturally neighboring areas of meaning in two different languages is striking. Another observation worth adding here is that the distributive use of the Greek preposition *ana* in conjunction with numbers, *ana dyo,* "two each," seems somewhat removed from the original meaning of this preposition, "upwards," but corresponds exactly to the Akkadian preposition *ana.*[20] Is this a kind of Syrian business slang, similar to the French *à* used in a similar sense in German accounting?

To return to what is definite and generally recognized: In the sphere of the craftsman the word *kanon* appears as the clearest example of borrowing. Of course the general word for reed or cane, *canna,* is current in the whole of the Mediterranean world; but the specialized use of this term for measuring stick, *qan mindati* in Akkadian, *q'neh hammiddah* in Hebrew, is less natural, but so well attested that no one will hypothesize that the Greeks hit upon this use of "reeds" entirely on their own.[21] The appearance of the term in Greek, however, means that a basic tool and concept of building construction has been imported. In addition there are the terms *titanos,* lime,[22] and *gypson,* plaster,[23] but above all even the clay brick, *plinthos,* which seems to come from the Akkadian **libintu, libittu.*[24] Thus the basic term of Mesopotamian architecture has made its way to Greece. Just as the Germans apparently first learnt how to build a solid wall from the Romans, *Mauer* derived from Latin *murus,* as opposed to a loose partition, *Wand,* made from wands, so the Greeks learnt the art of building walls to measure from bricks, lime, and plaster from the eastern craftsmen. Even the word for axe, *axine,* coincides with Akkadian *haṣṣinnu;*[25] and that word for booth, barracks, or tent which was to have a brilliant career, *skana/skene*—hence scene—is most probably an Assyrian-Aramaic *maškanu,*[26] from the most common root *šakanu,* "to set up"; whether the word was introduced in the sphere of the craftsman or the soldier remains in question. As to craftsmen, the characteristic expression "sons of craftsmen" constitutes another common element.[27] It is also possible that the noble-sounding word *cheironax* for the craftsman, literally "lord of hands," is borrowed indirectly, being translated from Hittite.[28] The name *solos* for the metal ingot points in a similar direction, to "Late Hittites" of Cilicia.[29]

Thus in the sphere of craftsmanship a picture arises even from linguistic data which ties in with the archaeologically demonstrable influx of oriental skills and products in the eighth century. For the influence of oriental iconography one should bear in mind that not only the lion—*lis*[30]—bears a Semitic name, but also the bull—*tauros*—has a clear Semitic correspondence.[31] Still the example *plinthos–libittu* shows how much transformation, even bowdlerization can occur with loan-words: It is the object rather than the phonetic correspondence which makes the borrowing plausible. Much remains in the gray area of the unprovable, especially as the technical vocabulary of early craftsmen is only patchily known to us even in Greek.

The same is true of another area in which there were prolonged and close contacts: the military sphere of mercenaries. In the pertinent vocabulary there are a number of suggestive resonances, but none of the supposed borrowed words has met with general recognition. One could name the word for scimitar, *harpe,* next to the Aramaic *ḥarba,* sword;[32] or perhaps *skylon* for looted weapon and *sylan* for looting,[33] or even *macha,* battle, with *machessasthai,* "to fight," corresponding to the general Semitic word for "to hit," *mahaṣu* in Akkadian, together with Aramaic *maha,* battle: The highly irregular formation of the root, irregular from the point of view of the Greek, could indicate external influences.[34] In addition the Greek warcry *alala* could be categorized with the corresponding Akkadian cry of *alala*—and finally even with Hallelujah.[35] These are serious possibilities, but they will generally meet with derision; for many it would be unacceptable to think of Hellenic warriors depending on Semitic prototypes even in their language. Still, from a historical point of view, the militarization of the Assyrians preceded the Greek *polis,* and, as far as the technology of weaponry is concerned, in particular the hoplite shield, the influence of the East is obvious.[36]

The search for oriental borrowings in names from Greek myth stands, as is to be expected, on particularly uncertain ground.[37] Great caution should also be exercised with the terminology of ritual practice. References to possible borrowings in this field will be given in the next chapter as suggestive possibilities, for the sake of illustration, as it were; they cannot be used as independent arguments.[38] There remain unclear relationships, such as Greek *pallake,* concubine, next to Hebrew *pilägäš,* Aramaic *palqta.*[39] In any case, the kind of minimalism that rejects all connections with the Semitic which are not crystal clear remains, on the whole, the most unlikely of possible hypotheses.

CHAPTER TWO

"A SEER OR A HEALER"
Magic and Medicine from East to West

"Craftsmen of the Sacred": Mobility and Family Structure

Seers and doctors are the first enumerated by Homer as migrant "craftsmen," individuals whom a community would be concerned to attract. They are specialists of a particular kind, having their art—*techne*—which no one else can master. Seers and doctors appear closely connected, at least in the period preceding the "Hippocratic" era. The change is documented in the fifth-century treatise *On the Sacred Disease* attributed to Hippocrates, which scorns the cathartic healer in the name of nature; before that caesura, seer and healer might even be identical, as the concept of a life characterized by initiation and divination, *telestikos kai mantikos bios,* indicates.[1] A modern-day prejudice against all charlatans should not obscure the importance in ancient societies of therapies based on ritual and religion. Even today it is hardly disputed that, in individual cases, astounding success can be achieved by such means, and seers with a variety of *technai* enjoy good business.

"He who makes the sacred his craft [*techne*]" is the memorable description given in the Derveni papyrus of people who specialize in private initiations. In a similar vein Strabo refers to "the Dionysiac and Orphic crafts," whereas for the Hippocratic polemicist such a technician is rather "banausic."[2] But even this author admits that migrant seers and healers pose as bearers of some special knowledge. In fact successful charismatic specialists became, as they can today, widely sought-after personalities; they could cross frontiers even more easily and more often than other craftsmen with simpler skills. Being the mobile bearers of cross-cultural knowledge, the migrant charismatics deserve particular attention as to cultural contacts.[3] In fact they represent the intellectual elite of the time with a chance to achieve international status.

There is evidence of the mobility of magic-wielding seers already in the ancient Orient. The king of Moab summoned Bileam from the Euphrates to come and to curse Israel, but the spirit of God which came upon the seer made him pronounce blessings instead.[4] In the Amarna correspondence both physicians and seers are requested to be sent, by the king of Ugarit as well as by the king of the Hittites; one king of Alasia-Cyprus has need of an "eagle-diviner," a bird augur from Egypt.[5] King Muwatallis of Hattusa ordered a conjurer from Babylon.[6] In the more marginal regions where the power of the kings was less, the independence of the seer was correspondingly enhanced. He could travel freely on his own initiative, as is seen in both Greece and Israel.[7] As was the case with local craftsmen, free enterprise developed in the Greek world in particular. The special status a seer could achieve in a city is impressively shown in the case of Teisamenos, who claimed descent from the mythical seer Melampus: He could enforce his conditions on Sparta even against ancestral custom—and was finally considered the "victor" in the battle of Plataea (479 B.C.).[8] Plato, by contrast, speaks in tones of contempt of those "beggar-priests and seers" who tendered their sevices "at the doors of the rich"; and yet he reveals that they could convince "whole cities."[9] In about 600 B.C. Athens summoned Epimenides the Cretan diviner to purge the city of the Cylonian sacrilege;[10] similarly after 466 Sparta summoned necromancers from Phigalia because the inauspicious death of Pausanias had polluted the precinct of Athena.[11] Already around 670 Thaletas of Gortyn had delivered Sparta from a plague.[12] His teacher Onomakritos the Lokrian, we are told, had wandered as far as Crete, "staying there on account of his mantic craft"[13]—the term for a temporary sojourn, *epidemia*, typically used of migrant physicians, can equally be applied to seers. According to Plato, Diotima came to Athens from Mantinea and, "for those who made sacrifices as she directed, she achieved a delay of the advent of the plague for ten years."[14] In the purification poem of Empedocles the migrant life of the seer is given a basic existential dimension: "Banished from the gods and wandering about," this is Empedocles' own situation, and just for this reason he can pose as a god.[15]

Everyone who chose to take up a career of initiation and divination did so on his own account and at his own risk. There was no monasticism, there were no religious orders. And yet these people enjoyed a certain status recognized by tradition; they also claimed to rely on some definite filiation of doctrine or technique: Each of the migrant charismatics has his "father," be it his natural father or his teacher who, through the apprenticeship, has made him his son, indeed, who often formally adopted him. Greek seers tend to present themselves in family groups. The most famous were the Melampodidae, to whom Teisamenos was related.[16] The Iamidae from Olympia and the Klytiadae connected with them were no less proud of their ancestry, and their activities lasted for centuries. The Telmissians in Karia, too, were a "mantic family" (*genos*).[17] Even more enduring was the success of the priest-families in Eleusis, the Eumolpidae and the Kerykes, who officiated for about one millennium until the mysteries were finally outlawed by the Christian emperor.[18] It was possible for a member of the family to turn to travelling and to become successful in foreign parts as a specialist in sacred matters, as Timotheos did with the first Ptolemy in Alexandria.[19] But we see family lines developing even outside the established clans. A few details are supplied by the trial speech *Aiginetikos* of Isocrates:[20] Polemainetos the successful seer—"Praised in War," a telling name?—himself childless, chose Thrasyllos to be his successor and bequeathed him his "art," his books, and his money. Thrasyllos "made use of the art," became very highly regarded, and amassed such a large fortune that the children from his various marriages continued to litigate over it long after his death. He had married into a noble family on Siphnos, and this was apparently the end of the seer tradition in his line. But such an art could be revived when necessary: The mother of Aeschines the orator, caricatured by his bitter enemy Demosthenes as a witchlike priestess of arcane mysteries, was, according to an inscription, descended from a family of seers in the tradition of Amphiaraos; both father and brothers were practicing seers, and evidently she herself did what she could to support the family financially through her special "craft." [21] A decree of King Ptolemy Philopator around 210 B.C. summoned all those who practiced the Dionysiac mysteries in Egypt to register in Alexandria and to declare "from whom they have received the sacred things, up to three generations." [22] We see that a practitioner of the telestic craft not only had to legitimate himself by giving the name of his immediate teacher, but also had to know who his spiritual grandfather and great-grandfather were. One may also compare the fact that the city Magnesia on the Maeander summoned three maenads from Thebes, from the family of Ino—that is, according to myth, the original maenads who had tended Dionysus—to organize the new Dionysian mysteries. [23]

The requirement that secret knowledge be passed on only to an actual son appears in alchemical writings and in the magical papyri. [24] However, this mandate already applied to the organizations of the early Greek physicians. Best known is the "family" of the Asclepiads, [25] although it was hardly unique. The famous Hippocratic Oath has obligations for the pupil which are the equivalent of a de facto adoption. [26] No less significantly, the Hippocratic *nomos* makes the transmission of the knowledge an initiation into mysteries: "Holy things are shown to holy men; such things are not permitted for the profane until they are initiated through the rites of knowledge." [27]

Precisely this connection of sacred skills with family tradition and the mandate of esotericism can already be found in cuneiform documents. These contain extensive information about many kinds of seers and practitioners of magic. Even in the ordinary crafts the son takes over the art from the father so that the true craftsman is called the "son of the master craftsman" (*mâr ummani*); the Codex Hammurapi makes the learning of a craft a de facto adoption.[28] On the Tyskiewicz bowl found in Italy, Phoenician artists sign as "sons of the foundrymen."[29] Correspondingly, a true seer is a "son of a seer"; in his incantation he presents himself as "the knowing one, son of the master craftsman."[30] "The secrets of *ašipu*-art, the knowing one shall show them to the knowing one; he who does not know does not see them; to your son whom you love, make him pronounce the name of god Asalluhi and god Ninurta, and show him": this is the prescription for the tradition of esoteric wisdom in incantation texts;[31] or, in other words: "The wise one makes his son . . . take the oath; he makes him learn."[32] Thus the peculiar practice of taking an oath to ensure that knowledge remains within the family is common to the Babylonian magicians and to the Hippocratics. Diodorus reports that with the Chaldaeans, too, the secret art of astrology is regularly acquired by the son from the father.[33]

A similar craft is found in the West in which the father-son line was preserved with particular zeal even when spreading to foreign areas, and this was part of its success: that of Etruscan *haruspices*.[34] In Rome this art was always left to the specialists from neighboring Etruria. Tacitus states expressly that the noble Etruscan families reserved this knowledge for themselves and passed it on only within the family; already Cicero takes this for granted.[35] It cannot seriously be doubted, even in the absence of direct documentation, that this practice goes back to the great period of Etruria—that is, back to the archaic period. According to the Roman historians, the *haruspices* officiated even in the age of the kings; they tell how Attus Navius took an apprenticeship with the Etruscans.[36] This ultimately leads back to the orientalizing period of Etruria.

It is true that such family-based practice can come into being in many places and cultures without contacts or dependence. Similar ties within the "family" are reported for Egyptian priests as well as for Iranian *magi* but may also easily be found elsewhere.[37] Nevertheless there is a linguistic peculiarity that appears to point to a narrower connection between Semitic and Greek usage: In the realm of craftsmen and of seers, of healers and physicians, there appears in Akkadian, Phoenician, and Hebrew on the one hand and in Greek on the other, the expression "sons of . . ." to designate the collective group:[38] "sons of Asclepius" but also "sons of painters" in Plato;[39] "sons of philosophers" became a common, slightly ironic expression later on. That the agreement between the Semitic and the Greek idiomatic expression is not just natural but significant can be measured by the fact that an expression such as "the children of Israel" will still be recognizable as a Semitism. It is true that we also find "sons of the Achaeans" in Homer, hence also "sons of the Lydians" and similar terms in Herodotus and later to designate nations. This too is fully equivalent to eastern practice.[40] The Christian Gnostics borrowed a corresponding expression afresh from the Semitic side.[41] We have much less direct evidence for the earlier periods; but the general situation strengthens the hypothesis of cultural transfer even at that time.

Hepatoscopy

That the Etruscan *disciplina* of taking omens from liver inspection (*hepatoscopy, haruspicina*) shows remarkably close correspondence to the form of divination developed in Mesopotamia and that this can best be explained as the transmission of a "school" from Babylon to Etruria has been established since the decipherment of cuneiform.[1] However, this correspondence has barely been discussed within the general framework of a cultural exchange. There are indeed specific problems of comparison even here: The cuneiform material is overabundant, but much of it still lacks definitive publication.[2] The Etruscan material, on the other hand, is lost and can be reconstructed only piecemeal from Latin and Greek texts. The correspondence between Etruscan and Assyrian hepatoscopy became evident as soon as the Etruscan bronze liver found at Piacenza[3] was compared with the Assyrian clay model of a liver in the British Museum (Figure 3);[4]

Figure 3. TOP: *Liver model in clay, with cuneiform inscription, from Mesopotamia, eighteenth century* B.C. BOTTOM: *Liver model in bronze, with Etruscan inscription, from Piacenza, third century* B.C.

further examples have subsequently come to light. The age-old practice of animal slaughter brings with it many unforeseeable and uncanny details; the liver in particular, with its complicated and changing form, seems to invite attempts at oracular interpretation. For this reason the direct connection between the oriental and Etruscan lore has been brought into doubt again.[5] And yet to build a system specifically on the slaughter of sheep, to manufacture demonstration models of sheep livers from clay and metal and to provide them with inscriptions for the sake of explanation, is something peculiar found precisely along the corridor from the Euphrates via Syria and Cyprus to Etruria. It can even be shown that both the Assyrian and the Etruscan models diverge from nature in a similar way;[6] that is, they are derived not directly from observation but from common traditional lore.

Models of livers are the concrete archaeological evidence for the diffusion of Mesopotamian hepatoscopy. Besides Mesopotamia such models have been found since the Bronze Age with the Hittites of Asia Minor; in Alalakh, Tell el Hajj, and Ugarit in Syria; in Hazor and Megiddo in Palestine; and also on Cyprus. Assyrian hepatoscopy was practiced at Tarsos in Cilicia in the time of the Assyrians.[7] By contrast, the Etruscan examples, so far as is known, date from the third and second centuries B.C. Thus, the presumption that we are dealing with contacts in Hellenistic times[8] cannot be ruled out. Nevertheless, the balance of probabilities speaks against it: At that time, the golden age of Etruria lay far in the past. But the internal tradition of the Etruscan *disciplinae* goes back to the seventh century, as is seen from their system of *saecula*[9]—that is, to precisely that period whose glory is reflected in so many oriental imports.[10] The esoteric family tradition of the *haruspices* guaranteed the preservation of the knowledge unaltered. If that knowledge ever arrived from elsewhere, it must have done so at an early period which was still receptive, before the *disciplina* became fixed.

This fact is confirmed from the Greek side. It seems that hepatoscopy had no place in the older strata of Homeric epic, but it makes its appearance in the final version we have, dating to around 700 B.C.: Calchas, Agamemnon's seer, is the best of the "bird-diviners," and by virtue of this art he has "led" the army.[11] But a "sacrifice-diviner" (*thyoskoos*) is mentioned in the twenty-fourth book of the *Iliad* and has his role in the *Odyssey*.[12] Of course there are various ways to practice divination at sacrifice, but the observation of the liver is by far the most predominant; the name of the Etruscans, Tusci, was subsequently derived from *thyoskoos* by Greek speculation.[13] Greek iconography shows the seer examining the liver from about 530 B.C.;[14] after the Persian Wars Greek literature has hepatoscopy fully developed as the dominant form of divination. From Plato we learn that hepatoscopy enjoyed greater prestige than bird augury.[15]

It is interesting enough that there is a special tradition which points to Cilicia and Cyprus: The priest clan of the Tamiradae at Paphos claimed to have brought this art with them from Cilicia, and to have passed it on to the Cinyradae there.[16] With the oracle priests of Carian Telmessos liver augury enjoyed a special status;[17] this too may point to that epoch when Carian mercenaries went to the Orient, just as Greeks would do soon after them.

For all we know, liver models did not get as far as Greece itself. But another curious object related to the examination of entrails is the "Humbaba face," a grotesque human visage that can be made entirely from lengths of intestine.[18] It is familiar from finds made in Mesopotamia, but a characteristic example has also been unearthed at the acropolis of Gortyn, in a sanctuary where the presence of oriental craftsmen and seers in the eighth century is evident from the architecture as well as from the relics of foundation sacrifices.[19] The Humbaba face is also imitated in some of the grotesque masks from the Ortheia sanctuary at Sparta, confirming the spread of paraphernalia of the eastern art of divination to the West.

What is more, there is a remarkable correspondence between the Babylonian and the western terminology of hepatoscopy. The Etruscan language has been lost, so for us, Greek and Latin must take its place. The systems are not exactly identical: There is a strict order of examination of ten parts of the liver in the

Assyrian school[20] which has no parallel in the West. However, a whole string of Greek terms looks like a translation from the Akkadian. Here as there, the liver has a "gate," a "head," a "path," and a "river."[21] If one looks at the naming of the variously shaped lobes of the liver as a kind of Rohrschach test, the most divergent projections and interpretations might come to the fore: The correspondence between East and West can hardly be accidental. In addition, there is a special binary logic in the system which can be shown to exist in the Akkadian as well as in the Greek, and above all in the Etruscan-Latin branch of the science: There are "auspicious" and "hostile" sections of the liver according to which the import of the observations alters: what is normal is good in the auspicious section and dangerous in the hostile section; malformation in the hostile section is good, and vice versa.[22] Less telling proofs for interconnections are general imaginative associations, such as a missing "head," indicating catastrophe of leader, king, or country; or two "heads" indicating two rival powers. Even this parallel connects the factual Mesopotamian reports to fantastic scenes elaborated by Roman poets.[23]

What would seem to be the strongest argument for the Assyrian–Etruscan axis is, in fact, the most uncertain: that of linguistic borrowing. Alfred Boissier, who was the first to work systematically on Babylonian liver-omen texts, saw that *liver* in these texts was consistently written with the Sumerian ideogram *ḪAR;* and he at once concluded that this was the etymology for the Latin word *haruspex,* the first part of which had always defied explanation, while the second part must mean "seer of"; "seer of liver" would perfectly match its use in reference to those Etruscan specialists officiating in Rome.[24] This is as suggestive as it is surprising; but serious doubts must remain. Even if the transmission of knowledge from Mesopotamia to Etruria seems to be beyond dispute, there was no transmission of cuneiform script anywhere in the West. In oral instruction, however, something such as *ḪAR* was most unlikely to have been pronounced. The sign *ḪAR* is used as an ideogram for what, in Akkadian, should sound *amutu.*[25] Moreover the Etruscans, the actual specialists, had their own, completely different word for this type of seer, *netsvis*.[26] How should the Romans come by a Sumerian name for something which was practiced by the Etruscans? One is thus forced to take Boissier's etymology as an example of how a coincidence of linguistic homonymy can lead us astray. It is perhaps no less suggestive that the sign which the seer had to interpret is called *tertu* in Akkadian; its plural, *teretu,* sounds remarkably like the *terata/teirata* with which a seer such as Teiresias was to deal.[27] But even here a curious coincidence cannot be ruled out.

Cicero writes that it is unthinkable that Etruscan, Greek, Egyptian, and Punic diviners should meet for consultation and reach a common consensus in problems of hepatoscopy; they would never agree, because "there is not a single science for all of them," but only diverging sectarian views.[28] Skeptics could draw the conclusion that the whole thing was nonsense; the historian, however, finds the clearest evidence of cultural diffusion precisely in correspondences of details that seem most absurd and unnatural, and hence least likely to be arrived at independently. It is only to be expected that individual aberrations will creep in, and of course individual forms tend to adapt themselves to the prevailing cultural context. Thus Greek divination characteristically proceeds far more from a visual-associative basis, without the almost scholarly ballast of the Etruscan *disciplina,* which, on the other hand, has preserved more of its eastern origins. The similarities are nevertheless indicative of a common source, of some historical connection which binds all the individual forms together. The spread of hepatoscopy is one of the clearest examples of cultural contact in the orientalizing period. It must have been a case of East-West understanding on a relatively high, technical level. The mobility of migrant charismatics is the natural prerequisite for this diffusion, the international role of sought-after specialists, who were, as far as their art was concerned, nevertheless bound to their father-teachers. We cannot expect to find many archaeologically identifiable traces of such people, other than some exceptional instances: a model liver or a Humbaba face.

Still the migrant diviners have left their mark in Greek mythology. One name which links the Orient and Greece is that of the seer Mopsos. According to the Greek version, which was fixed above all in the Hesiodic Melampodia,[29] he was a nephew of Teiresias; he first founded the oracle of Claros and eventually emigrated to Cilicia, where the city of Mopsuestia carried his name. Surprisingly, the name Mopsos appears in a Hittite report, as *Muksus;*[30] in addition, the famous bilingual inscription from Karatepe in Cilicia from the eighth century introduces a King Azitawadda from the "house of Mopsos";[31] the hieroglyphic Luwian text indicates the name to be *Moxos,* a name preserved also in Lydian tradition,[32] whereas the Phoenician version has *Mopsos (mps).* How these testimonia should be combined to reconstruct the real history of one King Mopsos and his progeny in Asia Minor is a problem which cannot be discussed here. It suffices to state that a name from the Hittite-Cilician tradition is used in Greek myth to identify one of the great seers who was, in the Greek view, connected with Cilicia. The Cilician origins of the seers of Paphos should not be forgotten. Next to Mopsos there stands, with a pure Greek name, Amphilochos, the son of Amphiaraos. Mopsos and Amphilochos together are honored as the founding heroes of the famous oracle of Mallos in Cilicia, a place where, once more, oriental and Greek traditions meet in a special way.[33] In any case, Greek myth establishes a connection between Greece and Cilicia precisely around the figure of the migrant seer. Not too far away is Tarsos, where Greek ceramics as well as cuneiform documents with divinatory contents have been found. The "Hesiodic" text about Mopsos may come close in time to the Karatepe inscription, that is, to the Assyrian period. The spread of the art of the seer from the Euphrates to Greece and the Etruscans as indicated by the other evidence presents the plausible background for the development of the Mopsos myth. It is true that the Greek narrative has reversed the circumstances, as the Greek Mopsos is made to emigrate to Cilicia, although according to the local documents his "house" had been established there and not in Greece. It is interesting that the myth has Mopsos defeat Cal-

chas "the best bird augur" in a contest of seers; the foreign origin of the art is, however, suppressed.

Let us not forget that a whole range of other forms of divination are common to the Hittite and Semitic Orient and the
Greeks; next to the interpretation of many other portents,[34] bird
augury played a notable role in Babylon. Different kinds of lecanomancy also constituted a special art, whether in the pouring
of oil onto water or the sprinkling of flour onto liquid.[35] "To
pour vinegar and flour into the same glass" and to watch their
movements is mentioned once by Aeschylus; Farnell took this
to be a clear example of Mesopotamian influence.[36] Such practices did not, however, become as prominent as liver augury.
The fact that *lekane* is an Aramaic word is probably just another
coincidence.

Foundation Deposits

To make offerings on the occasion of the construction of build-
ings on the very spot is a widespread practice, well known to
both ethnologists and folklorists. However, there are culturally
specific forms which can develop into fixed traditions. In the
Near East, where there are pertinent texts as well as archaeological finds, various forms emerge according to place and period.
There are guardian figures which are interred under the building; there are stone tablets with inscriptions buried likewise.
There are also less specific sacrificial rituals involving animal
sacrifice and libations. In addition there is the practice, particularly widespread among the Assyrians, of interring valuable objects, different kinds of precious metal and precious stones,
under temples or palaces.[1] One relevant ritual text for the erection of a new house has been preserved in Hittite; it specifies
how gold, silver, and bronze and other objects are to be deposited in specific places to the accompaniment of prayers.[2]

There are comparable albeit not identical foundation offerings
in the Minoan world: colored pebbles from the sea, small vessels, seals, even, in one case, animal bones, buried under the
floor or the threshold of a sacred room.[3] A deposit of eastern

style, consisting of bronze objects deliberately interred, has come to light under the Late Bronze Age Temple IV in Kition on Cyprus; the excavators were immediately reminded of the Mesopotamian practice, although the inhabitants of Kition at that time may have been Mycenaean Greeks.[4]

The next find, closer to Greece proper, dates from around 800 on Crete: A family of goldsmiths which had immigrated from Syria buried a deposit of gold nuggets, half-worked pieces, and other jewelry in a re-used tholos tomb at Knossos, rededicating it for their own use.[5] Thus we find religious practice directly imported from the East along with the skilled craft of foreign specialists.

From the subsequent period, two rich deposits excavated under two famous temples have attracted a great deal of attention. One was found at the wall and partly under the wall of the earliest temple of Artemis on Delos and is dated around 700: Small Mycenaean and contemporary valuables, already partly fragmented, had been interred together; a pit containing some animal bones and charcoal, traces of sacrifice, is closely connected.[6] The other deposit, which belongs to the temple of Artemis at Ephesos, is particularly rich, consisting of about a thousand objects; it has long been famous and controversial, since its date is tied in with the dating of the oldest electron coins. The options used to fluctuate between 650–630 and 600. Yet recent excavations yielded the result that it belongs to the temple built by Croesus, about 560 B.C. Similar deposits of valuables are known from one of the temples at Perachora, from the temple of Poseidon at Isthmia, and from the temple of Athena in Priene.[7]

The foundation offerings which were discovered at the temple on the acropolis of Gortyn are simpler and of a different type: two pits had been dug next to the temple wall in which there were the remains of animal bones, of some kind of libation in the form of a vegetable paste and various small vessels; the whole had been carefully covered with stone slabs on which a fire had been lit.[8] Here we have sacrificial ritual in a form familiar from later Greek and Latin texts: First, sacrifice is made "into the pit" (*bothros*); then this is covered over and a permanent marker, a boundary stone, or a god is erected above it.[9] A pit with foundation offerings, carefully covered before the erection of the building, has also been identified under one of the treasuries—previously called Temple D—in the Hera sanctuary of Samos; it is dated to 510–500 B.C.[10] In the earlier case, at Gortyn, the archaeologists who excavated the temple found the architecture—dated by them to around 800—similar to Late Hittite techniques, and they indicated a similar provenience for the foundation offerings. Animal sacrifices and libations are attested as construction offerings in Mesopotamia, too, though in a less specific form.[11]

The interment of small valuables, in particular pieces of metal, provides more specific evidence of the spread of a Mesopotamian practice, with the decisive leap across the Aegean linked to the emigration of craftsmen to Crete around 800. Admittedly this practice would not have brought much of a spiritual world with it: no pantheon, no myths; the practice itself is not even explained in the eastern texts.[12] What seems to suffice is the conviction, inherent in the act, that valuable offerings will ensure the permanent and undisturbed possession and safety of the building. One thing, however, is stated explicitly by the eastern texts: However much the builder may wish to come to the fore, the foundation succeeds "according to the message of the art of the conjurer"; the charismatic specialist could not be left out.[13] One is led to imagine that, even at the building in Gortyn, where workers from North Syria were probably involved, and no less at the beginnings of temple building on Delos or in Ephesos, together with the masons and carpenters there had also been a craftsman of the other kind, a migrant seer, in attendance.

Purification

Although the correspondence between Mesopotamian and Etruscan hepatoscopy has long been a subject of discussion, the no less significant similarities between eastern magic and the cathartic rituals of the Greeks have rarely been considered in detail. The situation is parallel, though, insofar as the practice of purification which is common in later periods does not yet appear in Homer—a fact noticed already by the ancient commentators on Homer. But the cyclic epic *Aithiopis* narrated the purification of Achilles after he had killed Thersites.[1] This is generally taken to represent a more recent stage in the development of Greek civilization: Concern about purification appears to be characteristic of the archaic period.[2] It is taken for granted that the influence of the oracle of Delphi was operative in this growing concern. Possible contacts with Scythian shamanism have also attracted attention since the work of Karl Meuli.[3] The role of Babylon was scrutinized by Lewis Richard Farnell alone, who found such significant differences between East and West that the cathartic system of the Greeks could not have been borrowed from Babylon; at least Farnell insisted that certain borrowings could not antedate Homer.[4] This has had a soothing effect on Hellenists—although one should realize that Farnell dated Homer to the tenth century and thereby left the eighth and seventh centuries open to all sorts of "influences"; indeed in some cases he was the first to acknowledge their existence.

As to the sources available, the situation is similar to that of hepatoscopy: On the Greek side we are dependent on isolated allusions and brief references and often have to rely upon later reports. Akkadian literature, in contrast, has a whole corpus of magic-ritual texts which have been known for a long time, although definitive editions are still lacking in quite a few cases.[5] These are often bilingual, Sumerian-Akkadian texts, a fact which speaks for their age; they were collected in a systematic way in the library of Ashurbanipal. Derivatives reached as far as Tarsos.[6] Among the practitioners of the rituals there are two main types: the seer (*barû*), who was responsible for divination; and the actual magician-priest (*ašipu*), whose main task was the healing of the sick.[7] The latter is the focus of discussion here.

The cathartic practice of the Greeks appears to concentrate on the purification of murderers from blood guilt: blood is purified through blood.[8] The standard example is that of Orestes, although Aeschylus does present Ixion as the original paradigm.[9] In the case of Orestes, Aeschylus gives us more graphic indications of how the actual procedure was carried out: In order to "wash away the stain," a piglet must be slaughtered in such a way that its blood pours over the polluted man; the blood is then washed off with running water; in this way the pollution "has been driven out by piglet-killing purifications."[10] We already know from the *Iliad* that the dirty water (*lymata*) must then be disposed of in turn.[11] An Apulian bell *krater* in the Louvre has an impressive representation of the purification of Orestes inspired directly by the Aeschylean text. Apollo himself is holding the piglet directly over the head of Orestes, who is seated; its blood will flow directly over his head. But then it can be made to disappear: Guilt "can be washed away."[12]

There is no evidence in Babylonia for this kind of purification of blood through blood, as Farnell was right to state.[13] However, the very ritual with the sacrificial piglet being held over the head of a person, to be slaughtered and to drench the patient with blood, is represented dramatically in another vase painting, on a *krater* found at Canicattini; yet the objective in this case is not to purify a murderer, but to cure the daughters of Proetus of their "madness."[14] This madness had been caused by some ritual transgression by the girls which varies in different versions of the myth; the cure is directed against the manifest sufferings which have resulted from it. Compared with this even the case of Orestes takes on a double meaning: Orestes too has become mad; he is manifestly suffering from his illness. So is it atonement or just healing that has to be procured by purification ritual? To raise the question is to see the irrelevance of this distinction. That social and physio-psychic ills were not clearly differentiated in archaic societies, that administration of justice and healing can be seen to fuse, has often been brought out and discussed in more recent anthropology. An offense is the source of illness, illness is the result of an offense, be it in the personal, the social, or the religious sphere. Even in Greek the word *nosos,* illness, embraces both, the physical and the social disturbances, ailments and sufferings.[15] The effect of the therapy which the "knowing" specialist is able to apply is no less broad. In other words, the purification of Orestes could equally well be understood as the healing of an illness, even before Euripides brought this interpretation onstage in his tragedy *Orestes*. Orestes was both mad and guilty and had to be cured at both levels. Then, however, the boundary between the Babylonian and the Greek becomes much less distinct.

A bilingual ritual text from the collection "Evil Demons of Illness" (*Asakki marṣuti*) has the following prescription for the exorcist—it is presented as a command issued from the sky god Anu to his son Marduk:

> [Take] a suckling pig [and . . . at] the head of the sick man [put it (?) and] take out its heart and above the heart of the sick man [put it], [sprinkle] its blood on the sides of the bed, [and] divide the pig over his limbs and spread it on the sick man; then cleanse that man with pure water from the Deep [*Apsu*] and wash him clean and bring near him a censer [and] a torch, place twice seven loaves cooked in the ashes against the outer door, and give the pig as his substitute, and give the flesh and the blood as his blood: they [the demons] shall take it; the heart which thou hast placed upon his heart, as his heart give it: they shall take it. [lacuna] [that the] pig may be his substitute . . . May the evil spirit, the evil demon stand aside! May the kindly spirit, the kindly demon be present![16]

This ritual is not identical with the one we are to envisage for Orestes and the Proetids from the Greek representations, but the similarity is undeniable: the condition of sickness, the knowledgeable specialist, the sacrificial piglet, slaughter, contact with blood, and the subsequent cleansing with water. The torch and the incense bowl belong to the apparatus of Greek purification priests, too.[17]

What is peculiar in the Mesopotamian text is the emphasis on substitution, to which we shall return. In this respect it most closely resembles a ritual described by Ovid in the context of the Roman festival Carmentalia, a ritual against magical birds, *striges,* said to feed on babies at night—that is, de facto against children's disease. Once more the sacrifice of a suckling pig occurs, performed by the goddess Carmenta herself as a mythical model, with the explicit formula of substitution: "Take the heart for the heart, the intestines for the intestines, we give this life for a better one." [18] Is this a case of a spontaneous parallel arising from general "elementary ideas" of the human mind, or is it simply the case that in the lower realm of witches and magic the cultural barriers are more permeable than at the level of higher literature?

If one regards Orestes as a case of sickness (*nosos*), then sickness appears personified to a remarkable degree: It is described as an attack by demons. The Erinyes are imagined as beasts of prey, "dogs" who want to suck his blood, leech the life-force from him. Remarkably enough, already in Homer sickness is once described as an "attack by a hateful demon." [19] The magicians ridiculed by the author of the Hippocratic treatise *On the Sacred Disease* also speak of attacks (*ephodoi*) of demons or gods. The concept of savage, rapacious, carnivorous demons who cause sickness is common if not fundamental in Mesopotamian healing magic. But there is also the less personalized concept of the curse of murder, which has to be eliminated by a ritual in the "wash house." [20]

In spite of these similarities, however, it is clear that the peculiar function of atonement for murder for which Orestes is a model case, the system of purification current in archaic Greece, is not just some Babylonian import. Farnell was right to that extent. But this does not rule out cultural connections; on the contrary. In Mesopotamia blood guilt had been regulated by state law from early times, as the law codes attest; there was no problem left. Unaffected by law, however, were individual sufferings, those recurring sicknesses surmised to be caused by some guilt which could not be defined in legal terms, or some demon going astray. This was the sphere of the practitioners, the priest-exorcists. In archaic Greece, in fact, the corresponding practice would not only meet private needs of manifest sufferings, but also fill a vacuum covering "social illness"—disruption of the community through murder, through the shedding of blood. Written laws were to appear only gradually with the development of the *polis,* and were difficult to enforce. In the meantime magic "therapy" had a chance to gain public significance to a degree which was unthinkable in the sphere of eastern governmental bureaucracy. The Greeks lacked straightforward institutions of monarchic power and law, uncertainty being the touchstone of freedom. Thus "sickness" might involve an entire city which needed healing atonement: After the Cylonian sacrilege, Athens summoned Epimenides from Crete, and he restored order through ritual.[21] The difference between the eastern civilizations and Greece corresponds to the specific levels of culture attained in different regions. This does not obviate influence, transfer, or adoption; but any import would win a new function and thus develop some new forms in its new context. The ritual practice itself as it had for a long time been conducted by eastern exorcists, the sacrifice of a suckling pig, hardly had to change.

To keep themselves "clean" is an elementary need of human beings; no wonder cleansing ceremonies play their role worldwide in profane as well as in religious varieties. Similar procedures and similar formulas are to be expected: "Begone, Evil! Come in, Well being!" is one of the most common exhortations. It is still remarkable that it is attested both in Mesopotamia, as a common inscription on magical figurines, and in Greek apotropaic ritual.[22] In both cultures, too, mere contact with an unclean person or unclean matter is to be feared. "He has come into contact with a woman of unclean hands . . . or he has come into contact with a man of unclean hands . . . or his hand has touched one of unclean body": these are some of the conjectures made by the exorcist when dealing with a case of sickness. One should not talk to a man who is carrying guilt, nor eat and drink with him, the Akkadian prescription warns; the same warning applies to dealing with a murderer in Greece: only after Orestes' purification was "contact without damage" possible.[23]

Branches also are of special use in purifications, alongside piglet blood, torches, and water from the sea. In the Akkadian poem *I Will Praise the Lord of Wisdom* the man celebrating his healing portrays a dream of hope: "And in [my dream] I [saw] a remarkable young [man . . .] holding in his hand a tamarisk rod of purification . . . the water he was carrying he threw over me, pronounced the life-giving incantation, and rubbed [my body]." Compare the legend of the origin of Apollo's cult at Didyma: Branchos, the Apollonian seer, freed the Milesians of the plague: "he sprinkled the people with laurel branches . . . the people spoke the responses"; Callimachus has Branchos speak a formula two or three times which the people do not understand.[24] Is there a foreign language involved here? One tempting association: *branchia* means gills of fish in Greek; Branchidai is the name of the "family" of priests who ran the sanctuary of Didyma down to the Persian era. Now, a characteristic representation in the context of Mesopotamian healing magic is a man with the head of a fish, worn like a mask over his head, carrying an instrument of purification in his right hand and a water bucket in his left; the figure can be identified as representing an *apkallu,* a "wise man" from olden times. Figures of this kind definitely reached northern Syria.[25] Did some healer bring this requisite as far as Didyma, thus causing the nickname Branchidai, "gills family," to be given to his clan?

Another, drastic purification procedure is that of "wiping off" (*apomattein*). Demosthenes uses the term in his invective against the mother of Aeschines, the priestess of purifications and initiations; the commentary says that the person to be purified was plastered all over with mud and chaff which was then scraped off. A "purifier of the army, the one who knows the things for wiping off" is mentioned in Sophocles.[26] Wiping off (*kuppuru*), generally with flour paste (*lišu*), is, however, also a well-documented practice of purification priests in Mesopotamia.[27] The importance of the practice is reflected in the fact that the root of this word came to mean purification in general in Hebrew, even without the corresponding practice: Yom Kippur is the "Day of Purification." The practice itself links the Akkadian with the Greek. A purifying substance which is often mentioned in eastern texts is asphalt (*kupru* in Akkadian); *asphaltos,* however, is also one of the materials used by the witches of Sophron, or by Melampus in the comic's parody.[28] Even more surprising is the use of onions for purification. Akkadian texts describe the procedure in detail—the onion is peeled layer by layer, until nothing is left; in Greek we find just the passing mention of the magical onions; one sort of onion is specifically named after Epimenides the famous purifier.[29]

Anything left over from the purification must be carefully disposed of: "They threw the *lymata* into the sea," the *Iliad* says (1.314). The Babylonian exorcists may throw away the water with "all the evil";[30] then other persons should take care not to come into contact with it. Better still to use a pot in which everything, including previously manufactured magic figurines, can be securely enclosed.[31] Correspondingly, in Greece a pot called a *pharmake* would be made available for "those who purify the cities."[32] In Mesopotamia the remains, including the cinders from the sacrificial fire, are "thrown onto a barren place," "buried in abandoned wastelands," "deposited in the steppe under a thornbush."[33] The Hippocratic text *On the Sacred Disease* reports on the magical healers: "And they hide the remains of the purifications partly in the earth, part they cast into the sea, part they carry away to the mountains where no one can touch them or step on them."[34] In Mesopotamia, putting one's foot "in some unclean water," the residue of some purification ceremony, was thought to be one of the possible causes of illness; it was not different in the West even in Roman imperial times: "In which residue from purification did you step at the crossroads at night?" suffering Encolpius is asked in Petronius' romance. Within the framework of much older Roman ritual, the ritual of *devotio,* a substitute image was buried, and in consequence "no Roman official was allowed to get to that place."[35] It would be still better to let birds carry off the evil plague; this was done in Thessaly, but also in the Mosaic law.[36]

Another striking detail: Epimenides, the most famous priest of purification, received a miraculous food from the nymphs which allowed him to get by without ordinary sustenance, a no-hunger drug (*alimon*). He kept it in a cow's hoof[37]—as if ordinary containers were not able to hold it. The text of an Akkadian exorcism prescribes: "You fill a cow's hoof with water, throw in bittercorn meal, strike it with a reed in face of the sun god, you pour it out: the dead will be kept away."[38] The effect is different, but the prescription is clearly related. According to the *Alexander* romance, the poison of Antipater which brought about the death of Alexander the Great in Babylon was carried in a mule's hoof.[39]

Skeptics can still doubt the existence of direct cultural contact and insist on the possibility of spontaneous parallels rising again and again within general forms of "superstition." Yet it is precisely with the name Epimenides that the historical horizon of the orientalizing period comes into play. It is archaic Crete which, according to the Greek texts, is the home of "cathartic" knowledge. Epimenides in particular is connected with the cult caves of Crete, with a cave of Zeus—tradition varies as to which of the famous caves was concerned—where he experienced his initiation in a sleep that lasted for decades. He assumes the function of initiator in turn at the cave of Zeus on Mount Ida.[40] If the historical Epimenides ever did seek out this cave he would have stood face to face with the Assyrian-style tympanon there which was probably made for the cult of Zeus by eastern craftsmen.[41] Even before Epimenides, Thaletas of Gortyn had been active as a charismatic musician; he cured a plague in Sparta.[42] Gortyn was no less a center of orientalizing craftsmanship. We are led back into the realm of myth with Karmanor of Crete, the priest who purified even Apollo after the god had slain the Delphic dragon.[43] The name does not appear to be Greek. In any event, Crete is not only the ancient center of Minoan culture but also—after Cyprus—the area most closely connected with the Semitic East in the geometric and early orientalizing period. There are strange ritual connections of Apollo himself with Semitic culture, above all in the celebrations of the day of the new moon and of the seventh day of the month.[44] In this light the assumption of pure coincidence becomes the most unlikely of hypotheses.

The question remains whether linguistic borrowings can provide key proof for cultural ties with the East. There is little to be gained from non-Greek proper names such as Karmanor or even Branchos and Rhakios.[45] It carries more weight that the root *kathar,* to clean/to purify, has no Indo-European etymology but ties in with a Semitic root in the sphere of purification: *qatar,* to fumigate.[46] One cleansing substance in this context is sulphur: Fumigation with sulphur is used in Homer for both practical and ritual means. No less suggestive is the similarity of the sound of the Akkadian word for "dirty, polluted" and "to stain, to pollute," *lu"u* or *luwwu,*[47] to the word for the dirt to be cleansed in Greek ritual, *lymata* or *lythron.* Here we encounter a word root without Indo-European etymology provided with two alternative Greek suffixes. The Greeks would somehow associate this word with either *lyein,* to solve, or rather with *louein,* to wash, but the rules of normal word formation do not permit the one, and they allow the other only with difficulty. There are similar problems with the Latin word *lustrum* in the context of purifications, which the Romans would tend to associate with *lux,* light. It is true that both word groups, *lymata* and *kathairein,* appear in Homer. *Kathairein* and *katharos* are quite common: They had risen above the status of foreign words. Such a claim would apply even more to a third homonymy in this sphere: *ara* means prayer and curse; it is Chryses the *areter* who can summon up a plague with his prayer or rather curse the Greeks and banish the plague again. In Akkadian the word "to curse" is *araru;* the order given to Bileam by the king of Moab is, in Hebrew, *ara!,* "curse!" A Greek would undoubtedly have understood this word in this situation, if not grammatically then at least its meaning in context. What creates difficulties is the fact that the Greek word originally had the form *arwa,* as its derivatives in the various dialects indicate.[48] This does not go together with *araru,* which has no *w* in its root.

To sum up, there are suggestive possibilities, but no incontrovertible proofs of linguistic borrowing in the sphere of purification ceremonies. It would, however, be no less bold to deny their existence altogether. The continuum from the Mesopotamian culture to the Mediterranean is there.

Spirits of the Dead and Black Magic

The evil forces against which purification is supposed to assist are conceived of as malevolent, carnivorous demons.[1] Next to the various fantastical names which are invoked in this connection, the spirit of the dead, *eṭemmu,* plays an unpleasant role, too.[2] Spirits of the dead are regarded with fear even in Greece, as Erwin Rohde in particular has brought to attention.[3] In Homer this kind of dread is suppressed rather than not yet known.

The hypothesis of animism as a universal stage in the evolution of human civilization, which influenced Rohde, precluded rather than encouraged culturally specific comparisons. Nevertheless, the extent to which the Homeric concept of Hades corresponds to the Mesopotamian is striking: a realm of mud and darkness that leaves no hope for mortals. It is described in a famous scene of *Gilgamesh* when the ghost of Enkidu meets his friend, a scene which may have links with Homer even on a literary level.[4] Ritual appeasement of the dead is achieved in very similar ways by Mesopotamians and by Greeks, preferably through various kinds of libation: "water, beer, roasted corn, milk, honey, cream, oil" in Mesopotamia;[5] "milk, honey, water, wine, and oil" in Aeschylus.[6] Even more peculiar is the importance of pure water as an offering to the dead: "cool water," "pure water."[7] The insertion of pipes into a grave for precisely this purpose is unusual in Greece,[8] but there is direct literary evidence of the practice in Mesopotamia.[9]

Those dead who show themselves capable of affecting the living are called *heroes* in Greek. A fragment of Aristophanes shows in a particularly lively and entertaining way just how these heroes have the power to bring down all manner of illnesses on the living if they are not appeased.[10] The Akkadian *eṭemmu* can equally be the cause of many kinds of sickness, so he is met with similar fears. Again we have extensive Sumero-Akkadian incantation texts for documentation:[11] "When the spirit of a dead person has taken possession of a man," or "the hand of a spirit of the dead,"[12] then exorcism is due. The sick person believes himself to feel this grip, and he prays: "If it is the spirit of a member of my family or my household or the spirit of one slain in battle or a wandering spirit . . ."[13] It is indicative of the psycho-social constraints involved in sickness that the spirits of closely related persons are especially to be feared: "The hand of the spirits of his father and his mother has seized him."[14] No less dreaded is the anger of those who have not met with a natural death, the *biaiothanatoi,* as the Greeks would say: The one "killed in battle" and the unburied "who lies in the wilderness without the covering of the earth," "whose body was thrown onto the steppe . . . : his spirit wanders restlessly over the earth."[15] Even a "foreign spirit," "whose name no one knows," can be the active cause behind the torments of the sick.[16]

The Greek term for this wrath of the dead is *menima.* It appears in a significant context as early as in Homer: Hector, dying, threatens Achilles, who is to refuse him a proper burial, saying that he could become a "cause of wrath [*menima*] of the gods" for him, on that day when Achilles will be killed himself. In a less dramatic way, deceased Elpenor, meeting Odysseus in the underworld, demands a decent burial so that he will not become a *menima.*[17] These are the critical, dangerous cases, somebody "killed in battle" or else unburied and hence restlessly wandering about. Plato states expressly that "ancient *menimata*" manifest themselves in "great sufferings" which affect "particular families," arising "out of old, uncleansed wrongdoings"; they are to be cured with ceremonies of purification and initiation involving madness.[18] In his *Laws,* Plato wants to emphasize the moral factor, but he cannot help but mention purifications. Again the old and renowned specialist in this type of purification is Epimenides, who prophesied "not over that which was to come, but over that which was past."[19]

There was, of course, no lack of people who were willing to make use of the wrath of the spirits of the dead in order to direct it against personal enemies, through black magic. The most direct practice, well known throughout antiquity, is to make an image of the person to be harmed and to bury it in a grave. In this way the victim will fall prey to the dead and to the gods of the underworld. Such figurines are usually referred to as "voodoo dolls" today—an indication that the same practice may occur in widely different civilizations. Such a voodoo doll from the Periclean era has been found in the Kerameikos cemetery at Athens. But the same practice was also employed by evil witches in Babylonia. Thus the sick person complains: "You have handed figurines of me to a corpse," "my image has been placed in a tomb"; "if figurines of a man have been entrusted to a dead man behind him," the man will experience a loss of vitality.[20] Magic countercharms are contained above all in the *Maqlû* collection.

This is not the only form of black magic to appear in both Greece and Mesopotamia. The "making of an image," "taking saliva, hair, the hem of a robe, footprints,"[21] may well be thought simply to represent universal forms of magic. The "hem of the robe" is also used in the *Pharmakeutria* of Theocritus.[22] There are also Akkadian love charms which use figurines.[23] The *Pharmakeutria* refers specifically to a "foreigner from Assyria" who supplied a particularly potent substance.[24] This is Hellenistic; but already Plato portrays the uncanny effect on the citizens of a town "when they catch sight of wax models outside a door or at a crossroads or on a tomb, perhaps that of their own parents":[25] These magical practices have already been with the Greeks for a long time. In the same way in Babylon people are frightened by "fabrications which show up," indicating that "life has been cut" by someone.[26] Countermagic is urgently necessary in such a case.

A powerful rite of annihilation is to melt down wax effigies. This is done by the sorceress in Theocritus as it is practiced in Mesopotamia. In Egypt the use of wax figures in magic is attested as early as the third millennium.[27] From the eighth century we have a relevant Aramaic text, the treaty text of Sfire—a rare opportunity to document what lay in between Babylonia and Greece. This is an international contract concluded by solemn oaths and curses; in this context it is said: "As this wax is

consumed by fire, thus . . . (N.N.) shall be consumed by fire."
In the seventh century the same formula appears in a contract
made between the Assyrian king Esarhaddon and his vassals;
much earlier it is found in a Hittite soldiers' oath.[28] It corresponds to the oath of the Cyreneans as set out in their foundation decree, transmitted through a fourth-century inscription;
whether this is an authentic document from the seventh century
remains controversial: "They formed wax images and burned
them while praying that anyone who did not keep the oath but
flouted it might melt and flow away like the images."[29] At any
rate the practice is well attested for the archaic period through
the parallel from Sfire, and oath-taking rituals of international
character have the best chances to cross cultural borders.

There is one name in the sphere of black magic which definitely travelled from Sumer into Hellenistic Egypt and on to
Carthage: Ereshkigal is the Sumerian name of the terrible goddess of the underworld, and Ereskhigal is the name of an infernal goddess which commonly appears in later Greek defixions
and magical papyri.[30] This is one of the most exact transcrip-
tions from Sumerian into Greek: Coincidental homonymy in
the case of such a sequence of syllables is out of the question. So
far only texts from the imperial era with this name seem to have
been published. But given that the influence of Babylon had
long since ceased and cuneiform had been forgotten, the period
of borrowing may well be much earlier. In the realm of magic,
though, exact chronology may be less important than elsewhere. In any case the name Ereshkigal is proof of the far-
reaching influence of Mesopotamian magic, as is the "Assyrian"
in Theocritus.

Another text from Cyrene should be considered in this context: In the fourth century B.C. an extensive sacred law on purification rites as sanctioned by the Delphic oracle was recorded
at Cyrene; to judge from the contents, it could be much older.[31]
We are concerned here with the section headed *Hikesion*. The
word *hikesios* is believed to be well understood, meaning "he
who has reached" in the sense of suppliant; so the first commentators had no doubt that it is the treatment of suppliants nor-

mally called *hiketai* which is being dealt with here. Yet under
this assumption the individual prescriptions made in the text
must seem highly abstruse. It is no coincidence that John Gould,
in his exemplary treatment of *hiketeia,* did not consider the Cy-
renean text.[32] Three cases are set apart in the sacred law from
Cyrene: first a *hikesios* "sent from elsewhere," *epaktos.* The main
problem with this fellow seems to be to establish who has
sent him:

> If he has been sent to the house, if [the owner] knows from
> whom he has come on him, he will call his name, pronounc-
> ing it three times a day; if he has died in the country or was
> lost elsewhere, if he knows the name, he will pronounce him
> by name; if he does not know [he will pronounce]: "Oh you
> man, whether you are man or woman"; he will make effigies,
> [one] male and [one] female, from wood or clay; he will re-
> ceive them [in his house] and present [them] with a portion
> of everything. When you have done what is customary, then
> take them into an uncultivated wood and cast them into the
> ground, the effigies and their portions [of the meal].[33]

It is strange that this ritual could ever have been held to be the
purification and acceptance of a suppliant: No one is seen to care
for such a person who should be present and in need of protection; the concern is about some individual, known or unknown,
who is clearly absent but is presumed to have sent the *hikesios;*
and one obviously wishes urgently to get rid of this again. If
one looks for a counterpart of this practice as described in the
passage quoted, the closest parallel is provided by Akkadian
magic literature. Here, once more for the healing of a sick person, an effigy of "everything evil" is produced, placed on the
roof next to the sickbed, and tended for three days. Then, to the
accompaniment of incantations, the effigy is enclosed in a pot,
taken away, and buried in "an abandoned wilderness."[34] The
correspondence between the procedures—the making of a figurine, the tending of it, its disposal in the wilderness—is perfect;
and thus the word "sent" in the Greek text becomes clear:
"Sending upon" (*epagoge*) is a well-known term of black magic;

in Plato it ranks directly next to the *defixio*.³⁵ A sorcerer "sends" evil "onto the head" of his enemies. That is why it is so important to find out who is behind it in order to strike at the root of the evil, or rather, in the sense of appeasement, to come to some solution by agreement. For this reason the effigy of everything evil is first fed and then energetically disposed of. The conclusion is that, in Cyrene, *hikesios* does not mean suppliant, but an evil spirit who "comes upon" a house or person.³⁶

The hypothesis must stand or fall in the light of the other two paragraphs in Apollo's sacred law for Cyrene, covering other cases of *hikesioi* and how to deal with them.³⁷ The second section is preserved almost completely intact, but its understanding is made difficult by the unclear meaning of three terms, applied here in a special, technical way unknown from other documents: *teliskesthai, ateles/tetelesmenos,* and *propheresthai.* In addition, the archaic style often does not identify the subject of the verb; nor do we know what the "public shrine" (*damosion hieron*) of Cyrene was. The following analysis attempts to render the structure of the law without the benefit of more information, taking *telein* in the general sense of "performance of a ritual."³⁸ The "other" *hikesios,* either with or without performance of ritual, has "taken his seat at the public shrine"; if there is a "pronouncement," then ritual is to be performed on the terms pronounced; if there is no pronouncement, then an annual offering of fruits of the field accompanied by libation has to be made in perpetuity. If one should forget that, double offerings are due the next year; if a descendant should omit it, forgetting it, and there is a pronouncement for him, he will pay to the god and sacrifice whatever will be revealed to him by the oracle—if he knows, to the father's god; otherwise the oracle is to be consulted.

It is clear that this text is about setting up and maintaining a cult. Interpreters who take this to refer to a human suppliant must make three additional assumptions: It is dealing with the case of a murderer—although only the third section of the law speaks of killing; the cult is for the benefit of the victim of murder; the pronouncement is made by a priest: "[the priest] lays down," and "performance of ritual" means acceptance to citizenship, "to be initiated."[39] But with these assumptions, the very first line of the text would be absurd: the ritual can "either be performed or not," and it seems that it can be repeated. Further, the priest would be free either to set the terms or not as capriciously as he wishes; precisely if he(?) "does not pronounce," sacrifices shall be made in perpetuity, whereas in the other case the atonement is made once and forever. Above all, if a problem arises in a subsequent generation, why should first a priest and then, in addition, an oracle "establish" the sacrifice? The directives are different and much clearer indeed if one decides to imagine that some powerful spirit is asserting himself, whether in a dream or in the form of visions or auditions; under these circumstances there will be a religious procedure, "according to command" (kat' epitagen), as it is so often expressed in inscriptions. The term pronouncement (propheresthai) then recovers its well-established meaning of "to reproach, to complain": it means the same as "to express a menima"; it is also close to the term "to give a sign of divine will," episemainein. If there is no precise manifestation, if the spirit has only inflicted wordless horror on people, then the usual form of appeasing sacrifice for the dead applies: fruits of the earth and libations for the dead. Children and children's children are affected insofar as the cult of the dead is mostly a cult of ancestors. Thus a forgotten ancestor can express his displeasure and "complain": "The spirit of a member of my family has laid hold of me," as an Akkadian text would put it. In case of doubt one must consult an oracle to find out the correct offerings to be made. These should be made to the family god if he is known—"they make their sacrifices to Zeus Karios," states Herodotus of the family of Isagoras in Athens;[40] otherwise the oracle will also establish who this should be. Thus the text makes sense, if only in the sense of what we call superstition. Teliskesthai then means the ritual establishment of a cult. That the public sanctuary of Cyrene should have been particularly connected with the cult of heroes is an attractive assumption.

The third section in the law of Cyrene is unclear as to the decisive term concerning the third variety of hikesios, autophonos:

"one who killed with his own hands" or "one who killed himself"? Here the intrusion of the one who "came on" is met by a counter-rite of "making him who arrives go," *aphiketeuein*.[41] This vocabulary makes it clear again that we are not dealing with the acceptance of a suppliant in the community, but rather with someone one desires to get rid of. The text has some lacunae, however, supplements of which remain doubtful. The person affected has to "announce" the ritual; he makes somebody sit on a fleece on the threshold[42] and anoints him. Then he will go out with attendants onto the public highway while all who meet him keep silent, receiving the harbinger, until—there is a gap here; that "sacrifices and other" (rites?) take place is still legible. If this text were dealing with the purification of one stained with murder, then a final act of integration, with admission to the city's shrines, would have to be assumed; editors have proposed their supplements accordingly. The part of the text which is preserved, however, speaks of leading "away," "going out," "passing by"; and it mentions a marginal region where "three tribes meet" (*triphylia*);[43] silence is appropriate in the presence of "more powerful beings";[44] this is a ritual not of integration but of riddance, in all probability involving demons rather than living people.[45]

The counterargument remains that the word *hikesios* in some other Greek texts clearly carries the meaning "suppliant," and never else occurs with the meaning "haunting spirit." However, there is an exact parallel in the dual meaning of the word *prostropaios,* meaning literally "he who turns to somebody." Since Aeschylus we find this word in use not only for a suppliant but also for a demon who attaches himself to one. Nevertheless this meaning has often been mistaken, particularly in the Liddell–Scott lexicon, even though expressions such as "the *prostropaios* of Myrtilus [murdered treacherously] followed him" in Pausanias or the combination of *prostropaios* with "Erinyes and spirits of vengeance" in Polybius is clear enough.[46] The threatening invocations of the *prostropaios* of the dead in Antiphon the orator and already in Aeschylus are to be understood correspondingly.[47] The "one who approaches" can be an unclean person or an evil spirit of the dead; the same ambivalence is peculiar to both Greek words. It is true that in this interpretation the document from Cyrene shows Apollonian religion more deeply involved in "superstition" than some Hellenists have been willing to accept. They will hardly be delighted at the fact that a parallel from a Mesopotamian ritual text is found helpful for establishing the meaning of a purely Greek word. The borderlines between the eastern and the Greek are seen to melt away.

Substitute Sacrifice

In a situation of pursuit, seized by panic, human beings are naturally relieved if another creature suffers that fate in their place. Substitute sacrifices are widespread.[1] They were particularly common in Mesopotamia because basic anxieties were conventionally given shape there in the forms of demonic carnivores.[2] This was less common in Greece. All the more notable, then, is one particular account, a cult legend from the sanctuary of Artemis of Munichia at Athens.

Once again it is a pestilence in which the anger of the goddess is made manifest. The cause is said to be the killing of a sacred bear. For atonement, the goddess demands the sacrifice of a young girl. "Embaros promised to do this on the condition that his family would be granted the office of priest for their lifetime. He dressed up his daughter, but hid her in the temple, dressed up a goat with a garment as his daughter, and sacrificed that." This is the text of Pausanias the Atticist; the version in the collection of proverbs of Zenobius is very similar. Embaros was mentioned in the comedies of Menander.[3]

It is clear that this anecdote describes a ritual, a substitute sacrifice performed in the cult of Artemis for the lifting of a pestilence. The myth of Iphigenia's sacrifice at Aulis obtrudes itself as a parallel, where the goddess herself is said to have finally substituted a hind for the virgin. But the Munichia legend portrays the actual manipulations much more graphically. To what extent this can be taken as evidence for actual cult is by no means certain, though. There is no other information about a family of Embaros or a priesthood of Embarids in the Attic prosopography. But to assume that we are dealing with pure invention would make the proverbial status of Embaros even less explicable.

There are well-documented rituals elsewhere in which an animal is substituted for a human being; a remarkable instance is the provision in the old Law of the Twelve Tables in Rome: *aries subicitur,* "a ram is substituted."[4] The closest parallel, however, is provided by a Mesopotamian incantation text.

This text deals with the healing of a sick person. It bears the title "Substitution of a Man for Ereshkigal." Ereshkigal is the Sumerian-Akkadian goddess of the underworld. The substitute is an "unmated goat." It is put into bed with the sick person and is supposed to spend the night with him. At dawn the conjurer arrives, throws the goat and the sick person out of the bed onto the floor, touches the throat of the sick person with a wooden knife, and then cuts the throat of the goat with a real knife. The slaughtered goat is then stuffed with spices, it is dressed in a robe and given shoes, its eyes are adorned, the headgear of the sick person is wound round its head, and it is tended "as if it were a dead man" while the sick person leaves the house. The conjurer speaks an incantation, raises the lamentation for the dead over the body, brings offerings for the dead, makes libations of water, beer, roasted corn, milk, honey, cream, and oil; finally, with offerings for the "spirit of the dead of the family" and the goat, he buries the animal. In this way the sick person is delivered.[5]

The differences between the two rituals should not be overlooked. In Munichia a sacrifice at the altar of a sanctuary is described, whereas, in the East, dying at home in bed is acted out. The similarity of the charade, which in both cases has a sacrificial goat dressed up in human clothes, is striking nevertheless; and the Munichia legend is concerned with the healing of sickness, too. Gellius states that in the Roman cult of Veiovis a goat is sacrificed *ritu humano;* this may well point to a somewhat similar form of ritual.[6] On Tenedos, in the cult of Dionysus Anthroporraistes the "Smasher of Men"—once more within the ideology of human sacrifice—the calf sacrificed to the god is provided with buskins, while the butcher has to flee.[7]

We see there is no lack of parallels. Direct contact could be proved by linguistic borrowings, but, nevertheless, it remains a "perhaps." The name Embaros—with the long *a*—does not sound Greek, at least not Attic. Pausanias and subsequently other lexicons give the name Baros as a variant. This sounds even more exotic but corresponds precisely to the Akkadian word for seer, *barû*.[8] One could assume that there lies behind the legend an actual event when a seer of eastern origin employed a substitute sacrifice to lift a pestilence with apparent success. The cult and shrine of Artemis at Munichia is linked to the month Munichion in the Attic calendar and, like other festivals of Artemis, has the aura of Greek girls' initiations; this can hardly be an oriental import in its entirety. Furthermore, the evidence for the form *Baros* is weak: The Menander texts, which are the oldest documents we have and on which the lexicons rely, clearly have *Embaros*. However, additional rituals are not excluded even in established cults, and all sorts of accidents may befall imported words. Even if the exact path of tradition cannot be established, the East-West parallel of ritual substitute deserves notice.

Asclepius and Asgelatas

Three small bronze statuettes from the Hera sanctuary on Samos provide the strongest evidence of Babylonian imports to Greece as regards sickness demons and healing gods. Two of them, first published in 1979, were excavated from levels dated to the seventh century (Figure 4).[1] These bronzes represent a man standing at prayer with a large dog. As confirmed by similar finds from Babylonia and also by cuneiform texts, these figures are connected with the Babylonian goddess of healing, Gula of Isin, the "great physician," *azugallatu*. Dogs were sacrificed in her cult: A whole series of dog burials has come to light at her shrine at Isin.[2]

If several figurines of this type were dedicated to Hera on Sa-

Figure 4. Babylonian bronze figurine, "dog and dog-leader," from the cult of the Babylonian healing goddess Gula, found in the Hera sanctuary at Samos.

mos, they cannot be merely coincidental souvenirs. It is more likely that Hera is being approached as a goddess of healing, too; such assistance was requested from practically all the gods but especially from the goddesses. Whether the dedication of these bronzes originated with eastern merchants who had reached Samos or whether they had been brought from the East by Greeks such as Alcaeus' brother Antimenidas, who—somewhat later— served as a mercenary at Babylon, cannot be established. What sickness means can easily be understood across the language barriers; and if a particular talisman seems to be efficacious against it, this will be accepted with equal ease.

But this is not the whole story. We are led to go further by the striking role of the dog in the cult of the main Greek god of healing, Asclepius. A dog was standing next to the chryselephantine statue of Asclepius in his temple at Epidaurus; a dedicatory relief from there has dogs alongside the sons of Asclepius.[3] Myth relates that as a child Asclepius was exposed on Mount Kynortion, where he was nourished by a bitch and found by huntsmen with dogs[4]—*kynegetai,* dog-leaders, in Greek; in addition, actual cult comes to the fore with the requirement of a *lex sacra* from the shrine of Asclepius at Piraeus: Who seeks healing, it is stated, must make preliminary sacrifice of three cakes to Maleatas, Apollo, Hermes, Iaso, Akeso, and Panakeia, and finally to "dogs and dog-leaders," that is, huntsmen.[5]

These dogs and dog-leaders can be explained by reference to myth; but the bronzes from the shrine of Hera present a much more direct and graphic explanation: Here dogs and dog-leaders are seen in effigy. One can easily assume that figures of this type were also to be seen at the shrine of Asclepius at Piraeus; they were treated with respect, just like the other gods and powers in the retinue of Asclepius, and thus had their part in the ritual. Dogs and dog-leaders as recipients of a preliminary sacrifice also appear in a grotesque parody of cult in a piece by the comic poet Plato.[6] This, therefore, was a well-known, somehow remarkable detail of a certain cult. It becomes comprehensible as soon as one considers the statues of the Samian Hera sanctuary: By their very existence, they indicate a peculiar East–West understanding in the realm of healing gods.

From another place we are induced to a leap forward into the linguistic evidence. Gula, the goddess of healing, patroness of dogs and dog-leaders, is called *azugallatu,* "the great physician," in Akkadian.[7] On the Cycladic island Anaphe near Thera, however, and only there, Apollo is worshipped as Asgelatas and celebrated with a festival, Asgelaia.[8] The name, which does not sound Greek, has repeatedly attracted attention, particularly as it has a ring not too dissimilar from the name of Apollo's son Asklapios/Asclepius, which equally defies explanation.[9] *Az(u)gallat(u)* and *Asgelat(as)* sound perfectly identical, if the variable morphemes are omitted; the sequence of syllables is complicated enough to exclude sheer coincidence, and the meaning fits: Being a physician is one of the most important honors of Apollo, who is expressly called physician (*ietros*) in other cults.[10] It is true that in consequence the name of the festival, Asgelaia, must be secondary, reconstructed from the name Asgelatas as if this had the normal Greek suffix *-tas, -tes.* If the equation Azugallatu/Asgelatas is accepted, it follows that there must once have been a healer on this island who invoked the name of the Mesopotamian *azugallatu* against a pestilence and ostensibly succeeded in driving the disease away. From that time Apollo Asgelatas was worshipped there, as Apollo Epikurios at Bassae was credited with succoring at the great plague[11]—or as Santa Maria della Salute was to receive worship much later at Venice. Apollo Asgelatas, then, provides the most direct proof of the infiltration of charismatic practitioners of the eastern tradition into archaic Greece, parallel to the Gula bronzes found on Samos.

The way in which the Greek language absorbs and suppresses these foreign terms is particularly evident in this case. The deceptively similar form *Aiglatas* is attested quite early on Anaphe, "Apollo of the radiant sky"; this epithet has also made its way into the myth of the Argonauts; it appears in dedications as early as the fifth century B.C.[12] Who could guess at the existence of Akkadian behind such crystal-clear Greek? It is a lucky chance that the strange but official names of the cult and the festival have been preserved in a few epigraphic documents. It is evident that Asgelatas is the *lectio difficilior,* hence older than Aiglatas. The name Asgelatas is, therefore, attributable to the archaic epoch at the latest. Thus the external evidence leads close to the orientalizing period, to which the Samian dog-leaders belong.

One further reference to a word from the sphere of Asclepius the physician: One word for headache or dizziness attested since the Aristotelian *Problems* is *karos.* It has no Greek etymology. But in Akkadian *kâru* means "to be dizzy," and in Aramaic *karah,* "to be ill."[13] Coincidence is quite possible with such a simple sequence of phonemes, but one can as well imagine that the term came to the Greeks with the eastern banqueting fashions, especially the introduction of couches on which to recline (*klinai*) in place of chairs, which is distinctive of the Greek symposium since the end of the seventh century but first makes its appearance with Ashurbanipal. There may be more loan-words of the kind in medical vocabulary; what is unusual is that *karos* escaped camouflage.

Ecstatic Divination

Divination is a strange art which only specialists can practice successfully under particular circumstances. Sometimes stress is laid on the outwardly technical, acquired apparatus of the diviner, which seems easy to learn; sometimes it is the particular state of mind that is seen to be all-important, be it called possession, trance, or madness. With the Greeks, the "raving" seer first appears onstage in Aeschylus' *Agamemnon,* in the great scene of Cassandra. But already earlier Heraclitus had spoken of the Sibyl prophesying "with raving mouth," and Herodotus presupposes ecstatic prophecy at the Ptoon oracle by 480.[1] Then Plato discusses divinatory madness at a highly philosophical level; in this context he clearly confirms that the most famous seer in Greece, the Pythia at Delphi, used to prophesy in a state of ecstasy.[2] Much later the Pythia's séance was described in some detail by Plutarch in his writings on Delphi,[3] a firsthand witness since he served for years there as a priest. Although the rationalizing hypothesis about volcanic vapors rising from the ground beneath the tripod in the temple at Delphi and thus chemically "inspiring" the Pythia has been geologically refuted, this should not serve to disprove the ecstatic state characteristic of Apollo's pronouncements at the place. A medium does not need chemistry. How ecstasy manifested itself in individual cases may have varied from person to person. There is nothing surprising in the fact that a suitable peasant girl could be chosen, as Plutarch affirms—although some scholars have found this disconcerting. Ecstatic prophecy is a specific gift which cannot be anticipated and only partially manipulated.

Farnell wrote in 1911 that, in contrast to Greece, ecstatic prophecy did not exist in Babylon;[4] but this has long since been refuted. Ecstatic priests and priestesses (*mahhu, mahhutu*) were in fact common in Mesopotamia. The most extensive evidence has appeared in Mari; but Wen-Amon's report has a case in Byblos, too.[5] In the time of Esarhaddon ecstatic women were active in Assyria; in particular, temple attendants of Ishtar of Arbela reported the direct communications of the goddess to the king. The deity was speaking directly through the mouth of a woman, in the first person: "I, Ishtar . . ."[6]

The tradition of the Sibyl or Sibyls reaches from Babylon to Cumae with a center of gravity in Asia Minor.[7] Admittedly widely divergent ideas about date and lifetime of Sibyls were current in antiquity, and it is difficult to reconstruct the older traditions out of the later sources. Heraclitus, our oldest witness, refers to the Sibyl and her ecstasy, as she utters unpleasant prophecies "with raving mouth," covering "1,000 years." Tradition dates the Sibyl of Marpessa before the Trojan War, but the Sibyl of Erythrae to the eighth century;[8] the Sibyl of Cumae is made a contemporary of Tarquinius Superbus in Rome.[9] This chronology should be given credit insofar as the Cumae tradition must extend back beyond the conquest of the city by the Oscans in the fifth century.

Eastern origins of the Sibyl have been considered since antiquity. To a certain extent the Sibylline books of late Hellenistic

and imperial times incorporate the "eastern" opposition to
Rome with strong Jewish elements. But in view of the widespread availability of mediumistic talents and prophecies, only
specific details or the name Sibyl itself could provide clear evidence of cultural diffusion in ancient times. There is a "Babylonian Sibyl"; but to link the name Sibylla directly to Siduri the
ale wife, *sabitu*,[10] who appears in the epic *Gilgamesh*—her role is
to show Gilgamesh the way to Utnapishtim, the hero of the
flood—is frivolous. Once the special name Sambethe is reported
for the Babylonian Sibyl, and she is said to have been present in
the ark as one of Noah's daughters-in-law;[11] this might in ear-
nest reflect the *sabitu* of *Gilgamesh*. The Babylonian Sibyl has
also been connected with Berossos, which indicates a dating in
the Hellenistic epoch.

As for the archaic period, it should give us pause that in quite
another context, that of astronomy and calendar making, connections appear to run from Mesopotamia specifically to Delphi. This interrelation was worked out by Martin Nilsson.[12] Already the early Greek calendar system with its intercalary
months seems to follow the principle of the Babylonian Oktae-
teris. The organization of "penteteric" games, in particular the
Olympiads, presupposes that the calendar had been fixed according to such an eight-year period. The traditional date of the
first Olympiad is 776 B.C.; the great rise of the Delphic sanctuary begins around this time. How many uncertain factors are
present in such combinations hardly needs to be stressed: Even
if the early list of Olympic victors is taken to be authentic, the
timetable of the early games remains in doubt—it has recently
been argued that the games started only in about 700 B.C.[13]—
and the relations to Delphi are not very clear. Nevertheless the
perspective introduced by Nilsson remains intriguing, especially if those correspondences in purification and healing rituals
are added which Nilsson did not take into consideration.

Thus the ecstatic prophecy of the Pythia can well be seen in a
similar context. In fact even the special ritual in which, before a
séance of the Pythia, a goat was sprinkled with water and its
reaction observed, has its parallel in Mesopotamia.[14] It seems

that, parallel to the spread of liver augury, the more direct art of mediumistic prophecy also came to supersede older and simpler methods of augury and bird observation. Did this establish Delphi's fame?[15] One should still resist the temptation to go so far as to derive the name of Apollo from Babylon.[16]

Lamashtu, Lamia, and Gorgo

Not only rituals and incantation texts but also amulets belong to the sphere of Mesopotamian magicians. There are simple, small cylinders as well as beads with pertinent inscriptions,[1] but also fantastic images such as the Pazuzu heads[2] and the Lamashtu tablets.[3] As with the model livers of hepatoscopy, these are spread as far as North Syria, Ugarit, and Cyprus. And as the Humbaba face reached Gortyn and the dog-leader figurines reached Samos, reflexes of Lamashtu iconography travelled as far as Italy.[4] It is certain that the Greeks of the archaic period occasionally saw such figures; the Mesopotamian demons did, in fact, leave various traces of themselves.

The horrifying figure of Gello, an object of terror for children, is mentioned as early as the work of Sappho; Gello was said to steal and eat little children. Traces of this figure have persisted to the present day.[5] Greeks will associate the name Gello with evil grinning, *gelan,* but neither the spelling of the word nor its meaning properly corresponds to this. Gallu is, on the other hand, one of the most common Sumerian-Akkadian names for an evil spirit. The correspondence has long been pointed out by Assyriologists and interpreted as a borrowing from Mesopotamia;[6] the testimony of Sappho would place it in the seventh century at the latest. That *a* is reproduced as *e* has a parallel in Azugallatu/Asgelatas and in the name of the letter *delta.*[7]

An even more popular horror figure than Gello is Lamia. She is already mentioned in the archaic period by Stesichoros[8] and has also persisted in modern folklore.[9] Lamia is grotesque, repulsive, and hideous beyond measure; however, there is no undisputed Greek representation of her. The main characteristic of

Lamia is that she steals children, perhaps even from their mothers' bodies.

In this especially Lamia resembles Lamashtu the demoness; the correspondence between the names was clouded for a while by the earlier reading of her name as *Labartu*.[10] Lamashtu was feared by pregnant women, by women giving birth, and by mothers. They protected themselves against her with magic: An ass or a ship was supposed to carry her away. Amulet tablets therefore were fabricated with corresponding images, to offer direct protection against Lamashtu. Such tablets have been found far beyond Mesopotamia, in Ugarit, Boghazköy, Carchemish, and Zincirli.[11] The western connections are stressed if on a seal we find a representation of an Assyrian demon combined with a Phoenician inscription; and at least one amulet with a Lamashtu-like representation comes from seventh-century Italy.[12] Demons similar to Lamashtu also appear in later Syrian magical beliefs:[13] There is no gap between Babylon and Greece. One Greek text states that Lamia is a daughter of the Phoenician Belos, thereby crediting the demoness with Semitic origins.[14]

Lamashtu has a particular iconography which is known both from the amulet tablets and from related texts: She is naked; she has a lion's head, dangling breasts, and the feet of a bird of prey; she lets a pig and a dog suck at her breasts; she often holds a snake in each hand; often she is represented with one knee bent, in *Knielauf* position, which presumably is meant to represent swift flight. There is usually an ass underneath her and beneath that a ship, all designed to carry her away (Figure 5). Sometimes the animals appear separated from the main figure, grouped to the right and left in the Mistress of Animals schema.[15]

As has often been discussed, Lamashtu shares a whole range of characteristics with the Greek Gorgon.[16] It is not so much the actual face of the Gorgon that is similar; the Gorgon face does incorporate lion features, yet the leonine is only one of the elements, and the Gorgon is always represented *en face,* whereas Lamashtu is always represented in profile. There is, however, a striking correspondence in the dangling breasts, the schema of

*Figure 5. Bronze plate from Carchemish: Lamashtu. Demoness with
lion's head, bird's talons, standing on a donkey, wielding snakes,
and suckling a pig and a dog.*

Knielauf, and, above all, the iconographic paraphernalia. We
may take as an example the famous representation of the Gorgon from the temple in Corfu: She appears in *Knielauf* between
two "lions" which are beasts of fantasy rather than zoology; two
snakes form her belt, while a horse and a human, Pegasos and
Chrysaor her "children," touch her right and left hands. Nearly

all these elements, with the exception of the human Chrysaor, have their counterparts in the image of Lamashtu. There may be a horse at her side, and both the Gorgon and Lamashtu are occasionally depicted holding two snakes. And yet, all these elements have been shaken up, taken out of their context, and placed in a new order. The basic concept remains the same: the fleeing monster—but the Greek myth has developed a whole new system with the myth of Perseus, Pegasos, Chrysaor. The steed and the warrior are indicative of a trial of initiation: It is the armed hero and not magic that overcomes the demon and petrifying fear. It cannot be doubted that some artists who created Gorgon compositions of this kind had seen Lamashtu tablets, but they took only the images and used them to construct something closer to their own traditions.[17]

The connection between the Perseus-Gorgon myth and the Semitic East is even more complex. On the one hand the Andromeda myth is located in Ioppe-Jaffa;[18] on the other, Perseus has a remarkable connection with Tarsos.[19] Iconographic models for Perseus' fight with the marine monster (*ketos*) appear on some eastern seals;[20] in Mesopotamia even the slaying of a one-eyed female monster by a youthful hero occurs.[21] However, finding names for the scenes in oriental seal art is by no means simple; the connection with the epic texts such as *Gilgamesh* can be established only in rare cases. One of these is the slaying of Humbaba by Gilgamesh and Enkidu, a scene which in turn is one of the models for representations of Perseus killing the Gorgon (Figure 6).

A strange oriental seal, now in Berlin, is particularly worthy of note.[22] It depicts an oversized, demonic creature shown *en face* and in *Knielauf* position. It has been seized by a young hero who is holding up a scimitar, a *harpe,* in his right hand, and, in doing so, he has apparently turned his face away from his opponent. He is wearing winged shoes; behind him is the representation of a large fish. This picture was reproduced in Roscher's *Dictionary of Mythology* as a clear illustration of Perseus fighting the Gorgon.[23] Pierre Amiet is no less decided about the framework of eastern mythology for this representation, recalling the Ugaritic

Figure 6. TOP LEFT: *Seal impression from Nuzi, about 1450 B.C.:
Gilgamesh and Enkidu struggling with Humbaba. From the left, a
goddess is handing a weapon to the champion.* TOP RIGHT: *Shield
strap, Olympia, about 560 B.C.: Perseus killing the Gorgon, with the
help of Athena, turning his face from the petrifying monster.*
BOTTOM: *Seal from Baghdad, seventh to sixth century B.C.: Perseus
fighting the Gorgon?*

myth of the fight between the goddess Anat and Mot, with no mention of Perseus and the Gorgon.[24] In contrast to the Gorgon, the monster has bird's claws, which is rather reminiscent of Lamashtu. There is not much point in arguing about the interpretation: Even the date of the seal is unclear; it may already be dependent upon Greek iconography; still less could we hope to find adequate texts for explanation. Even so, this picture is an important document illustrating the complex interrelations of Greek and oriental in the archaic period. Images and possibly even narrative motifs become ambiguous in the sphere of intercultural contacts; they are understood in different ways from different sides; they form new constellations. Creative misunderstanding might be considered to be more significant than the transmission itself in such cases. But the transmission remains a fact; the iconographic patterns remain preserved, in the instances of the combats of Perseus as in the case of Lamashtu and the Gorgon.

One difference is striking indeed: For the Greeks these demons are not really demonic; they do not carry the association of some *mysterium tremendum*. At best they are apt to frighten little children. For Greek men Perseus has set an example of how to deal with such creatures, weapon in hand, even if an element of magic and some help from the gods is not lacking. A similar transformation can be established in still another instance, in the image of the snake strangler. This is quite an old and apparently important image in the Mesopotamian repertoire: a master of animals, a shamanistic figure, who has seized two large snakes in his hands; this type probably has an apotropaic function.[25] The Greeks made this the first adventure of their Herakles, the heroic deed a baby performed in his cradle.[26] In everyday life of course Herakles is the averter of evil, *alexikakos,* whose amulets are used for protection.[27] But in myth, or rather in the accepted and representative form of Greek poetry, the fear of demons has been eliminated. The Greek hero is represented as trusting in his own strength, godlike even if in the shadow of death.[28] Magical figurines are transformed into practical robots, not awe-inspiring but simply a source of wonder.[29]

CHAPTER THREE

"OR ALSO A GODLY SINGER"
Akkadian and Early Greek Literature

From Atrahasis *to the* "Deception of Zeus"

Since the rediscovery of the Akkadian epics and of *Gilgamesh* in particular, there has been no shortage of associations between motifs in these and in the Homeric epics, especially the *Odyssey*.[1] These motifs can be highlighted and used to surprise, but hardly to prove anything: Approximately the same motifs and themes will be found everywhere. Instead of individual motifs, therefore, we must focus on more complex structures, where sheer coincidence is less likely: a system of deities and a basic cosmological idea, the narrative structure of a whole scene, decrees of the gods about mankind, or a very special configuration of attack and defense. Once the historical link, the fact of transmission, has been established, then further connections, including linguistic borrowings, become more likely, even if these alone do not suffice to carry the burden of proof.

Not until 1969 was the text of an Akkadian epic published for the first time in anything approaching its entirety: The story of Atrahasis "outstanding in wisdom"—a telling name in Akkadian—or rather a "Story of Mankind" beginning, as the opening line says, with the paradoxical primordial situation "when gods were in the ways of men."[2] Up until then it had been known only from a few not very characteristic fragments. The first version in three books is dated to the time of Ammiṣaduqa, a few generations after Hammurapi, in the seventeenth century B.C. Various Old Babylonian examples have survived in fragmentary form; the library of Ashurbanipal also contained other, slightly varying editions. A fragment of another recension has been found in Ugarit. We are therefore dealing with a text which had been in circulation and popular for over a thousand years, a text astonishingly original in conception. "When gods were in the ways of men" and there were no humans yet in existence, the gods had to do all the work themselves; this led to a rebellion by the younger gods against the senior gods and especially Enlil, the acting chief. Fortunately Enki the cunning god came to their aid, and together with the mother goddess he created men to act as robots for them: They should bear the burden of the work. But soon, "after 600 [and?] 600 years," these creatures became too numerous and a nuisance to the earth, and so the gods tried to destroy them. They made three attempts, apparently at formulaic intervals of 1,200 years, by sending first a plague, then a famine, and finally the great flood. However, the cunning god of the deep, Enki, in league with the man "outstanding in wisdom," Atrahasis, frustrated these attacks. He played the gods off against one another, and finally had Atrahasis build his ark. The final part of the text, as can now be seen, is an older parallel version to the famous Tablet XI of the *Gilgamesh* epic, the well-known story of the flood,[3] which in turn influenced the story of Noah in the first book of Moses. The *Atrahasis* text, however, far from being an example of Old Testament piety, is imbued with a remarkably human, if not a slightly cynical optimism: Whether for or against the gods, mankind, for all the hard work and all the afflictions it has to bear, is indestructible. "How did man survive in the destruction?" the great god Enlil finally asks, baffled as he is (III vi 10). Beyond doubt, survive he did.

At the beginning of the *Atrahasis* text, the Babylonian pantheon is introduced systematically: "Anu, their father, was the king; their counsellor was the warrior Enlil; their chamberlain was Ninurta; and their sheriff Ennugi." These verses are copied in the *Gilgamesh* epic, but not the following lines: "They grasped the flask of lots by the neck, they cast the lots; the gods made the division: Anu went up to heaven." A second god—there is a lacuna in the text here—"took the earth, for his subjects"; and "the bolts, the bar of the sea, were set for Enki, the far-sighted."[4] Enlil, the most active of the gods, surely belongs in the lacuna, which produces the usual trinity of Anu, Enlil, and Enki: the sky god, the wind god, the water god. The *Atrahasis* text returns repeatedly to the division of the cosmos into the three parts given over to the different gods, particularly when Enlil undertakes a total blockade of the human world while sending the famine.[5] A different version, Tablet X, has Anu and Adad—sky god and wind god—for the heavens, Sin and Nergal—moon god and god of the underworld—for the earth. The underworld is clearly included in the concept of the earth. The realm of Enki, the Lord of the Deep, is fixed, not as the salt sea, but the potable ground and spring waters—these are also the realm of Poseidon in Greece.

In Homer's *Iliad,* however, there are those famous, oft-quoted verses in which the world is divided among the appropriate Homeric gods; Poseidon speaks: "For when we threw the lots I received the grey sea as my permanent abode, Hades drew the murky darkness, Zeus, however, drew the wide sky of brightness and clouds; the earth is common to all, and spacious Olympus."[6]

This differs from the system of *Atrahasis* in that the earth together with the gods' mountain is declared to be under joint dominion; Poseidon insists on his right to become active on the plain of Troy. Still the basic structure of both texts is astonishingly similar: There are three distinct areas of the cosmos—heaven, the depths of the earth, and the waters—and these three areas are assigned to the three highest gods of the pantheon—all of which are male. And in both instances the division is said to have been made by drawing lots. This is not normally the practice among Greek gods: according to Hesiod, Zeus dethroned his predecessor—who was also his father—by force, and then the other gods asked him to become their king.[7] From another point of view, too, this passage, when looked at in more detail, is unique in Greek myth: In other passages of the old epic, when the parts of the cosmos are being enumerated, there is either a trinity of heaven–earth–underworld or of heaven–sea–earth, or even a combination to make four, heaven–earth–sea–underworld, but not heaven–sea–underworld as assigned to the three brothers.[8] Furthermore, the trinity of the sons of Kronos and their realms does not have any further part to play in Homer, nor is it rooted in any Greek cult. By contrast, the corresponding passage in the *Atrahasis* text is fundamental to the narrative and is referred to repeatedly.

There is hardly another passage in Homer which comes so close to being a translation of an Akkadian epic. In fact it is not so much a translation as a resetting through which the foreign framework still shows. One may still believe this to be a misleading coincidence. However, the passage stands in a very special context in relation to the overall structure of the *Iliad*. The scene belongs to the section which the ancients called the "Deception of Zeus" (*Dios Apate*). Its peculiarities have often been commented upon in Homeric studies. Albrecht Dihle listed linguistic peculiarities and found so many deviations from the normal, traditional use of Homeric formulas that he concluded that this section of the *Iliad* could not belong to the phase of oral tradition, but was a written composition.[9] This result has not been generally accepted; but it must be acknowledged that in this part of the *Iliad* we are dealing with a text which is linguistically unusual, isolated in its content, and, in a way, quite "modern."

There is, above all, a peculiarity of content which was noted even by Plato and may also have been noticed and exploited before Plato by the pre-Socratics:[10] This is the only passage in the Homeric canon where, quite unexpectedly, a cosmogonic theme comes to the fore. Hera, in her deception speech, says she wants to go to Oceanus, "origin of the gods," and Tethys the "mother"; Oceanus is also called "the origin of all" in another verse. Oceanus and Tethys, the primeval couple, have withheld their conjugal rights from each other for a long time, separated as a result of strife, *neikea*.[11] This sounds like an anticipation of the Empedoclean *Neikos* cosmogony. The genesis of the gods has come to an end. It is true that in the Iliadic narrative all this is made up by Hera, a patent lie, as it were; but the motifs used radiate beyond those speeches. The very climax of this song of Homer—Zeus and Hera making love within a golden cloud on the summit of Mount Ida, from which resplendent drops are falling—shows divinity in a naturalistic, cosmic setting which is not otherwise a feature of Homeric anthropomorphism. Thus the division of the cosmos into three parts in Poseidon's speech somewhat later, when Zeus has reawakened, is the third motif which involves the gods in the origin and function of the natural cosmos.

Aristotle, following Plato, found in the Oceanus cosmogony of Homer the very beginning of natural philosophy, the inspiration for Thales, usually considered the first philosopher. Modern research has drawn attention to antecedents of Thales' water cosmogony among the Egyptians, the Phoenicians, and, not least, the Babylonian epic of creation, the *Enuma Elish*.[12] The Babylonian epic begins: "When above" the heavens did not yet exist nor the earth below, Apsu was there, the freshwater ocean, "the first, the begetter," and with him Tiamat, the saltwater sea, "she who bore them all." They "were mixing their waters."[13] This came to an end when Apsu was put to sleep and killed by Ea, and Tiamat was vanquished by Marduk in a dramatic fight. Then Marduk established the cosmos as it now exists.

Thus Hera's incidental inventions closely correspond to the beginning of *Enuma Elish*. Apsu and Tiamat equal Oceanus and Tethys as the original parental couple. But Tethys is in no way an active figure in Greek mythology. In contrast to the sea goddess Thetis (with whom she was sometimes confused even in antiquity), she has no established cults, and no one had anything further to tell about her. She apparently exists only by virtue of the Homeric passage; how she came to achieve the honored position of the mother of all remains a mystery. But now the "rhyming of the names" finally comes into play. *Ti-amat* is the form normally written in the text of *Enuma Elish* for the mother "who bore them all." The Akkadian word which lies behind this, however, is just *tiamtu or tâmtu,* the normal word for the sea. The name can also be written in this more phonetic orthography; but in the *Enuma Elish* we also find the form *taw(a)tu.*[14] If one proceeds from *Tawtu,* then *Tethys* is an exact transcription. The different reproductions of the dentals, *t* and *th,* might disturb the purist; but Sophilos wrote *Thethys,* which, in normal Greek orthography, would automatically yield Tethys. In fact the *Enuma Elish* became known to Eudemos, the pupil of Aristotle, in translation;[15] here we find Tiamat transcribed as *Tauthe,* which is still closer to the reconstructed form *Tawtu.* That the long vowel *a* is changed to *e* in the Ionian dialect even in borrowed words has parallels in *Kubaba* becoming *Kybebe, Baal* becoming *Belos,* and *Mada* known as *Medes.*[16] Thus the proof seems complete that here, right in the middle of the *Iliad,* the influence of two Akkadian classics can be detected down to a mythical name.

There can be no question of Bronze Age borrowing in this case. We are rather dealing, in the words of Martin West, with a "neo-oriental element." Four hundred years of oral tradition in Greece would have led to stronger distortions in the process of assimilation; and it is not at all clear whether the *Enuma Elish* can be given such an early date.[17] This argument accords with Albrecht Dihle's observations from the other side on the "young" character of this Homeric piece.

Once an orientalizing background is established for the "Deception of Zeus," further observations are bound to follow. Aphrodite has her Semitic connections anyhow, but the embroidered girdle (*kestos*) borrowed from her as a love charm by Hera seems to be oriental in a particular way. The catalogue of women once loved by Zeus—athetized by ancient commentators—has its counterpart in Gilgamesh's enumeration of the lovers of Ishtar.[18] The famous oath of the gods which Hera is made to swear, ending "by the River Styx," is, in fact, a cosmic oath: heaven, earth, and the waters of the underworld are called upon to bear witness. It is precisely such a cosmic formula which concludes the enumeration of divine witnesses in the only Aramaic treaty text which has survived from the eighth century: "Heaven and earth, the deep and the springs, day and night."[19]

Zeus the weather god makes love to his wife at the top of the mountain within the thunderstorm; the weather god together with his wife unveiling herself on their storm dragons is a motif frequently represented on eastern seals, and the marriage of heaven and earth is a mythical theme set out explicitly in Akkadian literature.[20] But even a famous wooden statuette of Zeus embracing Hera from the Hera sanctuary on Samos, a representation most probably inspired by the text of the *Iliad,* is iconographically dependent on eastern prototypes.[21]

More specific is the question of the Titans. Of the five Homeric passages in which the previous gods, held prisoner in the underworld, are mentioned, three belong in the context of the "Deception of Zeus." The other two also belong to divine scenes, being proclamations of Zeus, the father of the gods.[22] Since the *Kumarbi* discovery it has been well known that the concept of ancient, fallen gods connects Greek mythology with the Hittites, the Phoenicians, and the Babylonians. The details of the evidence, however, remain more complicated in the Greek as well as in the eastern settings. In Greek tradition the concept of the Titans as a collective group is not easily reconciled with the very special personality of Kronos; on the other side we find, besides Kumarbi the hero of the Hurrian-Hittite myth of succession, apparently other "ancient gods," always mentioned collectively in the plural. We learn that the weather god—who corresponds to Zeus—banished them to the underworld.[23] The corresponding deities in Mesopotamia are the "defeated" or "fettered gods," *ilani kamûti.*[24] They, too, have been banished beneath the earth by the victorious god or gods. In the *Enuma Elish* these have been the supporters of Tiamat; in other texts they are the evil "Seven" who have been bound by the god of the heavens. Note that in Orphic tradition the Titans, sons of Heaven and Earth but "bound" in the netherworld, are precisely seven in number.[25]

The evil Seven belong above all in the realm of exorcism and protective magic. This fact leads to a further possible connection: In protective magic, figurines—some friendly, but mostly hostile—are often fabricated but then destroyed. The most common material is clay, Akkadian *ṭiṭu*. This word reached Greek as *titanos*, plaster.[26] Later Greek authors have taken precisely this word to provide an etymology for the name of the Titans: When the Titans attacked the child Dionysus they disguised their faces with plaster; hence their name.[27] In the Greek language, however, this etymology fails as a result of the fact that the *i* of *Titanes/Titenes* is long, whereas that of *titanos* is short. The Semitic base word, however, has a long *i,* so that with the hypothesis of borrowing the ancient etymology becomes plausible again. A ritual context then would be possible: The Titans bear their name of *ṭiṭ*-people[28] because eastern magicians used to fabricate clay figures—*ṣalme ṭiṭ* in Akkadian[29]—to represent the defeated gods who were used for protective magic or as witnesses in oaths. This daring hypothesis, however, lacks specific material for verification; other possibilities remain open.

A hypothesis of literary transmission is perhaps preferable. Both passages which resonate so notably in the "Deception of Zeus"—Apsu and Tiamat mingling their waters, and the three gods casting lots for the partition of the universe—come from the very beginnings of the respective texts, *Enuma Elish* and *Atrahasis,* mythological texts which were particularly well known and frequently used. It is attested that these texts were used in school curricula in particular.[30] In such a situation the emphasis falls naturally on the opening section: Many will recall *arma virumque cano,* but not much more of Virgil from their schooldays. A Greek desirous of education might well have been exposed to precisely these sections of "classical" eastern literature, either directly or possibly indirectly via Aramaic versions, even if he did not progress very far with his studies. A scholastic tradition, if only on an elementary level, is inherent in the transmission of the alphabet to Greece.[31] Anyhow, the various channels of transmission to be considered—the ritual, the iconographic, and the literary—are in no way mutually exclusive, but may have overlapped and reinforced one another in many different ways. Be that as it may, the conclusion is that Homer's *Iliad* bears the mark, at least at one probably "late" stage, of the orientalizing impact.[32]

Complaint in Heaven: Ishtar and Aphrodite

The "apparatus of the gods" which accompanies the sequence of events narrated in the *Iliad* and, in a modified form, in the *Odyssey* has more than once been called a "late" element in the tradition of Greek heroic epic.[1] There has also been an awareness of oriental parallels with precisely these scenes involving the gods.[2] It is true that the double stage of divine and human actions, which is handled so masterfully by the composer of the *Iliad,* is not found in this extensive form in the Mesopotamian epics. Still, *Atrahasis* and *Gilgamesh* repeatedly introduce the gods interacting with the deeds and sufferings of men; and kings are made to win their heroic battles in direct contact with their protective gods.

In *Gilgamesh* in particular, there is a famous meeting between deity and man: When Gilgamesh has killed Humbaba and cleansed himself of the grime of battle, Ishtar "raised an eye at the beauty of Gilgamesh": "Do but grant me of your fruit!" she says, and she offers fabulous goods for him. But Gilgamesh scornfully rejects her, reciting the catalogue of all her partners whom she once "has loved" only to destroy or to transform subsequently. "If you would love me, you would [treat me] like them." Whereupon

> Ishtar, when hearing this,
> Ishtar was enraged and [went up] to heaven.
> [Forth went Ishtar before Anu, her father;
> before Antum, her mother [her tears were flowing]:
> ["Oh my father! Gilgamesh has heaped insults upon me!
> Gilgamesh has recounted my insults,
> my insults and my curses."
> Anu opened his mouth to speak,
> he said to glorious Ishtar:
> "Surely you have provoked [the King of Uruk],

and (thus) Gilgamesh recounted your insults,
your insults and your curses."[3]

Compare this with a scene from the *Iliad*:[4] Trying to protect Aeneas, Aphrodite has been wounded by Diomedes; her blood is flowing. "But she, beside herself, went away, she felt horrible pain." With the help of Iris and Ares she reaches Olympus. "But she, glorious Aphrodite, fell into the lap of Dione, her mother; but she took her daughter in her arms, stroked her with her hand, spoke the word and said: Who has done such things to you, dear child?" Aphrodite replies: "Wounded has me the son of Tydeus, high-minded Diomedes." Mother sets out to comfort her with mythical examples; Athena her sister, less sympathetic, makes a scornful comment; but Zeus the father smiles: "He called golden Aphrodite and said to her: 'My child, not for you are the works of war! But you should pursue the tender offices of marriage . . .' " In other words: It's partly your own fault.

The two scenes parallel each other in structure, narrative form, and ethos to an astonishing degree.[5] A goddess, injured by a human, goes up to heaven to complain to her father and mother, and she earns a mild rebuke from her father.

Of course this may be called a universal scenario from the realm of children's stories. The scene repeats itself with variations in the battle of the gods later in the *Iliad*.[6] Artemis, after being beaten by Hera, climbs weeping onto the knees of father Zeus. He pulls her to him and asks, laughing: "Who did this to you?" And she replies: "Your wife beat me." The scene from the Diomedes book is simpler in that both parents appear as a refuge, the stepmother being left out, with the father taking the stance of slightly distant superiority. This corresponds exactly to the *Gilgamesh* scene.

But what is more: The persons involved in both scenes are, in fact, identical, the sky god and his wife, and their common daughter the goddess of love. Aphrodite is in general the equivalent of Ishtar; she has offered herself to a mortal man, Anchises the father of Aeneas, and Anchises suffered some strange fate as a result of his contact with the goddess—another case of what Gilgamesh is blaming on Ishtar. It is possible that the name Aphrodite itself is a Greek form of western Semitic Ashtorith, who in turn is identical with Ishtar.[7] And by force of an even more special parallelism, Aphrodite has a mother who apparently lives in Olympus as Zeus's wife, Dione; Hera seems to be forgotten for a moment. Dione at Olympus makes her appearance in the context of the Diomedes scene, and only there. The contrast with Hesiod's account of Aphrodite's birth from the sea, after Uranos had been castrated, has been found disconcerting since antiquity. Dione is attested in the cult of Dodona; scholars have also referred to the Mycenaean goddess Diwija.[8] In any event, the mother of Aphrodite is given here a name which is crystal clear in Greek, being just the feminine form of *Zeus*. Such a system of naming is unique in the Homeric family of gods, where couples enjoy complicated private names. But it is this very detail which has its counterpart in the Akkadian text: Antu mother of Ishtar is the usual, obviously feminine form of *Anu,* Heaven. This divine couple, Mr. and Mrs. Heaven, is firmly established in the worship and mythology of Mesopotamia. Homer proves to be dependent on *Gilgamesh* even at the linguistic level, forming the name Dione as a calque on Antu when recasting an impressive scene among the gods. This may be seen as a counterpart to the relation Tethys/Tawtu, though rather at the level of narrative structure and divine characters than of cosmic mythology.

A few observations may be added about Diomedes in relation to the Aphrodite scene. Diomedes belongs to Argos, as the catalogue of ships has it; it is at Argos that we find a ritual corresponding to the Iliadic narrative, the shield of Diomedes carried in a procession with the image of Pallas Athena on a chariot.[9] But Diomedes also belongs to Salamis on Cyprus; it is said that there was human sacrifice for Diomedes and Agraulos, performed in the sanctuary of which Athena had her share, in the month of Aphrodisios; the victim was killed with a spear and burnt.[10] Thus we find Diomedes, Athena, and Aphrodite in strange company combined with spear-killing; some have found the Cypriote holocaust reminiscent of Semitic practice.[11] At any rate an aspect of the Diomedes legend, which seems somehow to tie in with the Aphrodite scene in Homer, points to that island where Hellas and the Semitic East enjoyed their closest contact and where precisely in the Homeric period the Assyrian kings commemorated their power in inscriptions.[12] In this perspective the connection between the Homeric and the Akkadian epic hardly appears astonishing any more.

Still, among all the similarities it is important to keep sight of the differences. Ishtar's meeting with Gilgamesh is firmly anchored in the structure of the *Gilgamesh* epic; it constitutes the narrative link from the Humbaba theme to the next heroic deed, the vanquishing of the bull of heaven. Glorious Ishtar, in her revenge, has the bull of heaven make his attack, thus giving Gilgamesh and Enkidu the opportunity to overcome the bull and thus establish sacrifice. The ritual background is clear even in details. Gilgamesh's rejection of Ishtar corresponds to the hunters' taboo: It is sexual restraint that ensures a successful hunt. Hence the denial of love causes the bull to appear.[13] Also the transformations of Ishtar's lovers as reported in Gilgamesh's catalogue have their special meaning and function, being basically myths about the installment of culture: In this way the horse was bridled.[14] What has remained in Homer is the narrative thread of a genre scene, all the more carefully presented because it is, on the whole, functionless. It has its own charm and aesthetic merit in the framework of the *Iliad,* but it does not carry the same weight either in the narrative or in terms of ritual background as in the Akkadian epic. The manner in which Akkadian demons have been turned into fantastic monsters, more amusing than frightening—Lamashtu transformed into the Gorgon—has its counterpart on the level of epic poetry about the gods.

The influence of *Gilgamesh* may also be detected in a scene from the *Odyssey.* The *Odyssey* once describes a form of prayer which historians of religion have found confusing: When Penelope learns about the risky journey undertaken by Telemachos and the suitors' plot to kill him, she first bursts into tears and laments. Then, calming down, she washes and dresses in clean clothes, goes to the upper story with her maids, taking barley in a basket, and prays to Athena for the safe return of Telemachos; she ends with an inarticulate and shrieking cry.[15] Both the basket with barley and the cry (*ololyge*) have their proper place in blood sacrifice; their use in this scene is unparalleled elsewhere. So scholars either spoke of an "abbreviation of sacrifice" or of an otherwise unknown ritual of bloodless offering or of an invention of the poet, if not incompetence of the "redactor."[16] But look at *Gilgamesh:* When Gilgamesh together with Enkidu is leaving his city to fight Humbaba, his mother "Ninsun enters her chamber, she takes a . . . [special herb], she puts on a garment as befits her body, she puts on an ornament as befits her breast . . . she sprinkles water from a bowl on earth and dust. She went up the stairs, mounted the upper storey, she climbed the roof, to Shamash [the sun god] she offered incense, she brought the offering and raised her hands before Shamash"; thus she prays, full of distress and sorrow, for a safe return of her son.[17] The situation, mother praying for an adventurous son, is not a special one. Yet in its details the scene from the *Odyssey* comes close to being a translation of *Gilgamesh;* in fact it is closer to the *Gilgamesh* text than to the comparable scene of Achilles' prayer in the *Iliad.*[18] Whereas the ritual is odd in the *Odyssey,* none of these oddities is found in the passage of *Gilgamesh:* Burning incense on the roof is a well-known Semitic practice,[19] and it is especially appropriate when turning to the sun god. Ceremonial prayer in the women's upper story is otherwise unheard-of in Greece. It seems the poet knew that burning incense was out of place in the heroic world, so he took as a substitute the female part in normal sacrifice, that is, throwing of barley (*oulochytai*) and *ololyge.* Even the use of religious ritual as an effective motif in epic narrative has its antecedent in the oriental tradition.

The Overpopulated Earth

The basic concept of the ancient Babylonian *Atrahasis* epic is almost disconcertingly modern. Humans multiply, the land feels oppressed by their multitude, the outcome can only be catastrophe to annihilate mankind; yet man survives the attempts at destruction; and so, ultimately, the only effective method is found: birth control. To achieve this, though, the poem has only one method to offer: the institution of priestesses who are not allowed to bear children.[1]

The suffering of the earth is expressed in verses which recur at the beginning of each new act of *Atrahasis*: "Twelve hundred years had not yet passed, when the land extended and the peoples multiplied. The land was bellowing like a bull. The gods got disturbed with their uproar. Enlil heard their noise and he addressed the great gods: 'The noise of mankind has become too intense for me, with their uproar I am deprived of sleep . . .' "[2] Hence he proceeds to orchestrate the catastrophes of plague, famine, and flood.

This cannot but remind of a passage of Greek epic, of an extremely prominent text in fact, the very beginning of the Trojan cycle, which tells about the ultimate cause of the Trojan War. This is the opening of the *Cypria,* an epic that was still quite well known in the classical period but subsequently fell into disregard and got lost; already Herodotus doubted the authorship of Homer, which Pindar still accepted. The opening lines have been preserved as a fragment, albeit in a corrupt textual form. They are quoted in order to explain the "decision of Zeus" mentioned right at the beginning of the *Iliad.*

The *Cypria* began in the style of a fairy tale:

Once upon a time, when countless people moved on the face
  of the earth . . .
[lacuna; they oppressed?] the breadth of the deep-chested
  earth.
Zeus saw this and took pity and deep in his heart
He decided to relieve the all-nourishing earth of mankind
by setting alight the great conflict of the Ilian War.[3]

In the same scholia there is also a prose narrative:[4]

Earth, being oppressed by the multitude of men, since there was no piety of men, asked Zeus to be lightened of this burden. And first Zeus caused at once the Theban War by which he destroyed many men thoroughly. Afterwards he caused again the Trojan War, consulting with Momos—this is called the "decision of Zeus" by Homer; he could have destroyed them all with bolts of lightning or floods, but Momos prevented this and suggested rather two measures to him, to marry Thetis to a human and to generate a beautiful daughter.

Thus Achilles and Helen are born and, with them, the seeds of the Trojan War.

The two texts cannot directly be combined. In the verses quoted, Zeus reacts directly to the conditions on the earth, "seeing" and feeling pity at her plight, and immediately plans the Trojan War. As the excerpts from the *Cypria* in Proklos indicate,[5] Zeus discussed further details with Themis. In the prose version, however, the earth is not a dumb object of pity, but a speaking partner. The decision involves first the Theban War, and this is followed by a remarkable discussion with Momos. We are clearly dealing with two competing versions. In fact a third version comes from the end of the Hesiodic *Catalogues*. Here Zeus makes his decision all alone which the others "did not yet fully comprehend." His aim is to bring an end to the confusion of the human and divine spheres and thereby to bring the age of heroes to a close. "He sought to destroy the greater part of mankind" through the catastrophe of war.[6] According to Hesiod's *Erga* it was both the Theban and the Trojan wars that mark the end of the age of heroes (163–165). The text of the *Catalogues* is so badly preserved in this section that it is not fully comprehensible; but it is clear that the catastrophe is linked to Helen.

Here are, therefore, three variations on the basic concept of a catastrophe affecting mankind through the decision of the ruling god. Both the *Cypria* and the *Catalogues,* even if we cannot give them an exact date, must belong to the archaic period, whereas the source of the prose version can hardly be fixed in time. Yet it is precisely the prose version which has a particular affinity with the *Atrahasis* text. Here plans for different catastrophes, though not carried out, are still considered in a systematic fashion, and, somewhat surprisingly, it is the flood which appears as the most radical measure. What is strange is the role of Momos, the personification of Reproach, as it seems; he is introduced only here as an advisor of Zeus to reject two suggestions—much poetic investment with little effect. Or is it his role to reproach mankind? What is even more curious is that, at the beginning of *Enuma Elish*, Apsu, "the first one, the begetter," distressed by the noise of the younger gods, who are depriving him of his sleep, makes plans to kill them all, and doing so he has an advisor, Mummu, "giving counsel to Apsu."[7] Is Momos the same as Mummu? If so, the Greek text would present a contamination of motifs from *Atrahasis* and *Enuma Elish*, as appears to be the case in the context of the "Deception of Zeus" too. This possible connection still does not allow us to place this text securely within the framework of Greek literature. In the case of Typhon-Typhoeus, to take another example, a prose text preserved in the library of Apollodorus provides the most striking parallel with the Hittite myth of Illuyankas the dragon; it may come from a Hellenistic source.[8]

As regards the *Cypria*, the *Atrahasis* text shows in any case that the motif of the oppression of the earth and the plan of destruction of mankind by the highest of the gods, the weather god, is extremely old. This discourages one from simply finding some "post-Homeric invention" in the opening of the *Cypria*.[9] In addition, there is a reference to the East even from the Greek side: The remarkable title *Cypria* can be understood only as a reference to the island of Cyprus,[10] however skeptical we may be about the later information that makes Stasinus of Cyprus the author of the poem. An indication that at least the main contents of the *Cypria* were known around 650 B.C. is provided by the representation of the Judgment of Paris on the Chigi vase.[11] However, these observations must then point to that epoch when Cyprus, though rich and powerful, was still formally under Assyrian domination. The flavor of this period on Cyprus appears to be a mixture of eastern luxury and Homeric life style. The burials are as lavish as that of Patroklos; in the chamber tombs there is elaborate eastern furniture; before their entrances horses were sacrificed and interred along with their chariots; even a sword with silver nails, as known from Homeric diction, has been found.[12] This does not explain why it was the Homeric theme of the Trojan War which caught the imagination of Cyprians to result in the production of "the Cyprian epic." But it is a fact, evidenced by the current title *Cypria*. No less clear than the Homeric connections of Cyprus at the time were those to Syria and Mesopotamia; the commemorative steles of Assyrian kings were erected in the cities of Cyprus.

Among the splendid objects of art produced on Cyprus in this period are two silver bowls with relief decoration, unique insofar as the outer band of reliefs evidently illustrates a continuous story: A prince in his chariot leaves the city to go out hunting; he alights from his chariot and kneels down to shoot at a stag; he follows the bleeding animal; he flays the corpse; he makes offerings to his god, represented as a winged sun disk above the scene; a wild man from the woods attacks the prince with a stone; but a winged female divinity lifts the prince up with her arms and saves him; the prince mounts his chariot and pursues the wild man; the prince kills the wild man with his axe; the prince returns to his city. One of these bowls reached Italy through trade and was found in the lavish Bernardini tomb at Praeneste/Palestrina (Figure 7); the other is preserved in only fragmentary condition.[13] It has been proposed that works of art like this provided the Greeks with the incentive for inventing their own mythology.[14] Today the reverse hypothesis seems more attractive: The artists who decorated these pieces, Phoenicians on Cyprus or Greeks trained by Phoenicians, were illustrating a Greek tale, a "song" current on Cyprus.[15] It is clear how easily the tale whose contents we can follow in the frieze could be transformed into Homeric hexameters, especially the intervention of the divinity to save her protégé: "And here Aineias, prince of men, could well have perished, had not the daughter of Zeus sharply noticed this . . ."[16] In this perspective the Praeneste bowl and its counterpart allow the notion of Homeric poetry on Cyprus around 700 B.C.

Another possible reflection of *Atrahasis* in the *Iliad* should be

*Figure 7. Cypriote silver bowl, about 700 B.C., found in the
Bernardini tomb, Praeneste: a hunting adventure,
including a fight with a wild man.*

mentioned: One of the most dramatic episodes right at the beginning of the Babylonian poem is the attack of the lower gods
on Enlil, their chief. They are tired of doing all the toilsome
work of digging dikes; so they burn their implements and that
night they gather in front of the house—the temple—of Enlil in

order to start a revolt. Enlil becomes alarmed and quickly sends a messenger to Anu in the heavens and to Enki in the depths of the waters. Both come at his call and give their advice, the outcome being the creation of the human robots.[17] In the first book of the *Iliad*, Thetis tells a story which does not otherwise appear anywhere else, "how the other gods of Olympus wanted to bind Zeus"—there is no reason given for the revolution. In this instance Thetis acted as messenger and fetched from the depths of the sea the powerful Briareos-Aigaion, who sat down at Zeus's side and with his ferocious aspect scared the other gods away.[18] The correspondence with *Atrahasis* is not very detailed; stories of disputes among the gods are not unusual. Yet if connections between eastern and Greek epic texts are established already, they allow us to take into consideration the eastern model even in this case. Once more we find what had been an integral element of the main story in *Atrahasis* devolved into a casual motif, an unconnected improvisation without precedent or consequence.

Further threads lead from cunning Atrahasis to the Prometheus myth. But these are less specific when set in the context of the very common trickster figure.[19]

Seven against Thebes

History is, to a great extent, the history of war; and wars give the impression of reality. The war of the "Seven against Thebes" is usually accepted as an actual historical event of the Late Bronze Age; this seems even less controversial than the historicity of the Trojan War, which should have happened one generation later: "There is no reason to suppose that the tale was not based on historical fact."[1] A destruction level at Thebes towards the end of Late Helladic III B—that is, in the thirteenth century—has been established archaeologically, although its exact chronological relationship with the fall of Pylos and Mycenae and the destruction of Troy VII A is disputed.[2] At Thebes the destruction would be linked to the attack by the Epigones, who belong to the same generation as the heroes who fought at Troy. In the catalogue of ships in the *Iliad* it is presupposed that Thebes has been destroyed and only some small *Hypothebai* has been left.[3] One usually assumes that Thebes lay in ruins still in the eighth century, and that its rise to hegemonic power in Boeotia occurred later.[4]

No archaeological trace can be expected of the war of the Seven against Thebes, which enjoyed far greater literary fame than that of the Epigones. The seven gates and the walls of Thebes were not stormed at this time, tradition says; on the contrary, the attack proved disastrous for the assailants. The epic poem which dealt with these events evidently was the core of the Theban cycle. Its contents are presupposed in more than one passage of the *Iliad*. In particular, the formula "seven-gated Thebes" could have been taken from the Theban epic.[5]

Yet it is here that the problem of reality arises. It is difficult to imagine a seven-gated city in the Bronze Age; it is nonsense to think of a fortified palace in the style of Mycenae with seven gates. In 1891 Wilamowitz calmly declared that the seven gates existed for the sake of the seven assailants in the saga only: a narrative symmetry which bore no relation to reality. The later Greek city extended some distance over the plain and was correspondingly walled. In fact the hill upon which the current city of Thebes lies and where, in the central section, finds from the Mycenaean palace have come to light, is large enough for a city of that period. Local archaeologists, in their maps, have long put the seven gates on the boundaries of that hill.[6] As a result of constant overbuilding, there are no corresponding archaeological finds. Others have insisted that the hill always had and still has three and not seven natural approaches. Sarantis Symeonoglou, in his recent and authoritative reinvestigation of Theban topography, agrees that the Late Bronze Age city can have had only three or four gates—he decides on four—but then attributes the seven gates to the smaller, earlier settlement of the Middle Bronze Age, finding confirmation in what Pausanias wrote some 1,600 years later, undaunted by the consequence that, if he were right, the putative historical "Seven" of the Late Bronze Age could never have found their proper seven gates. This paradox finally should vindicate Wilamowitz' skepticism.

The Seven themselves are a strange group. Their names vary in different versions, and it is impossible to reconstruct the oldest one with any certainty. It is not even clear whether the leader, Adrastos, and the instigator of the enterprise, Polyneikes the exiled king of Thebes, should be counted in with them.[7] Some of the heroes, as we know them from Aeschylus, have a story and hence some individuality of their own, including Amphiaraos the seer, who had his sanctuary and his cult afterwards,[8] and Tydeus, father of the immortal Diomedes. Others appear as stock figures to fill out the list. To call one of them Eteoklos, vis-à-vis Eteokles the brother of Polyneikes, appears to be the almost desperate invention of a faltering poet. But seven they were. Polyneikes and Eteokles have telling names which refer to precisely this war: "much strife" against "true glory," the assailant against the protector of the city. It is absolutely impossible that both the war and the names of the commanders should be historical, that is, coincidental. These names are inventions to fit a specific concept.

This and similar considerations led Ernst Howald to a radical thesis presented in 1939—which has, since then, found hardly any echo. He claimed that the tale of the seven evil assailants who are fortunately repulsed, led by Adrastos the "inescapable" on his magic horse, is pure myth in its essence: Originally these were seven demons, an "outbreak from Hell." Adrastos betrays his infernal status even through the tragic choruses by which he was honored at Sikyon, as we are told by Herodotus; his horse Arion, born of Erinys, is an infernal steed; Adrastos' followers are seven demons from the underworld, including Tydeus with his cannibalistic desires.[9] Later and secondarily the underworld myth was transformed into a heroic epic linked to the actual city of Thebes. This has created "history," accepted as such right up to *The Cambridge Ancient History*.

What Howald did not know was that the story of the attack of the evil Seven from the underworld under the command of a terrifying god exists in fact, in the form of an Akkadian epic text: the story of Erra, the plague god. It was first published in a virtually complete form in 1956, with an improved version appearing in 1969.[10] It is unique insofar as it is the work of an individual poet named Kabti-Ilani-Marduk, who introduces himself at the end of the text. The god Erra himself, he says, revealed the complete text to him in a dream. In contrast to *Atrahasis,* this work is relatively "young." It has been dated to the ninth or eighth century B.C.[11]

Kabti-Ilani-Marduk introduces the Seven *(Sibitti)* as the sons of heaven and earth, "champions without peer"—this expression is used as a formula—and absolutely terrifying; each of them is assigned his special destructive "fate" by father Anu. They call on the god Erra, the god of war and plague, to destroy mankind. Marduk, the highest god of Babylon, leaves his throne and abandons the world to its destruction. Foreign peoples begin to invade Babylonia, only to be themselves attacked by the Seven. The cry goes up on every side: "Erra has killed." But then the god, who has demonstrated his power so irresistibly, calms down, and, before mankind is completely destroyed, he withdraws together with his Seven. The epic concludes with a blessing for the land of Akkad and praise for the powerful god.

This is a very short summary of a complicated composition. It cannot be claimed that this text is simply and directly the original version as postulated by Howald. There are, nevertheless, remarkable parallels: the seven "champions without peer," whose number is used as their very name in this text, with an ineluctable god at their head; an attack and great danger; and then, finally, the retreat which means salvation for those under threat. A significant difference between the Greek and Babylonian versions is that the Greek saga concentrates on the city of Thebes while in the other the action is set in a worldwide framework; and whereas the Babylonian poet combines plague and war, the Greek story portrays pure heroic battle.

Erra is an unusual epic in that the literary text soon came to assume magic functions. It appeared suited to serve as a mythical model to reverse the attacks of that very plague god and thereby to act as a form of exorcism. The text, or parts thereof, were written on amulets to protect against sickness.[12]

In fact the evil Seven are well known in a whole range of Akkadian incantation texts, from different collections.[13] Occasionally they are listed individually and given various demonic names, such as *asakku, namtaru, utukku, alu, eṭemmu, gallu, ilu limnu* (evil god),[14] but also South Wind, Great Dragon, Panther, Snake, Slime Beast, Whirlwind, Evil Wind.[15] What remains constant is their number, which is repeated almost compulsively: "They are seven, they are seven." They live in the depths of the earth, they rise up from the earth;[16] they "kill," they bring diseases of all kinds; it is they who attack the moon god and thus cause the eclipses of the moon. Fortunately the exorcist priest has good, strong helping spirits to counteract their influence.

Among the texts in which the Seven appear is an incantation text from the series *Bit meseri,* "the house surrounded by protecting spirits."[17] This also deals with the healing of sickness. The evil powers of disease are represented by the Seven, the "Seven with terrible wings." In the ritual they are represented in effigy, perhaps even drawn on the wall. "I placed the picture of Nergal at their heads." Nergal is the god of the underworld and of plague who is very close to Erra in function. But then unusual figures of twins are named: two images of "twins brought together" at the head of the sick to the right and the left, "twins fighting each other made of plaster" in the center of the doorway, similar twins made of asphalt on the door frames to the right and to the left. In addition, the gods Ea and Marduk are placed as guardians to the right and left in the center of the door. The use of figurines, produced ad hoc and then destroyed, is not an uncommon feature in the practice of exorcism,[18] but the twins appear only in this particular text. There follows an incantation of the "Seven before whom there stands the image of Nergal"; but then the exorcist turns to other "Seven gods who carry weapons" and calls upon them to destroy enemies and evil forces and to grant life.

Seven terrible beings therefore are present, with the god of plague and death at their head; seven divine combatants are supposed to overcome the evil; and in addition there are the twins fighting each other in the doorway.[19] The situation is uncannily close to that of the *Seven against Thebes* as known from Aeschylus: Seven evil and frightful assailants are enumerated, led by one whose name is "inescapable"; seven armed heroes are pitted against them; and the decisive battle is between the two brothers who are to fight and kill each other at the seventh gate.

In addition there is a remarkable iconographic bridge from East to West. Among the orthostate reliefs from the palace of Tell Halaf, which, along with Carchemish and Zincirli, are important examples of Late Hittite monumental art, there appears side by side with lions and griffins a couple of almost identical men, twins, who have seized each other by the forelock and are simultaneously running each other through with their swords (Figure 8). This is iconographically parallel to the representations of Eteokles and Polyneikes in mutual fratricide as became popular in Etruria from approximately 600 onward.[20] There are no known intermediary links; a possibility would be lost metal reliefs. Instead of images, however, there is a text from Palestine to fill the gap, from the second book of Samuel: During the civil war between Saul's successor and David, events lead to a tournament between twelve hand-picked warriors from each side. "But each seized his opponent by the forelock and thrust his sword into his side so that all fell together."[21] This episode has also been compared with the fight of the Horatii and the Curiatii in Roman tradition.[22] In Greek myth there appear the two powerful brothers, Otos and Ephialtes, the Aloadae, who would have been invincible had they not accidently shot each other when aiming at a doe which leaped between them.[23] Mythological imagination stubbornly keeps portraying what, in reality, would be the most unlikely event. This seems to be the ideal of absolute and autogenous annihilation; no outsiders are involved, and the conflict eliminates itself. Perhaps it is for this reason that the Etruscans found it appropriate to use this image so often as a reference to death, again and again decorating their funerary

Figure 8. Orthostate relief from the palace at Guzana–Tell Halaf, ninth century B.C.: twins killing each other.

urns with the fight of Eteokles and Polyneikes. But the apotropaic function which the Tell Halaf relief must have possessed can well be understood in this sense, too, and finally also the miniature figurines used by the magicians officiating in the *Bit meseri* ritual fall into place. The conflict eliminates itself, after which harmony and health will return.

More perplexing is the question of what an exorcism of this type can possibly have to do with an epic about Boeotian Thebes. Yet several answers come to mind. Boeotia had its orientalizing period too; it lies close enough to Euboea, the center of East-West trade in the eighth century. Boeotian fibulae from around 700 B.C. have the earliest mythological representations we know in Greece, including the Trojan horse but also Herakles fighting the seven-headed snake. This motif clearly has to do with the Semitic East, as does the lion fight.[24] Thebes, however, lay in ruins and had been replaced by Hypothebai, if the catalogue of ships can be taken as evidence of the geometric or early archaic period. The Kadmean hill had been laid to waste until the rebuilding began, which still allowed some of the Mycenaean ruins to stand as sacred relics, such as the "House of Kadmos." It can be taken for granted that seers were involved in such a new beginning. The prominence of liver divination and the occasional occurrence of foundation deposits show that specialists from the East knew how to outdo the native bird-diviners.[25] Thus all the elements are there to allow us to entertain the idea that, to avert evil forces from the new foundation, a migrant practitioner carried out some form of *Bit meseri* ritual; and that a poet, inspired with many ways of song by the god, took the plot of the seven evil assailants and the seven protectors together with the twins as represented in the figurines to make it the central thread of an epic song: It was this city of Thebes which, in olden times, once was attacked by the dreadful seven but successfully rebuffed them all, even though the royal brothers killed each other simultaneously at the gate. That details of local tradition such as Amphiaraos and Tydeus and, most important of all, Oedipus, the uncanny father of fratricides, were incorporated in the web of poetry is not too astonishing.

There is also a second possibility. Disease is a universal problem; epidemics do not pause at language barriers. It has been argued that there was a catastrophic drought in Greece toward the end of the eighth century;[26] but this is far from certain. Famine and pestilence would easily go hand in hand—reason enough to seek out even unfamiliar, foreign remedies, providing an opportunity for migrant charismatics. Similarly to the way in which Asgelatas reached Anaphe, some after-effects of Mesopotamian magical practice may have remained in Boeotia, admittedly transformed almost beyond recognition into the form of a heroic song. It has been asked why, judging by the archaic imagery, the tale of Thebes was so much more popular with the Etruscans than it was in Greece, and the answer given has been that this was because of the special role given to the seers and to divination in this epic.[27] Perhaps the lost *Thebaid* bore more traces of such interests than the few fragments preserved allow us to recognize.

If the poem of the *Seven against Thebes* is an invention of the orientalizing period, it must still have been quite a success and spread rapidly. Even in primitive times this would not have taken more than a few years, and the combination with the Trojan theme, with Tydeus/Diomedes above all, could also have occurred very quickly. The *Iliad* presupposes the existence of the Theban theme if not necessarily the written text which later came to the Alexandrian library. It seems that towards the end of the geometric period a more ancient tomb was discovered at Eleusis and fitted out afresh for a cult of heroes. This presumably is the grave which subsequently was called the Tomb of the Seven, even though no direct evidence has been found to identify that tomb.[28] It fits in with other examples of heroic cult established under the influence of the epic since the eighth century.[29] This gives a terminal date for the fame of the Thebes theme. The text of our *Iliad* may well come from the first half of the seventh century.[30]

Much remains obscure and uncertain for us even after the end of the "dark ages." All the more reason, then, to draw on all the indications which point to likely connections. Whoever resists the idea that the Seven against Thebes have to some extent a Mesopotamian pedigree should nevertheless not overlook that a similar provenience must be accepted for the seven-headed Hydra as well as for the Seven Sages.[31] Seven gods or demons were also known among the Aramaeans in the eighth century.[32]

Common Style and Stance in Oriental and Greek Epic

Ever since the mythological texts from Hattusa and Ugarit have attracted the attention of classicists, parallels from Hesiod and

Homer in motifs and narrative techniques have been collected, occasionally also touching on Mesopotamian materials. Recently, Luigia Achillea Stella has presented an extensive catalogue of correspondences.[1] She pleads decisively for the Bronze Age cultural bridge. But comparisons by themselves do not provide specific indicators for either an earlier or a later borrowing, indeed for any borrowing at all in contrast to the chances of parallel development. In any case, uncertainties about the date of "influence" should not distract us from acknowledging how extensive these correspondences are.

In a sense, of course, Greek epic is a very self-sufficient flowering. The formulaic system, which Milman Parry discovered and explained in terms of its necessary function within an oral tradition, is tied to the Greek language.[2] From this point of view Homer has become the model example of an oral tradition.[3] By contrast, the eastern epic, at least in Mesopotamia, is based in a fixed tradition of writing and schools of scribes spanning more than two millennia. Within this tradition tablets are copied and recopied again and again, and sometimes also translated within the cuneiform systems.

One should expect therefore to encounter quite different principles of style in the East and in the West. Yet anyone who cares to consider both sides will be struck by the similarities. The most important of these have been indicated long ago; a partial listing follows.

In both cases "epic" means narrative poetry which employs, in form, a long verse which repeats itself indefinitely, without strophic division. As to content, the tale is about gods and great men from the past, often interacting. Main characteristics of style are the standard epithets, the formulaic verses, the repetition of verses, the typical scenes.

Epithets have always appeared to be a special characteristic of Homeric style. We are familiar with "cloud-gathering Zeus," "Odysseus of many counsels," "Odysseus of many sufferings." But in Akkadian epic, too, the chief characters have characteristic epithets. The chief god, Enlil, often appears as "the hero Enlil,"[4] the hero of the flood is "Utnapishtim the far-away,"[5] and the dangerous Seven in the Erra epic are "champions without peer."⁶ Similarly the Ugaritic epics have fixed formulas such as Baal "the rider of clouds," "the Virgin Anat," and "Danel the Rephaite."⁷ What sounds even more Homeric is the designation of a combatant as "knowledgeable in battle."⁸ It is less clear why the "mistress of the gods" is "good in shouting,"⁹ but it was also unclear even to Greeks why Kalypso as well as Kirke should be "a frightful goddess using speech," *deine theos audeessa*. Be that as it may, an epic poet cannot do without epithets: The earth is "the broad earth,"¹⁰ and a god of heavens can be called "father of gods and men."¹¹ The epithets are decorative insofar as they are neither essential to the actual context of the current situation nor modeled specially for it. Among other things, they are extremely helpful to fill out a half-verse.

In formulaic verse what is most striking is the complicated introduction of direct speech. The lavish use of direct speech, the representation of whole scenes in the form of dialogue is, indeed, a peculiarity of the genre. In Akkadian, the introductory formula is, in literal translation: "He set his mouth and spoke, to . . . he said [the word]."¹² The simple meaning of *speak* is expressed in three synonyms—just as with the well-known Homeric formula "he raised his voice and spoke the winged words." It is perhaps even more remarkable that characters in *Gilgamesh,* reflecting on a new situation, "speak to their own heart." "Consulting with her heart she spoke, indeed she took counsel with herself"—direct speech follows.¹³ In a similar way Homeric heroes speak to their own "great-hearted *thymos*" or to their "heart." When Gilgamesh is travelling, the new day is always introduced with the same formula: "Barely a shimmer of the morning dawned,"¹⁴ reminiscent of Homer's famous line "But when early-born rosy-fingered Eos appeared." It is natural for a narrative to move on from day to day, but to employ stereotyped formulas for sunrise and sunset, pause and action is a specific technique used in *Gilgamesh* as in Homer.

Among the repetitions which cover a whole sequence of verses a striking feature is the exact verbal correspondence between command and performance, reporting and repetition of the report. The Mesopotamian scribes, weary of wedges, occasionally used a "repeat" sign, which the Homeric scribes did not permit themselves.

Among typical scenes the assembly of the gods is prominent. Akkadian has a fixed expression for it, *puhur ilani;* the designation is the same in Ugaritic, and the respective scene is also fully elaborated in the Hittite *Song of Ullikummi.*[15] That in the assembly of the gods it is often decided to send out a messenger is natural and still worth noting.

Similes are a popular device in the Akkadian epic as in related poetry; details need not be given here.[16] What seems more remarkable is that in *Gilgamesh,* the longest and highest-ranking text, more complicated forms of narrative technique are being tried out, as is the case especially in the *Odyssey.* In the eleventh tablet of *Gilgamesh* a distant but particularly gripping piece of action, the great flood, is incorporated through direct speech by the main participant, Utnapishtim the far-away. The dual action at the beginning of the epic which has to bring together Enkidu and Gilgamesh is set out in such a way that the narrative first follows Enkidu's adventures and his transformation to civilization and then recounts Gilgamesh's preparations for the meeting through direct speech which the prostitute addresses to Enkidu (I v 23–vi 24). Thus even the narrative technique of the poet of the *Odyssey,* who incorporates most of Odysseus' adventures in a first-person speech by Odysseus himself to the Phaeacians and devises a double plot to bring Odysseus and Telemachos together, is not totally isolated. The similarity between the openings of *Gilgamesh* and the *Odyssey* has struck readers too: Attention is called to the hero who wandered wide and saw many things while his name is intentionally withheld.[17]

Foreshadowing the *Iliad,* as it were, *Gilgamesh* in particular exhibits a certain ethos of the mortality of human beings. The main theme of the poem is, in its own words, the "fates of humanity" (*šimatu awilutim),* which means death, in contrast to the life of the gods, which only Utnapishtim succeeded in winning for himself. Before his fight with Humbaba, Gilgamesh draws the heroic consequence: "The gods, with Shamash [the sun god] they sit forever; as for mankind, numbered are their days . . .

But you here, you fear death? . . . I will go ahead of you . . . If I myself were to fall, let me still set up my name." [18] Thus, precisely because man is denied eternity, all that remains for him is to win fame through risking death, fame which survives beyond death; imperishable glory (*kleos aphthiton*), in contrast to mortal men, these are the concepts set out in the *Iliad* in Greek. "Yes, dear friend! If, having escaped from this war, we were to live forever ageless, immortal, even I would not fight among the front ranks . . . But now, as the demons of death stand before us anyhow . . . Let us go! whether we bring glory to another man or someone gives glory to us"—this is Homer. [19] This insight into the limits of the human condition does not, however, lead to caution in relation to the gods. Far from it, aggressive outbursts may occur. Enkidu throws the hind leg of the bull of heaven to Ishtar and shouts: "If I caught you, like this I would do to you." [20] "Indeed I would take revenge if I only had the power," cries Achilles to Apollo, who has deceived him. [21]

But man is weak and changeable. "Of such a kind is the insight of mortal men, as the day which the father of gods and men brings on" states one of the most famous passages of the *Odyssey*. [22] Practically identical is a sentence about mortals from the Akkadian composition *I Will Praise the Lord of Wisdom:* "Their insight changes like day and night. When starving, they become corpses; when replete, they vie with their gods." [23]

Closer comparisons could also be made of actual battle scenes. One notable example is the Egyptian poem about Ramses II in the battle of Qadesh. The hero finds himself alone amidst the enemies, he prays to his father the god, the god hears him, whereupon the hero attacks and kills all the enemies. [24] Another suggestive text is incorporated in the *Annals of Sennacherib* and refers to the battle of Halule in 691 B.C.; it tells how the king takes up his armor, mounts his chariot, and with the assistance of his god knocks down the enemies; so finally "my prancing steeds, harnessed for my riding, plunged into the streams of blood as into a river; the wheels of my chariot, which brings down the wicked and the evil, were bespattered with blood and filth"²⁵—note the standard epithets; and just like Ramses the Egyptian, the Assyrian king, too, is represented fighting from his Bronze Age chariot. We are irresistibly reminded of the *Iliad:* "Thus under greathearted Achilles his one-hoofed horses stepped on corpses and shields together; with blood the whole axle was bespattered, and the rails around the seat, which the drops from the hoofs of the horses were hitting . . ." Considering the date of the Assyrian text, one might even toy with the idea that some Greek singer had arrived in Assyria together with the mercenaries, and that he composed this song on the battle of Halule which so much pleased the king that it was incorporated in the official annals, where it forms a strange contrast to the standard dreary and dull list of battle and plundering.²⁶ But more systematic research into this genre would be due. The "Song of Deborah and Barak" should not be forgotten in this context; it has, among other stirring events, a remarkable "battle at the river."²⁷

Some further connections in detail between East and West, though striking, have remained a mystery. This applies to the "Word of Tree and Stone" as it appears in Ugarit, in Jeremiah, and in Homer and Hesiod; it seems to be connected with a myth about the origin of man in the Old Testament and in the *Odyssey,* but is used as a less lucid saying in Ugarit as in the *Iliad* and in Hesiod.²⁸

Less surprising is that the blessing of the land under the rule of a good king is established in Mesopotamia, but it also appears in Homer and Hesiod: The earth brings forth her crops, the trees their fruit, the animals thrive, and "people thrive under him" the good king; compare Ashurbanipal on himself in his own account: "Since the gods . . . benignly made me take my seat on the throne of my father, my begetter, Adad released his torrents of rain, Ea opened his springs, the ears of the crops grew five ells high . . . the fruits of the field flourished . . . the trees brought their fruits to an abundant growth, the cattle bred successfully. During my reign there was abundance, during my years good things overflowed."²⁹

Enough of parallels. Style is hardly separable from content. For stylistic elements, direct dependence is hard to prove: Each language has its own laws and its own life. In Homer we cannot ascertain the presence of "younger," additional elements against the older epic tradition in the characteristics discussed so far, in contrast to the mythological concepts found in the context of the "Deception of Zeus," the opening of the *Cypria,* or the *Seven against Thebes.* For the style of battle scenes we definitely reach the Bronze Age with Ramses' account. Still, considering the fact that we are dealing with spatially and chronologically linked spheres of civilization anyhow, to insist on completely separate developments and purely coincidental parallels is begging the question. One has to reckon with multiple contacts, to be set against both the general human background and common tendencies of historical-social developments. What was in fact a heritage of the Bronze Age could also be revitalized by new incentives. It is probably symptomatic that besides the traditional Greek loan-word for lion, *leon,* another word of clearly Semitic-Palestinian pedigree, *lis,* has been adopted in some Homeric similes.[30] In any event, the eastern evidence offers such closely related material that it should not be overlooked in the interpretation of Homer. This finding must set certain limits to assessments of purely "Indo-European" heroic tradition.

The establishment of the first Greek library—the *Iliad* written down on twenty-four(?) leather scrolls—and of the great library of Ashurbanipal at Nineveh, who ruled from 668 to 627, may well have taken place at about the same time. Even this may not be totally coincidental. The Semitic East still held the cultural lead until that date.

Fables

The genre of the animal fable has met with disdain since the end of the Enlightenment; and yet it is one of the most peculiar and enduring forms of folk literature.[1] One might be tempted to relegate it to the level of popular tale and thereby to some form of general and diffuse oral tradition. But more detailed research, particularly in the area of medieval and early modern fables, demonstrates repeatedly that it was the written anthologies, the translations and selections of Aesop, and further elaborations which were responsible for the diffusion of these stories. It is true that the fables entered into living folk tradition through children's experience at the level of elementary school, so that field workers would rediscover them as if they had always belonged to people's oral wisdom. But their literary crystallization lies much further back.

Aesop, the name with which the basic collection of Greek animal fables is connected, is not the beginning. It has long been known that animal fables existed not only in Egyptian,[2] but also in Sumerian and Akkadian[3] and, at least in the genre of plant fables, in Hebrew.[4] Hermann Diels wrote on "oriental fables in Greek clothing" as early as 1910; he was dealing with the newly discovered text of Callimachus, which presents the fable "The Laurel and the Olive Tree" as a tale of "the ancient-Lydians."[5] Babrius, who set down the fables of Aesop in verse, states expressly at the beginning of his second book that this type of "myth" is an invention of the ancient "Syrians" from the time of Ninos and Belos; Aesop was the first to relate them to the "sons of the Hellenes." Ninos (that is, Nineveh) and Belos are terms used since the histories of Ktesias to designate the Assyrian era. Babrius was writing in Syria or Cilicia for some minor prince.[6] He knows what he is talking about, even if we are not in a position to prove what his sources were for this thesis. For confirmation there is the fact that the story of Ahiqar was translated from the Aramaic into Greek and was made a part of the *Life of Aesop*—maybe just at the time of Babrius; but Callimachus' reference to "the ancient Lydians" would point to oriental contacts in the archaic period.[7]

For us Greek fable begins with Hesiod's *ainos* "the hawk and the nightingale" (*Erga* 203–212); then Archilochus presents his fables with moral appeal in a poignant and aggressive form. We know most about his poem which introduces "the eagle and the fox." Its point is quite clear: to warn high-ranking and insolent criminals of the revenge which even the weak may take someday. The fox and the eagle entered into a pact, but one day the eagle ate the fox's young and jeered at him from the inaccessible heights of his nest. The fox called on Zeus, the powerful guardian of *hybris* and *dike*—a section of direct speech in the poem. Retribution follows.[8] It has long been remarked that an Akkadian text has nearly the same story. This is not itself an independent fable, but rather an introduction to the myth of Etana, who flew up to heaven on an eagle. In this case it is an eagle and a snake who enter into a pact and jointly gather food, which they share until the eagle perpetrates the outrage and eats the snake's young. The snake turns to Shamash, the sun god, and, in direct speech, calls on him as the guardian of justice. Retribution follows, thanks to the cunning of the snake.[9] Admittedly the form of revenge is different in the two texts, and a snake is involved instead of a fox. The polarity snake–eagle has a respectable symbolic tradition and may, to that extent, be the original model.[10] Anyhow we are not dealing with a case of translation. And yet it is not just the basic idea and the sequence of the motifs, the strange pact, the transgression, the revenge, which the two texts have in common, but also a literary device, the direct speech in the pathetic appeal to the heavenly god as a guardian of right and punisher of those who transgress it. A prayer of this nature is not common in Greece at the time of Archilochus, as far as we know, whereas for the Easterners the sun god is performing one of his usual functions. That the solemn prayer is put in the mouth of an animal has a grotesque and memorable effect in both the Akkadian and the Greek texts. By the way, Etana being carried up to heaven on the wings of an eagle is often represented on oriental seals. It may easily be presumed that the myth of the rape of Ganymede by Zeus in the guise of an eagle has been influenced by such representations.[11] This still does not explain how Archilochus could have had knowledge of a Mesopotamian text. But a further surprising link has surfaced for Archilochus: The new Archilochus poem contained in the Cologne papyrus uses the adage of the "hasty bitch who consequently bears blind puppies."[12] A good thousand years before Archilochus this proverb makes its appearance in a royal letter from

Mari.[13] This may be called folk tradition elaborating on biological facts, but we should rather acknowledge a tradition of wisdom which transcends linguistic and cultural barriers, especially in the form of the animal fable. In the case of the Etana text, direct literary connection is not at all ruled out. Archilochus knew the leather scrolls of Phoenician-Aramaic type.[14]

A much more engaging motif appears to be folkloric and literary at the same time, and it is found in both Akkadian literature and later in ancient Greece: the story of the herb of rejuvenation, which has been lost to mankind because it was eaten by the snake. In *Gilgamesh* this is the dramatic conclusion to the journey to Utnapishtim. The search to evade death has been the incentive for Gilgamesh's travels; finally all has been in vain. Utnapishtim had indicated how Gilgamesh could fetch the plant of eternal youth from the depths of the sea. Gilgamesh does so, and he sets off for home with his precious find; but, while he is bathing in a cool spring, a snake comes, attracted by the aroma of the plant, and eats it. The snake then sheds its old skin—this skin of snakes was called *geras,* old age, by the Greeks. Gilgamesh can only lament his loss.[15] In the Greek version, Zeus gave mankind a drug against growing old as a reward for having informed against Prometheus. The drug is loaded onto an ass. The ass arrives at a spring and wants to drink, but a snake prevents him from getting to the water until the ass gives over whatever he is carrying on his back. Thus, the snake is able to rejuvenate itself while mankind is left empty-handed. In what we have of Greek literature the story first appears in the work of Ibycus.[16] Thus it was known to the Greeks in the archaic period.

One tends to think of oral narrative traditions at this point. The basic thought and general human experience behind the story are dramatically impressive and easy to comprehend. The structure and the details in Ibycus differ from those of *Gilgamesh:* another context, another motivation, another animal involved as bearer of the miraculous substance. That snakes shed their skin is a biological fact, and snakes tend to be close to water both in nature and in Greek mythology. Still, real snakes do not feed on herbs or drugs. It cannot be proved that the tale migrated directly from *Gilgamesh* to Ibycus. Yet the general framework of the orientalizing period and the connections of the Greek with the Mesopotamian animal fable in particular, this tale of lost immortality becomes yet another element in the shared cultural horizon of East and West.

Magic and Cosmogony

It remains to reflect on how much the connecting threads which have been followed here intertwine: Images, practices, and mythical tales are all mutually connected. Seals, scarabs, and amulets can be put to profane as well as magical use. Reinterpretation, however, can produce a purely mythical figure from protective symbols: Lamashtu becomes the Gorgon.[1] Mythical motifs can grow from images such as the combats with the lion and with the seven-headed snake: These turn into tales of the adventures of Herakles, localized at Nemea and Lerna;[2] another battle with the monstrous snake changes to become the deeds of Perseus;[3] and the representation of the death of Agamemnon connects with the Humbaba images.[4] In this way a system of indigenous meanings is projected on foreign materials to modify and reinforce Greek heroic mythology; misinterpretation proves to be creative, but it still follows the lead of the adopted forms.

The fact that myth and magic ritual can profoundly influence each other is well known.[5] Magical incantations tend to use mythical stories as exemplary precedents which predict the outcome and thus assist in achieving their aim. This holds true from the *Veda* to some old German charms, but it is no specialty of the Indo-European tradition; Mesopotamian texts provide examples which are no less telling. There is the myth of Adapa the fisher, who broke the South Wind's wings with a charm and was summoned to heaven in consequence; the Assyrian version of this myth turns, in the end, into an exorcism against sickness supposedly caused by the South Wind. The poem *Erra* ends with the god of war and pestilence luckily appeased; the text is therefore written on magic amulets to protect against pestilence.[6] The creation of mankind as told in *Atrahasis* is also used as a magical text to help at childbirth, and the tale of how drought was overcome, from the same text, becomes a rain-making charm.[7] Another incantation text recounts how the moon god Sin couples with a virgin, she as a cow, he as a bull; the god begets children in this way and then lends a helping hand to ease the birth: This is a transparent magic rite of child-birth, too. The story recalls the Greek myth of Zeus and Io, who has been transformed into a cow, and the birth of Epaphos by means of the father's helping touch (*epaphon*).[8] There are also cosmogonical texts which are used against headaches and tooth-ache.[9]

It is in this way that speculation and practice meet in the cos-mogonic perspective: A new and proper order has to be created or recreated from its very foundations. Something has gone wrong, as sickness and pain indicate; so one should begin afresh from the beginning. The cosmogonic epic *Enuma Elish* was of-ficially incorporated in the New Year's festival at Babylon to rebuild the just and sacred order, including all the privileges of the god and his city.[10] This means to act out the same idea which a magician tries as he is getting to the root of a particular sick-ness within the hugely enlarged framework of the city at the center of the world. "High" literature and practical incantations come together on the same level, at any rate in the East. It is the practicing priests who also control the literary texts, as is shown by the existence of priests' libraries in Ugarit, Emar, and Sultan-tepe.[11]

Turning from this to Greek civilization, we find the double aspect of cathartic practice and speculative mythology combined in Orphism in particular:[12] There are the migrant, mendicant priests with their initiations scorned by Plato;[13] there is the fa-mous and controversial myth about the origin of mankind from the ashes of the Titans who had torn apart Dionysus—which is why we carry the rebellious as well as the divine element in ourselves.[14] The necessary link between ritual and anthropo-gonic myth can be seen from the function of the charismatic healers: The sick person desperately asks what the source of the affliction might be, "whence it sprang, what the root of evil can be, which gods they should appease with sacrifice in order to find relief from their sufferings."[15] The answer must lie somewhere in the past: Thus Epimenides the seer "prophesied not about the future, but about the past."[16] But the most general answer which can be given, extending far beyond the individual case, is the interpretation of human existence as the consequence of an ancient crime, as a punishment going back to the oldest "wrath" of great gods. Empedocles, as late as the fifth century, is a migrant seer and healer himself who identifies his lifestyle with the fundamentals of human existence: Here I am, "banished from the gods and a wanderer."[17]

For classicists the fact that the Dionysiac-Orphic anthropogony as an explicit text is found only in Olympiodorus, that is, in the sixth century A.D., has repeatedly roused the suspicion that this is a "late invention." It is all the more astounding that the closest parallels are in fact provided by the Mesopotamian mythological texts, which go back well into the second millennium B.C. The *Enuma Elish* depicts the creation of mankind from the blood of a rebellious god condemned by the judgment of the other gods. Other texts offer variations on the theme.[18] More startling is the version of the creation of mankind as told in *Atrahasis:* The flesh and blood of a god must be mixed with clay (*ṭiṭ*) "that god and man may be thoroughly mixed in the clay: . . . let there be a spirit from the god's flesh: Let it proclaim living [man] as its sign; that he be not forgotten, let there be a spirit."[19] The word translated as "spirit" is *eṭemmu,* which otherwise refers to a spirit of the dead, often subject to exorcisms.[20] The *Atrahasis* passage evidently has a special, speculative point to make, though it has proved difficult to capture it. A possible interpretation is that the "god's flesh" within the clay is meant to account both for life in the living being and for the ghost who is left after death, "that he be not forgotten." Contrasted with "clay," this still marks the rudiments of a dualistic anthropology as early as a thousand years before Homer: "God" giving rise to life and "spirit" amidst some form of matter—this conception states the existence of opposite elements in man, violently yet "thoroughly mixed" in the act of creation. There is no anachronism at all in attributing similar lore to Orphics as early as the archaic period, the assertion of some divine element in man left from the god who was killed at the primordial act of creation. There may even have been direct links.[21] Of course the Orphic myth of Dionysus is not a translation from any eastern text. But we may well envisage the evolution of a continuous tradition through those "families" of wandering priests and seers for whose craft a myth of this type was so practical, nay almost necessary. This would prove once more that the East–West connections went beyond accidental contacts and borrowings and occasionally reached the level of basic anthropological ideas.

CONCLUSION

To sum up a long and often tortuous investigation: Emanating from the Near East, in connection with military expansion and growing economic activities, a cultural continuum including literacy was created by the eighth century extending over the entire Mediterranean; it involved groups of Greeks who entered into intensive exchange with the high cultures of the Semitic East. Cultural predominance remained for a while with the Orient; but Greeks immediately began to develop their own distinctive forms of culture through an astonishing ability both to adopt and to transform what they had received. Soon Greece was to take over the leading role in Mediterranean civilization.

It is safe to state that the East-West connections of this epoch were more intensive than the "Aegean *koine*" of the Bronze Age. There were the military advances from Babylonia to Cilicia and Cyprus involving Greek merchants, Greek mercenaries, and Greek cities; there were the settlements of the Phoenicians on Cyprus and in the West, of the Greeks in Syria and then also in the West. There were the massive imports of goods, especially metalwork, but also the transfer of manual craft skills into Greece. With bronze reliefs, textiles, seals, and other products, a whole world of eastern images was opened up which the Greeks were only too eager to adopt and to adapt in the course of an "orientalizing revolution." Along with other craftsmen, migrant seers and purification priests seem to have arrived in Greek cities; liver divination, foundation deposits, the practice of cathartic healing magic all bear the traces of this influence. Over and above all this there was the direct impact of written culture as shown by the alphabet, the writing tablet, the leather scroll, and the format of writing books. This impact is confirmed by extant passages of early Greek literature that clearly echo Mesopotamian classics. Homer's decisive role in forming the world view of the Greeks for subsequent ages was achieved by the force of written culture into which the Greeks finally allowed themselves to be drawn right at this period. Just as in the case of liver divination, the literary borrowings seem to belong only to the last phase of Greek epic poetry; it is post–Bronze Age works such as *Enuma Elish* and *Erra* which have left their mark. It is precisely the Homeric epoch of Greece that is the epoch of the orientalizing revolution.

Culture is not a plant sprouting from its seed in isolation; it is a continuous process of learning guided by curiosity along with practical needs and interests. It grows especially through a willingness to learn from what is "other," what is strange and foreign. A revolutionary period such as the orientalizing epoch provided this very opportunity for cultural development. The "miracle of Greece" is not merely the result of a unique talent. It also owes its existence to the simple phenomenon that the Greeks are the most easterly of the Westerners. Under the special circumstances of the eighth century, they could participate in every development at the time without falling victim to the concomitant military devastations, as did their neighbors in Syria and southern Anatolia. The miracle did repeat itself once again, when the Persian Empire reached but finally spared the Greeks. Later the catastrophes were to come from both the West and the East. Greece has remained in an uneasy intermediary position. Hellas is not Hesperia.

ABBREVIATIONS

Common periodicals cited in the notes are referred to by standard abbreviations. For full titles of classical works cited in abbreviated form in the notes, see *The Oxford Classical Dictionary*.

ABV   J. D. Beazley, *Attic Black-Figure Vase Painters* (Oxford 1956)

AHw   W. von Soden, *Akkadisches Handwörterbuch* (Wiesbaden 1965–1981)

ANEP   J. B. Pritchard, ed., *The Ancient Near East in Pictures Relating to the Old Testament,* 2d ed. with supplement (Princeton 1969)

ANET   J. B. Pritchard, ed., *Ancient Near Eastern Texts Relating to the Old Testament,* 3d ed. with supplement (Princeton 1969)

Atrahasis   W. G. Lambert and A. R. Millard, *Atra-ḫasīs, The Babylonian Story of the Flood* (Oxford 1969)
W. von Soden, "Die erste Tafel des altbabylonischen Atramḫasis-Mythus, 'Haupttext' und Parallelversionen," *ZA* 68 (1978) 50–94
Translations: Bottéro and Kramer (1989) 530–564; Dalley (1989) 9–38

BM   British Museum

CAD   I. J. Gelb et al., eds., *The Assyrian Dictionary of the Oriental Institute of the University of Chicago* (Chicago 1956–)

CAH   *The Cambridge Ancient History* (Cambridge 1924–)

CIS   *Corpus Inscriptionum Semiticarum* (Paris 1881–)

CT   Cuneiform texts from Babylonian tablets in the British Museum (London 1896–)

Enuma Elish   W. G. Lambert and S. B. Parker, eds., *Enuma Eliš* (Oxford 1967) (cuneiform text)
G. F. Steiner, *Der Sukzessionsmythus in Hesiods 'Theogonie' und ihren orientalischen Parallelen* (Diss. Hamburg 1959) 7–35 (transcription of Tablets I–VI)
Translations: *ANET* 60–72; Labat et al. (1970) 36–70; Bottéro and Kramer (1989) 604–653; Dalley (1989) 233–277

EPRO   *Etudes préliminaires aux religions orientales dans l'Empire romaine*, ed. M. J. Vermaseren (Leiden 1961–)

Erra   L. Cagni, *L'epopea di Erra* (Rome 1969) (transcription and Italian translation)
L. Cagni, *Das Erra-Epos* (Rome 1970) (cuneiform text)
Translations: Labat et al. (1970) 114–137; Bottéro and Kramer (1989) 681–707; Dalley (1989) 285–315

Gilgamesh   R. C. Thompson, *The Epic of Gilgamish. Text, Transliteration and Notes* (Oxford 1930)
Translations: *ANET* 72–99; Labat et al. (1970) 145–226; A. Schott, *Das Gilgamesch-Epos übersetzt und mit Anmerkungen versehen*, ed. W. von Soden (Stuttgart 1982); Dalley (1989) 50–153

HAL   *Hebräisches und Aramäisches Lexikon zum Alten Testament von L. Koehler und W. Baumgartner*, ed. W. Baumgartner, 3d ed. (Leiden 1967–1990)

HKL   R. Borger, *Handbuch der Keilschriftliteratur*, vols. I–III (Berlin 1967–1975)

KAI   H. Donner and W. Röllig, *Kanaanäische und aramäische Inschriften*, vols. I–III (Wiesbaden 1966–1969²)

KAR   E. Ebeling, *Keilschrifttexte aus Assur religiösen Inhalts*, vols. I–II (Leipzig 1915–1923)

KBo   *Keilschrifttexte aus Boghazköi*, vols. I–VI (Leipzig 1916–23), VII ff. (Berlin 1954–)

KTU   M. Dietrich, O. Loretz, and J. Sanmartín, *Die Keil-alphabetischen Texte aus Ugarit einschliesslich der keil-alphabetischen Texte ausserhalb Ugarits*, vol. I (Keve-laer 1976)

KUB   *Keilschrifturkunden aus Boghazköi* (Berlin 1921–1944)

LIMC   *Lexicon Iconographicum Mythologiae Classicae* (Zurich 1981–)

LSAM   F. Sokolowski, *Lois sacrées de l'Asie Mineure* (Paris 1955)

LSCG   F. Sokolowski, *Lois sacrées des cités grecques* (Paris 1969)

LSJ   H. G. Liddell, R. Scott, and H. S. Jones, *A Greek-English Lexicon* (Oxford 1925–1940)

LSS   F. Sokolowski, *Lois sacrées des cités grecques*, supple-ment (Paris 1962)

Lugal-e   J. Van Dijk, *LUGAL UD ME-LAM-bi NIR-GAL. Le récit épique et didactique des Travaux de Ninurta, du Déluge et de la Nouvelle Création*, vol. I (Leiden 1983) Translation: Bottéro and Kramer (1989) 340–368

Maqlû   G. Meier, *Die assyrische Beschwörungssammlung Maqlû* (Berlin 1937)

PGM   K. Preisendanz, ed., *Papyri Graecae Magicae* (Leipzig 1928–31[1], Stuttgart 1973–74[2])

RE   *Paulys Realencyclopädie der classischen Altertumswissen-schaft* (Stuttgart 1894–1980)

RlA   *Reallexikon der Assyriologie* (Berlin 1932–)

RML   W. H. Roscher, ed., *Ausführliches Lexikon der grie-chischen und römischen Mythologie* (Leipzig 1884–1937)

SAHG   A. Falkenstein and W. von Soden, *Sumerische und Ak-kadische Hymnen und Gebete* (Zurich 1953)

Shurpu   E. Reiner, ed., *A Collection of Sumerian and Akkadian Incantations* (Graz 1958)

SVF   H. von Arnim, ed., *Stoicorum Veterum Fragmenta* I-IV (Leipzig 1905–1924)

BIBLIOGRAPHY

Ahlberg, G. 1967. "A Late Geometric Grave-Scene Influenced by North Syrian Art." *Opuscula Atheniensia* 7, 177–186.

———. 1971. *Fighting on Land and Sea in Greek Geometric Art.* Lund.

Akurgal, E. 1968. *The Birth of Greek Art. The Mediterranean and the Near East.* London.

Albright, W. F. 1950. "Some Oriental Glosses on the Homeric Problem." *AJA* 54, 162–176.

———. 1972. "Neglected Factors in the Greek Intellectual Revolution." *PAPhS* 116, 225–242.

Amiet, P. 1976. "Introduction à l'étude archéologique de Panthéon systématique et des Panthéons locaux dans l'Ancien Orient." *Orientalia* 45, 15–32.

Arnaud, D. 1985/87. *Emar. Recherches au pays d'Aštata VI: Textes sumériens et accadiens.* Paris.

Assmann, E. 1912. "Titaia, Titanen und der Tartaros." *Babyloniaca* 6, 236–239.

Astour, M. C. 1965, 1967². *Hellenosemitica. An Ethnical and Cultural Study in West Semitic Impact on Mycenaean Greece.* Leiden.

Auffahrt, C. 1991. *Der drohende Untergang. "Schöpfung" in Mythos und Ritual im Alten Orient und in Griechenland am Beispiel der Odyssee und des Ezechielbuches* (= Religionsgeschichtliche Versuche und Vorarbeiten, 39). Berlin.

Bakhuizen, S. C. 1976. *Chalcidian Studies.* Vol. III: *Chalcis-in-Euboea: Iron and Chalcidians Abroad.* Leiden.

———. 1981. "Le nom de Chalcis et la colonisation chalcidienne."

In *Nouvelle contribution à l'étude de la Société et de la Colonisation Eubéennes* (Cahiers du Centre Jean Bérard 6). Naples, 161–174.

Bammer, A. 1985. "Spuren der Phöniker im Artemision von Ephesos." *AS* 35, 103–108.

Barnett, R. D. 1948. "Early Greek and Oriental Ivories." *JHS* 68, 1–25.

———. 1956. "Ancient Oriental Influences on Archaic Greece." In *The Aegean and the Near East: Studies Presented to H. Goldman.* Locust Valley, N.Y., 212–238.

———. 1960. "Some Contacts between Greek and Oriental Religions." In *Eléments,* 143–153.

Baumgarten, A. I. 1981. *The Phoenician History of Philo of Byblos: A Commentary.* Leiden.

Beloch, J. 1894. "Die Phoeniker am aegaeischen Meer." *RhM* 49, 111–132.

———. 1912/13. *Griechische Geschichte.*² Rev. ed. Vols. I 1, I 2. Strassburg.

Bérard, V. 1902/03. *Les Phéniciens et l'Odyssée.* Vols. I–II. Paris.

Bernal, M. 1987. *Black Athena: The Afroasiatic Roots of Classical Civilization.* Vol. I: *The Fabrication of Ancient Greece, 1785–1985.* London.

Biggs, R. D. 1967. *SA ZI GA: Ancient Mesopotamian Potency Incantations.* Locust Valley, N.Y.

Blecher, G. 1905. *De extispicio capita tria* (Religionsgeschichtliche Versuche und Vorarbeiten II 4). Giessen.

Blome, P. 1982. *Die figürliche Bildwelt Kretas in der geometrischen und früharchaischen Epoche.* Mainz.

———. 1984. "Lefkandi und Homer." *Würzburger Jahrbücher,* n.s. 10, 9–22.

———. 1985. "Phönizische Dämonen auf einem attischen Krater." *AA* 573–579.

———. 1991. "Die dunklen Jahrhunderte—aufgehellt." In *Zweihundert Jahre Homerforschung,* ed. J. Latacz. Stuttgart, 45–60.

Blome, P., ed. 1990. *Orient und frühes Griechenland. Kunstwerke der Sammlung H. und T. Bosshard.* Basel.

Boardman, J. 1957. "Early Euboean Pottery and History." *ABSA* 52, 1–29.

———. 1961. *The Cretan Collection in Oxford. The Dictaean Cave and Iron Age Crete.* Oxford.

————. 1965. "Tarsus, Al Mina and Greek Chronology." *JHS* 85, 5–15.

————. 1967. "The Khaniale Tekke Tombs, II." *ABSA* 62, 57–75.

————. 1970. "Orientalen auf Kreta." In *Dädalische Kunst auf Kreta im 7. Jh. v. Chr.* Hamburg.

————. 1980. *The Greeks Overseas.* New enl. ed. London.

————. 1990. "Al Mina and History." *Oxford Journal of Archaeology* 9, 169–190.

Boardman, J., and G. Buchner. 1966. "Seals from Ischia and the Lyre-player Group." *JdI* 81, 1–62.

Boardman, J., and M. L. Vollenweider. 1978. *Ashmolean Museum Catalogue of the Engraved Gems and Finger Rings.* Vol. I: *Greek and Etruscan.* Oxford.

Boehm, S. 1990. *Die "nackte Göttin." Zur Ikonographie und Deutung unbekleideter weiblicher Figuren in der frühgriechischen Kunst.* Mainz.

Boehmer, R. M. 1965. "Die Entwicklung der Glyptik während der Akkad-Zeit." *ZA* Suppl. 4.

Börker-Klähn, J. 1973. "Verkannte Neuassyrische Bronze-Statuetten." *BagM* 6, 41–64.

Boissier, A. 1905. *Choix des textes relatifs à la divination assyro-babylonienne.* Geneva.

Borell, B. 1978. *Attisch-geometrische Schalen. Eine spätgeometrische Keramikgattung und ihre Beziehungen zum Orient.* Mainz.

Borger, R. 1956. *Die Inschriften Asarhaddons, Königs von Assyrien.* Graz.

————. 1974. "Die Beschwörungsserie bit meseri und die Himmelfahrt Henochs." *JNES* 33, 183–184.

————. 1979. *Babylonisch-Assyrische Lesestücke.*² Vols. I–II. Rome.

Bottéro, J., and S. N. Kramer. 1989. *Lorsque les dieux faisaient l'homme. Mythologie Mésopotamienne.* Paris.

Bouché-Leclercq, A. 1879/82. *Histoire de la divination dans l'antiquité.* Vols. I–IV. Paris.

Bowra, C. M. 1952. *Heroic Poetry.* London.

Braun, T. F. R. G. 1982a. "The Greeks in the Near East." In *The Cambridge Ancient History.*² Vol. III 3. Cambridge, 1–31.

————. 1982b. "The Greeks in Egypt." Ibid. 32–56.

Bron, F., and A. Lemaire. 1989. "Les inscriptions araménnes de Hazaël." *Rev. d'Ass.* 83, 35–44.

Brown, J. P. 1965. "Kothar, Kinyras, and Kythereia." *JSS,* 10, 197–219.

———. 1968. "Literary Contexts of the Common Hebrew-Greek Vocabulary." *JSS* 13, 163–191.

———. 1969. "The Mediterranean Vocabulary of the Vine." *VT* 19, 146–170.

———. 1980. "The Sacrificial Cult and Its Critique in Greek and Hebrew (II)." *JSS* 25, 1–21.

Brown, R. 1898. *Semitic Influence in Hellenic Mythology.* London.

Brown, W. L. 1960. *The Etruscan Lion.* Oxford.

Buchner, G. 1978. "Testimonianze epigrafiche del VIII secolo a.C. a Pithekoussai." *PP* 33, 130–142.

———. 1982. "Die Beziehungen zwischen der euböischen Kolonie Pithekoussai auf der Insel Ischia und dem nordwestsemitischen Mittelmeerraum in der zweiten Hälfte des 8. Jhs v. Chr." Niemeyer, 277–306.

Bunnens, G. 1979. *L'expansion phénicienne en Méditerranée.* Brussels.

Burkert, W. 1972. *Lore and Science in Ancient Pythagoreanism.* Cambridge, Mass. (German ed. 1962).

———. 1975. "Rešep-Figuren, Apollon von Amyklai und die 'Erfindung' des Opfers auf Cypern. Zur Religionsgeschichte der 'Dunklen Jahrhunderte.'" *GB* 4, 51–79.

———. 1979. *Structure and History in Greek Mythology and Ritual.* Berkeley.

———. 1980. "Griechische Mythologie und die Geistesgeschichte der Moderne." In *Les études classiques aux XIXe et XXe siècles: Leur place dans l'histoire des idées,* ed. O. Reverdin (Entretiens sur l'antiquité classique 26). Vandoeuvres, 159–199.

———. 1981a. "Seven against Thebes: An Oral Tradition between Babylonian Magic and Greek Literature." In *I poemi epici rapsodici non omerici e la tradizione orale,* ed. C. Brillante, M. Cantilena, and C. O. Pavese. Padua, 29–48.

———. 1981b. "Glaube und Verhalten: Zeichengehalt und Wirkungsmacht von Opferritualen." In *Le sacrifice dans l'antiquité,* ed. O. Reverdin. (Entretiens sur l'antiquité classique 27). Vandoeuvres, 91–133.

———. 1982a. "Craft versus Sect: The Problem of Orphics and Pythagoreans." In *Jewish and Christian Self-Definition.* Vol. III:

Self-Definition in the Graeco-Roman World, ed. B. F. Meyer and
E. P. Sanders. London, 1–22, 183–189 (notes).

———. 1982b. "Literarische Texte und funktionaler Mythos. Zu
Ištar und Atraḫasis." In J. Assmann, W. Burkert, and F. Stolz,
*Funktionen und Leistungen des Mythos. Drei altorientalische Bei-
spiele* (Orbis Biblicus et Orientalis 48). Freiburg and Göttingen, 63–82.

———. 1983c. "Oriental Myth and Literature in the Iliad." In Hägg
(1983) 51–56.

———. 1983a. *Homo Necans: The Anthropology of Ancient Greek
Sacrificial Ritual and Myth.* Berkeley (German ed. 1972).

———. 1983b. "Itinerant Diviners and Magicians: A Neglected
Element in Cultural Contacts." In Hägg (1983) 115–119.

———. 1985. *Greek Religion, Archaic and Classical.* Oxford and
Cambridge, Mass. (German ed. 1977).

———. 1987a. *Ancient Mystery Cults.* Cambridge, Mass.

———. 1987b. "Oriental and Greek Mythology: The Meeting of
Parallels." In *Interpretations of Greek Mythology,* ed. J. Bremmer.
London, 10–40.

———. 1991. "Homerstudien und Orient." In *Zweihundert Jahre
Homerforschung,* ed. J. Latacz. Stuttgart, 155–181.

Canciani, F. 1970. *Bronzi orientali e orientalizzanti a Creta nell' VIII
e VII secolo a.C.* (Studia archeologica 12). Rome.

———. 1979. "Coppe 'fenicie' in Italia." *AA* 1–6.

———. 1984. Chap. N 2: "Bildkunst." In *Archaeologia Homerica.*
Vol. II. Göttingen.

Caquot, A., and M. Leibovici, eds. 1968. *Rites et pratiques religieuses.* Vol. I: *La divination.* Paris.

Carter, J. 1972. "The Beginning of Narrative Art in the Greek Geometric Period." *ABSA* 67, 25–58.

Castellino, G. R. 1977. *Testi Sumerici e Accadici.* Turin.

Chantraine, P. 1968/80. *Dictionnaire étymologique de la langue
grecque.* Paris.

Charbonnet, A. 1986. "Le dieu aux lions d'Erétrie." *AION* 8, 117–
173.

Cogan, M., and H. Tadmor. 1977. "Gyges and Ashurbanipal." *Orientalia* 46, 65–85.

Coldstream, J. N. 1960. "A Geometric Well at Knossos." *BSA* 55,
159–171.

————. 1968. *Greek Geometric Pottery. A Survey of Ten Local Styles and Their Chronology.* London.

————. 1969. "The Phoenicians of Ialysos." *BICS* 16, 1–8.

————. 1977. *Deities in Aegean Art before and after the Dark Ages.* Inaug. lect. 27 Oct. 1976. London.

————. 1982. "Greeks and Phoenicians in the Aegean." In Niemeyer (1982) 261–272.

Curtis, J., ed. 1988. *Bronzeworking Centres of Western Asia c. 1000–539 B.C.* London.

Dalley, S. 1989. *Myths of Mesopotamia.* Oxford.

Dirlmeier, F. 1955. "Homerisches Epos und Orient." *RhM* 98, 18–37 = Ausgewählte Schriften zu Dichtung und Philosophie der Griechen (Heidelberg 1970) 55–67.

Dodds, E. R. 1951. *The Greeks and the Irrational.* Berkeley.

Dornseiff, F. 1933. *Die archaische Mythenerzählung. Folgerungen aus dem homerischen Apollonhymnus.* Berlin.

————. 1934. "Hesiods Werke und Tage und das Alte Morgenland." *Philologus* 89, 397–415 = *Antike und Alter Orient*[2] (Leipzig 1959), 72–95 = *Hesiod,* ed. E. Heitsch (Wege der Forschung 44) (Darmstadt 1966) 131–150.

————. 1937. "Altorientalisches in Hesiods Theogonie." *AC* 6, 231–258 = *Antike und Alter Orient*[2] (Leipzig 1959) 35–69.

Duchemin, J. 1979. "La justice de Zeus et le destin d'Io. Regard sur les sources proche-orientales d'un mythe eschyléen." *REG* 92, 1–54.

————. 1980a. "Contribution à l'histoire des mythes grecs. Les luttes primordiales dans l'Iliade à la lumière des sources proche-orientales." In *Miscellanea di studi classici in onore di E. Manni.* Vol. III. Rome, 837–879.

————. 1980b. "Le Zeus d'Eschyle et ses sources proche-orientales." *RHR* 197, 27–44.

Dunbabin, T. J. 1957. *The Greeks and Their Eastern Neighbours. Studies in the Relations between Greece and the Countries of the Near East in the 8th and 7th Centuries B.C.* (*JHS* Suppl. 8). London. Repr. 1979.

Ebeling, E. 1918/19. *Quellen zur Kenntnis der babylonischen Religion I/II* (Mitteilungen der Vorderasiatischen Gesellschaft 23). Vols. I–II. Leipzig.

———. 1925. *Liebeszauber im Alten Orient.* Leipzig.

———. 1931. *Tod und Leben nach den Vorstellungen der Babylonier.* Vol. I. Berlin.

———. 1949. "Beschwörungen gegen den Feind und den bösen Blick aus dem Zweistromlande." *Archiv Orientalni* 17, 172–211.

Edwards, R. B. 1979. *Kadmos the Phoenician. A Study in Greek Legends and the Mycenaean Age.* Amsterdam.

Eissfeldt, O. 1934. "Der Gott des Tabor und seine Verbreitung." *ARW* 31, 14–41 = *Kleine Schriften* II (Tübingen 1963) 29–54.

———. 1939. *Ras Schamra und Sanchunjaton* (Beiträge zur Religionsgeschichte des Altertums 4). Halle.

———. 1952. "Taautos und Sanchunjaton." In *Sitzungsber. der Deut. Akad. der Wissenschaften, Kl. für Sprachen, Literatur und Kunst.* Vol. I. Berlin.

Elayi, J., and A. Cavigneaux. 1979. "Sargon II et les Ioniens." *OA* 18, 59–75.

Eléments. 1960. *Eléments orientaux dans la religion grecque ancienne. Colloque de Strasbourg 22–24 mai 1958* (Travaux du Centre d'études supérieures spécialisé d'histoire des religions de Strasbourg). Paris.

Ellis, R. S. 1968. *Foundation Deposits in Ancient Mesopotamia.* New Haven.

Eph'al, I., and J. Naveh. 1989. "Hazael's Booty Inscriptions." *Israel Expl. J.* 39, 192–200.

Faraone, C. A. 1987. "Hephaestus the Magician and Near Eastern Parallels for Alcinous' Watchdogs." *GRBS* 28, 257–280.

———. 1991. "The Agonistic Context of Early Greek Binding Spells." In Faraone and Obbink (1991) 3–32.

Faraone, C. A., and D. Obbink, eds. 1991. *Magika Hiera. Ancient Greek Magic and Religion.* New York and Oxford.

Farber, W. 1977. *Beschwörungsrituale an Ištar und Dumuzi.* Wiesbaden.

Farnell, L. R. 1911. *Greece and Babylon. A Comparative Sketch of Mesopotamian, Anatolian and Hellenic Religions.* Edinburgh.

Fehling, D. 1980. "Lehnübersetzungen aus altorientalischen Sprachen im Griechischen und Lateinischen." *Glotta* 58, 1–24.

Fittschen, K. 1973. Chap. N, Teil 1: "Der Schild des Achilleus." In *Archaeologica Homerica.* Vol. II. Göttingen.

Fitzmyer, J. A. 1967. *The Aramaic Inscriptions of Sefire* (Biblica et Orientalia 19). Rome.

Fleischer, R. 1973. *Artemis von Ephesos und verwandte Kultstatuen aus Anatolien und Syrien* (*EPRO* 35). Leiden.

Fossey, C. 1902. *La magie assyrienne* (Bibliothèque de l'Ecole des Hautes Etudes 15). Paris.

Frank, K. 1941. *Lamaštu, Pazuzu und andere Dämonen. Ein Beitrag zur babylonisch-assyrischen Dämonologie* (Mitteilungen der altorientalischen Gesellschaft 14,2). Leipzig. Repr. 1972.

Frenkian, A. M. 1960. "L'épopée de Gilgames et les poèmes homériques." *Studia et Acta Orientalia* 2, 89–105.

Fries, C. 1910. *Studien zur Odyssee.* Vol. I: Das Zagmukfest auf Scheria. Leipzig.

Fuhr, I. 1977. "Der Hund als Begleiter der Göttin Gula und andere Heigottheiten." In *Isin-Isan Bahriyat.* Vol. I: *Die Ergebnisse der Ausgrabungen 1973–1974* (Abh. München N.F. 79). Munich, 135–145.

Furlani, G. 1940. *Riti babilonici e assiri.* Udine.

Gabelmann, H. 1965. *Studien zum frühgriechischen Löwenbild.* Berlin.

Galling, K. 1971. "Tafel, Buch und Blatt." In *Near Eastern Studies in Honour of W. F. Albright.* Baltimore, 207–223.

Garbini, G. 1978. "Scarabeo con incisione aramaica della necropoli di Macchiabate." *PP* 33, 424–426.

Gehrig, U., and H. G. Niemeyer. 1990. *Die Phönizier im Zeitalter Homers.* Hannover.

Genge, H. 1979. *Nordsyrisch-südanatolische Reliefs. Eine archäologische Untersuchung, Datierung und Bestimmung.* Copenhagen.

Goetze, A. 1939. "Cuneiform Inscriptions from Tarsus." *JAOS* 59, 1–16.

Goldman, B. 1961. "The Asiatic Ancestry of the Greek Gorgon." *Berytus* 14, 1–23.

Gordon, C. H. 1955. "Homer and the Bible. The Origin and Character of East Mediterranean Literature." *Hebrew Union College Annual* 26, 43–108. Repr. as a monograph Ventor, N.J. 1967.

Graf, F. 1985. *Nordionische Kulte. Religionsgeschichte und epigraphische Untersuchungen zu den Kulten von Chiòs, Erythrai Klazomenai und Phokaia* (Bibliotheca Helvetica Romana 21). Rome.

Greifenhagen, A. 1965. "Ein Ostgriechisches Elfenbein." *Jahrbuch der Berliner Museen* 7, 125–156.

Gresseth, G. K. 1975. "The Gilgamesh Epic and Homer." *CJ* 70, 4, 1–18.

Grottanelli, C. 1982a. "Profezia e scrittura nel Vicino Oriente." *La ricerca folklorica* 5, 57–62.

————. 1982b. "Healers and Saviours of the Eastern Mediterranean in Pre-Classical Times." In *La soteriologia dei culti orientali nell'impero Romano,* ed. U. Bianchi and M. J. Vermaseren. Leiden, 649-670.

Gruppe, O. 1887. *Die griechischen Kulte und Mythen in ihren Beziehungen zu den orientalischen Religionen.* Vol. I: *Einleitung.* Leipzig.

Guarducci, M. 1967. *Epigrafia graeca.* Vol. I. Rome.

Gubel, E., and E. Lipinski, eds. 1985. *Phoenicia and Its Neighbours* (Studia Phoenicia 3). Leuven.

Gurney, O. R. 1954. *The Hittites.*[2] Harmondsworth.

————. 1977. *Some Aspects of Hittite Religion.* Oxford.

Guzzo Amadasi, M. G. 1967. *Le iscrizioni fenicie e puniche delle colonie in occidente.* Rome.

Haas, V. 1986. *Magie und Mythen in Babylonien.* Gifkendorf.

Hägg, R., ed. 1983. *The Greek Renaissance of the Eighth Century B.C.: Tradition and Innovation.* Stockholm.

Hägg, R., N. Marinatos, and G. Nordquist, eds. 1988. *Early Greek Cult Practice.* Stockholm.

Hanfmann, G. M. A. 1948. "Archaeology in Homeric Asia Minor." *AJA* 52, 135–155.

Harmatta, J. 1968. "Zu den kleinasiatischen Beziehungen der griechischen Mythologie." *AAntHung* 16, 57–76.

Helck, W. 1971. *Betrachtungen zur grossen Göttin und den ihr verbundenen Gottheiten* (Religion und Kultur der Alten Mittelmeerwelt in Parallelforschungen 2). Munich and Vienna.

————. 1979. *Die Beziehungen Aegyptens und Vorderasiens zur Aegais bis ins 7. Jahrhundert vor Chr.* (Erträge der Forschung 120). Darmstadt.

Hemberg, B. 1950. *Die Kabiren.* Uppsala.

Hemmerdinger, B. 1970. "De la méconnaissance de quelques étymologies grecques." *Glotta* 48, 40–66.

Herrmann, H. V. 1975. "Hellas." In *Reallexikon der Assyriologie und vorderasiatischen Archäologie*. Vol. IV. Berlin, 303–311.

Herter, H. 1967/68. "Griechenland und Orient." *Archeion koinoniologias kai ethikes* 10, 49–60.

Heubeck, A. 1955. "Mythologische Vorstellungen des Alten Orients im archaischen Griechentum." *Gymnasium* 62, 508–525 = *Hesiod,* ed. E. Heitsch (Wege der Forschung 44) (Darmstadt 1966) 545–570.

———. 1979. Chap. X: "Schrift." In *Archaeologia Homerica*. Vol. III. Göttingen.

Hiller, S. 1974/77. "Kretisch-orientalische Kulturbeziehungen." *AOF* 25, 301–305.

Hirschberg, H. 1932. *Studien zur Geschichte Esarhaddons*. Diss. Berlin.

Hölbl, G. 1979. *Beziehungen der ägyptischen Kultur zu Altitalien* (*EPRO* 62). Leiden.

Hogarth, D. G. 1909. *Ionia and the East. Six Lectures*. Oxford.

Hopkins, C. 1961. "The Sunny Side of the Greek Gorgon." *Berytus* 14, 25–35.

Howald, E. 1939. *Die Sieben gegen Theben. Rektoratsrede*. Zurich.

Hunger, J. 1909. *Babylonische Tieromina nebst griechisch-römischen Parallelen*. Berlin.

Imai, A. 1977. "Some Aspects of the 'Phoenician Bowls.'" Diss. Columbia University.

Immerwahr, H. R. 1990. *Attic Script. A Survey*. Oxford.

Jameson, M. 1990. "Perseus the Hero of Mykenai." In *Celebrations of Death and Divinity in the Bronze Age Argolid,* ed. R. Hägg and G. Nordquist. Stockholm, 213–223.

Jantzen, U. 1972. *Aegyptische und orientalische Bronzen aus dem Heraion von Samos* (Samos 8). Bonn.

Jastrow, M. 1905/12. *Die Religion Babyloniens und Assyriens*. Vols. I, II 1/2. Giessen.

Jeffery, L. H. 1961. *The Local Scripts of Archaic Greece. A Study of the Origins of the Greek Alphabet and Its Development from the Eighth to the Fifth Centuries B.C.* Oxford.

———. 1976. *Archaic Greece. The City-states c. 700–500 B.C.* London and Tunbridge.

———. 1990. *The Local Scripts of Archaic Greece*. Rev. ed. with suppl. by A. W. Johnston. Oxford.

Jensen, P. 1902. "Das Gilgames-Epos und Homer." *ZA* 16, 125–134.

———. 1912/13. *Leitsätze und Tabellen zu einem Kolleg über die babylonisch-palästinenischen Ursprünge der griechischen Heldensagen* (Gedrucktes Manuskript). Marburg.

———. 1924. *Gilgamesch-Epos, jüdische Nationalsagen, Ilias und Homer.* Leipzig.

Jeyes, U. 1978. "The 'Palace Gate' of the Liver. A Study of Terminology." *JCS* 30, 209–233.

———. 1980. "The Act of Extispicy in Ancient Mesopotamia: An Outline." *Assyriological Miscellanies* 1, 13–32.

Johnston, A. 1983. "The Extent and Use of Literacy: The Archaeological Evidence." In Hägg (1983) 63–68.

Johnstone, W. 1978. "Cursive Phoenician and the Archaic Greek Alphabet." *Kadmos* 17, 151–166.

Kantor, H. J. 1962. "A Bronze Plaque with a Relief Decoration from Tell Tainat." *JNES* 21, 93–117.

Kett, P. 1966. *Prosopographie der historischen griechischen Manteis bis auf die Zeit Alexanders des Grossen.* Diss. Erlangen.

Klengel, H. 1960. "Neue Lamaštu-Amulette aus dem Vorderasiatischen Museum zu Berlin und dem British Museum." *Mitteilungen des Instituts für Orientforschung* 7, 334–355.

———. 1963. "Weitere Amulette gegen Lamaštu." Ibid. 8, 24–29.

———. 1980. *Geschichte und Kultur Altsyriens.*² Munich.

Knudtzon, J. A. 1915. *Die El-Amarna-Tafeln.* Leipzig.

Kolbe, D. 1981. *Die Reliefprogramme religiös-mythologischen Charakters in neu-assyrischen Palästen.* Frankfurt.

Kopcke, G. 1990. Chap. M: "Handel." In *Archaeologia Homerica.* Vol. II. Göttingen.

Kranz, P. 1972. "Frühe griechische Sitzfiguren. Zum Problem der Typenbildung und des orientalischen Einflusses in der frühen griechischen Rundplastik." *AM* 87, 1–55.

Krause, W. 1970. "Griechisch-orientalische Lehnwortbeziehungen. Ein referierender Versuch." In *Festschrift Karl Vretska.* Heidelberg, 89–115.

Kunze, E. 1931. *Kretische Bronzereliefs.* Berlin.

Kyrieleis, H. 1979. "Babylonische Bronzen im Heraion von Samos." *JdI* 94, 32–48.

Kyrieleis, H., and W. Röllig. 1988. "Ein altorientalischer Pferdeschmuck aus dem Heraion von Samos." *MDAI* (Athens) 103, 37–75.

Labat, R. 1967. "Assyrien und seine Nachbarländer (Babylonien, Elam, Ionien) von 1000–617 v. Chr. Das neubabylonische Reich bis 539 v. Chr." In *Fischer Weltgeschichte*. Vol. IV: *Die altorientalischen Reiche III*. Frankfurt am Main, 9–111.

Labat, R., A. Caquot, M. Sznycer, and M. Vieyra. 1970. *Les religions du Proche-Orient asiatique. Textes babyloniens, ougaritiques, hittites*. Paris.

Lambert, W. G. 1960. *Babylonian Wisdom Literature*. Oxford.

Laminger-Pascher, G. 1989. *Lykaonien und die Phryger* (Sitzungsberichte der Oesterreichischen Akademie der Wissenschaften 532). Vienna.

Landsberger, B. 1948. *Sam'al, Studien zur Entdeckung der Ruinenstätte Karatepe*. Part I. Ankara.

Laroche, E. 1973. "Contacts linguistiques et culturels entre la Grèce et l'Asie mineure au deuxième millénaire." *REG* 86. xvii–xix.

Leibovici, M. 1971. *Génies, anges et démons* (Sources Orientales 8). Paris.

Lemaire, A. 1981. *Les écoles et la formation de la Bible*. Fribourg.

Lemaire, A., and J. M. Durand, 1984. *Les inscriptions araméennes de Sfire et l'Assyrie de Shamshi-Ilu*. Geneva.

Lerat, L. 1980. "Trois boucliers archaiques de Delphes." *BCH* 104, 93–114.

Lesky, A. 1950. "Hethitische Texte und griechischer Mythos." *Anzeiger der Oesterreichischen Akademie der Wissenschaften* 137–160 = *Gesammelte Schriften* (Bern 1966) 356–371.

———. 1954. "Zum hethitischen und griechischen Mythos." *Eranos* 52, 8–17 = *Gesammelte Schriften* (1966) 372–378.

———. 1955. "Griechischer Mythos und Vorderer Orient." *Saeculum* 6, 35–52 = *Gesammelte Schriften* (1966) 379–400 = *Hesiod*, ed. E. Heitsch (Wege der Forschung 44) (Darmstadt 1966) 571–601.

Lewy, H. 1895. *Die semitischen Fremdwörter im Griechischen*. Berlin.

Lipinski, E. 1976. "Apladad." *Orientalia* 45, 53–74.

———. 1988. "Les Phéniciens et l'alphabet." *Oriens Antiquus* 27, 231–260.

Luckenbill, D. D. 1926/27. *Ancient Records of Assyria and Babylonia*. Vols. I–II. Chicago.

———. 1933. "Iadnana and Iawan." *ZA* 28, 92–99.

Markoe, G. 1985. *Phoenician Bronze and Silver Bowls.* Berlin.

Masson, E. 1967. *Recherches sur les plus anciens emprunts sémitiques en grec.* Paris.

Mayer, M. L. 1960. "Gli imprestiti semitici in greco." *RIL* 94, 311–351.

Mayer, W. R. 1987. "Ein Mythos von der Erschaffung des Menschen und des Königs." *Orientalia* 56, 55–68.

Mazzarino, S. 1947. *Fra oriente e occidente. Ricerche di storia greca arcaica.* Florence.

McCarter, P. K. 1975. *The Antiquity of the Greek Alphabet and the Early Phoenician Scripts* (Harvard Semitic Monographs 9). Missoula, Mont.

Meier, G. 1941/44. "Die zweite Tafel der Serie bit meseri." *AOF* 14, 139–152.

Meissner, B. 1920/25. *Babylonien und Assyrien.* Vols. I–II. Heidelberg.

Meyer, J. W. 1985. "Zur Herkunft der etruskischen Lebermodelle." In Gubel and Lipinski (1985) 105–120.

———. 1987. *Untersuchungen zu den Tonlebermodellen aus dem Alten Orient.* Kevelaer.

Momigliano, A. D. 1934. "Su una battaglia tra Assiri e Greci." *Athenaeum* 12, 412–416 = *Quinto contributo alla storia degli studi classici e del mondo antico* (Rome 1975) 409–413.

Mondi, R. 1990. "Greek and Near Eastern Mythology." In *Approaches to Greek Myth,* ed. L. Edmunds. Baltimore, 141–198.

Moran, W. L. 1978. "An Assyrological Gloss on the New Archilochos Fragment." *HSPh* 82, 17–19.

Müller, V. 1929. *Frühe Plastik in Griechenland und Vorderasien.* Augsburg.

Muhly, J. D. 1970. "Homer and the Phoenicians: The Relations between Greece and the Near East in the Late Bronze and Early Iron Ages," *Berytus* 19, 19–64.

Murray, O. 1980. *Early Greece.* London.

Naveh, J. 1982. *Early History of the Alphabet.* Jerusalem.

Niemeyer, H. G., ed. 1982. *Phönizier im Westen* (Madrider Beiträge 8). Mainz.

———. 1984. "Die Phönizier und die Mittelmeerwelt im Zeitalter Homers." *JRGZM* 31, 3–94.

Nilsson, M. P. 1906. *Griechische Feste von religiöser Bedeutung*. Leipzig.

———. 1967. *Geschichte der griechischen Religion*.³ Vol. I. Munich.

Nougayrol, J. 1955a. "Nouveaux textes accadiens du palais d'Ugarit (Campagne 1954)." *CRAI* 141–146.

———. 1955b. "Les rapports des haruspicines étrusque et assyrobabylonienne et le foie d'argile de Falerii veteres (Villa Giulia 3786)." *CRAI* 509–520.

———. 1966. "La langue des haruspices babyloniens. A propos d'un foie d'argile inédit." *CRAI* 193–202.

———. 1968. "La divination babylonienne." In Caquot and Leibovici (1968) 25–81.

Oberhuber, K., ed. 1977. *Das Gilgamesch-Epos* (Wege der Forschung 215). Darmstadt.

Öttinger, N. 1981. "Probleme phraseologischer Interferenzen." *Glotta* 59, 1–12.

———. 1989/90. "Die 'dunkle Erde' im Hethitischen und Griechischen." *Die Welt des Orients* 20/21, 83–98.

Oppenheim, A. L. 1967/69. "Essay on Overland Trade in the First Millennium B.C." *JCS* 21/22, 236–254.

Parker, R. 1983. *Miasma: Pollution and Purification in Early Greek Religion*. Oxford.

Patzek, B. 1988. "Die mesopotamische Dämonin Lamaštu im orientalisierenden griechisch-kolonialen Kulturkreis." *Oriens Antiquus* 27, 221–230.

Pfiffig, A. J. 1975. *Religio Etrusca*. Graz.

Popham, M. R., L. H. Sackett, and P. G. Themelis. 1980. *Lefkandi. The Iron Age*. Vol. I: *The Cemeteries* (*BSA* Suppl. 11). London.

Poulsen, F. 1912. *Der Orient und die frühgriechische Kunst*. Leipzig.

Powell, B. B. 1991. *Homer and the Origin of the Greek Alphabet*. Cambridge.

Prinz, F. 1979. *Gründungsmythen und Sagenchronologie*. Munich.

Reiner, E. 1960a. "Fortune-Telling in Mesopotamia." *JNES* 19, 23–35.

———. 1960b. "Plague Amulets and House Blessings." *JNES* 19, 148–155.

———. 1966. "La magie babylonienne." In *Sources orientales*. Vol. VII: *Le monde du sorcier*. Paris.

————. 1978. "Die Akkadische Literatur." In *Altorientalische Literaturen,* ed. W. Röllig (Neues Handbuch der Literaturwissenschaften). Wiesbaden, 151–210.

Ridgway, D., and F. R. Ridgway. 1979. *Italy before the Romans. The Iron Age, Orientalising and Etruscan Periods.* London.

Riis, P. J. 1960. "Plaquettes syriennes d'Astarté dans des milieux grecs." *Mélanges de l'université Saint Joseph* 37, 193–198.

————. 1970. *Sukas.* Vol. I. Copenhagen.

————. 1982. "Griechen in Phönizien." In Niemeyer (1982) 237–255.

Rittig, D. 1977. *Assyrisch-Babylonische Kleinplastik magischer Bedeutung vom 13.-6. Jh. v. Chr.* Diss. Munich.

Rizza, G., and V. Santa Maria Scrinari. 1968. *Il santuario sull'Acropoli di Gortina.* Rome.

Rodriguez Adrados, F. 1979. *Historia de la fabula greco-latina.* Vol. I. Madrid.

Röllig, W. 1982. "Die Phönizier des Mutterlandes zur Zeit der Kolonisation." In Niemeyer (1982) 15–28.

Rohde, E. 1898. *Psyche. Seelencult und Unsterblichkeitsglaube der Griechen.*² Vols. I-II. Tübingen.

Saggs, H. W. F. 1963. "The Nimrud Letters, 1952—Part VI." *Iraq* 25, 70–80.

Salonen, E. 1974. "Ueber einige Lehnwörter aus dem Nahen Osten im Griechischen und Lateinischen." *Arctos* 8, 139–144.

Sass, B. 1988. *The Genesis of the Alphabet and Its Development in the 2nd Millennium B.C.* Wiesbaden.

————. 1991. *Studia Alphabetica.* Freiburg.

Sasson, J. M. 1968. "Instances of Mobility among Mari Artisans." *BASOR* 190, 46–54.

Schefold, K. 1964. *Frühgriechische Sagenbilder.* Munich.

————. 1967. *Die Griechen und ihre Nachbarn* (Propyläen Kunstgeschichte 1). Berlin.

Schrank, W. 1908. *Babylonische Sühneriten besonders mit Rücksicht auf Priester und Büsser untersucht.* Leipzig. Repr. 1968.

Sendschirli. 1893/1943. *Ausgrabungen in Sendschirli,* ed. F. von Luschan. Vols. I-IV. *Die Kleinfunde von Sendschirli,* ed. W. Andrae. Vol. V. Berlin.

Sinn, U. 1985. "Der sog. Tempel D im Heraion von Samos II. Ein archäologischer Befund aus der nachpolykratischen Zeit, mit einem Exkurs zum griechischen Bauopfer." *AM* 100, 129–158.

Starr, J. 1983. *The Rituals of the Diviner*. Malibu, Calif.

Steiner, G. 1959. *Der Sukzessionsmythos in Hesiods Theogonie und ihren orientalischen Parallelen*. Diss. Hamburg.

Stella, L. A. 1978. *Tradizione Micenea e poesia dell'Iliade* (Filologia e Critica 29). Rome.

Streck, M. 1916. *Assurbanipal und die letzten assyrischen Könige bis zum Untergang Niniveh's*. Vols. I–III. Leipzig.

Strøm, I. 1971. *Problems concerning the Origin and Early Development of the Etruscan Orientalising Style*. Odense.

Strommenger, E. 1962. *Fünf Jahrtausende Mesopotamien. Die Kunst von den Anfängen um 5000 v. Chr. bis zu Alexander dem Grossen*. Munich.

Stucky, R. A. 1981. "Eine bronzene Wandapplike aus Kreta." *AA* 431–439.

———. 1982. "Anlehnung-Imitation-Kopie. Zur Aneignung orientalischer Bildmotive auf Zypern." In *Griechenland und Etrurien. Archéologie au Levant. Recueil R. Saidah*. Lyon, 205–220.

Szemerényi, O. 1974. "The Origins of the Greek Lexicon. Ex oriente lux." *JHS* 94, 144–157.

Thompson, R. C. 1903/04. *The Devils and the Evil Spirits of Babylonia*. Vols. I–II. London.

Thulin, C. O. 1905/09. *Die etruskische Disziplin*. Vols. I–III. Göteborg.

Thureau-Dangin, F. 1921. *Rituels accadiens*. Paris.

Ugaritica VI. 1969. *Nouvelles études relatives aux découvertes de Ras Shamra*, ed. C. F. A. Schaeffer et al. Paris.

Ungnad, A. 1921. *Die Religion der Babylonier und Assyrer*. Jena.

———. 1923. *Gilgamesch-Epos und Odyssee*. Breslau.

van der Meer, L. B. 1979. "Iecur Placentinum and the Orientation of the Etruscan Haruspex." *BABesch* 54, 49–64.

Van Dijk, J. 1983. *LUGAL UD ME-LAM-bi NIR-GAL. Le récit épique et didactique des Travaux de Ninurta, du Déluge et de la Nouvelle Création*. Vol. I. Leiden.

van Loon, M. N. 1974. *Oude Lering, Nieuwe Nering. Het uitzwermen der Noord-Syriske Ambachtslieden in de late 8e Eeuw v. Chr.* Amsterdam.

————. 1991. *Anatolia in the Earlier First Millennium B.C.* (Iconography of Religions XV 13). Leiden.

Vermeule, E. 1971. "Kadmos and the Dragon." In *Studies Presented to G. M. A. Hanfmann.* Mainz, 177–188.

————. 1977. "Herakles Brings a Tribute." In *Festschrift F. Brommer.* Mainz, 295–301.

Verzár, M. 1980. "Pyrgi e l'Afrodite di Cipro." *MEFR* 92, 35–84.

Wäfler, M. 1982. "Zum assyrich-urartäischen Westkonflikt." *Acta Praehistorica et Archaeologica* 11/12, 79–97.

Walcot, P. 1966. *Hesiod and the Near East.* Cardiff.

Ward, W. A., ed. 1968. *The Role of the Phoenicians in the Interaction of Mediterranean Civilizations: Papers Presented to the Archaeological Symposium at the American University of Beirut, March 1967.* Beirut.

Ward, W. H. 1910. *The Seal Cylinders of Western Asia.* Washington, D.C.

Webster, T. B. L. 1956. "Homer and Eastern Poetry." *Minos* 4, 104–116.

————. 1958. *From Mycenae to Homer.* London.

Wells, B. 1988. "Early Greek Building Sacrifices." In Hägg, Marinatos, and Nordquist (1988) 159-266.

Wendel, C. 1949. *Die griechisch-römische Buchbeschreibung verglichen mit der des Vorderen Orients.* Halle.

West, M. L., ed. 1966. *Hesiod: Theogony.* Oxford.

————. 1969. "Near Eastern Material in Hellenistic and Roman Literature." *HSPh* 73, 113–134.

————. 1971. *Early Greek Philosophy and the Orient.* Oxford.

————, ed. 1978b. *Hesiod: Works and Days.* Oxford.

————. 1978a. "Hésiode et la Grèce de l'époque géométrique." *Association Guillaume Budé, Actes du Xe Congrès, Toulouse, 8–12 avril 1978.* Paris, 117 ff.

————. 1983. *The Orphic Poems.* Oxford.

————. 1985. *The Hesiodic Catalogue of Women. Its Nature, Structure and Origins.* Oxford.

————. 1988. "The Rise of the Greek Epic," *JHS* 108 (1988) 151–172.

Williams, R. J. 1956. "The Literary History of a Mesopotamian Fable." *Phoenix* 10, 70–77.

Wilson, J. R. 1986. "The *Gilgamesh* Epic and the *Iliad*." *EMC* 30, 25–41.

Winter, I. 1973. "North Syria in the Early First Millenium B.C. with Special Reference to Ivory Carving." Ph.D. diss. Columbia University.

Winter, U. 1983. *Frau und Göttin*. Freiburg.

Wirth, H. 1921. *Homer und Babylon*. Freiburg.

Wolff, H. N. 1969. "Gilgamesh, Enkidu and the Heroic Life." *JOAS* 89, 392–398.

Woolley, L. 1953. *A Forgotten Kingdom*. Harmondsworth.

Zimmern, H. 1901. *Beiträge zur Kenntnis der babylonischen Religion. Die Beschwörungstafeln Šurpu, Ritualtafeln für den Wahrsager, Beschwörer und Sänger.* Leipzig.

NOTES

Introduction

1. 2. 142.

2. See *The Oxford English Dictionary* VII (1933) 199; E. Littré, *Dictionnaire de la langue française* V (1857) 1125; J. Grimm, *Deutsches Wörterbuch* VII (1889) 1345. The antithesis *oriens–occidens* originated in Roman imperial administration and was taken up in Christian Latin literature; see *Thesaurus Linguae Latinae* IX 2, 2004.52 ff. The motto "Ex Oriente Lux" is modern.

3. The etymology of Kabeiroi from Semitic *kabir*, great, goes back to J. J. Scaliger, *Coniectanea in M. Terentium de Lingua Latina* (1565) 146 (I owe this reference to A. Kurmann); see Hemberg (1950) 318–320; *contra*, J. Wackernagel produced an Indian etymology, *ZVS* 41 (1907) 316–318, P. Kretschmer another etymology from Asia Minor, *ZVS* 55 (1928) 82–88. The idea of "great" gods expressed by the Semitic root *kbr* is now definitely attested for North Syria in the thirteenth century B.C.: The new texts from Emar have personal names such as Rašap-Kabar and Baal-Kabar, "Reshep" or "Baal is great," Arnaud (1985/87) no. 15, line 15; no. 20, p. 23 f. The equation of Kadmos with Semitic *qdm*, East, is traced back to 1646 by Edwards (1979) 58 n.60; that of *Europa* with *ʿrb*, sunset, West, is ancient: Εὐρώπη· ἡ χώρα τῆς δύσεως, Hsch.; cf. Edwards 78 f.; see also Burkert (1991). On Iapetos see Chapter 1, "The Problem of Loan-Words," note 37.

4. R. Pfeiffer, *History of Classical Scholarship from 1300 to 1850* (1976) 173 gives more precise information; see also E. Schröder, "Philologiae studiosus," *NJb* 32 (1913) 168–171; E. J. Kenney, *The*

Classical Text (1974) 98 n.1; H. Lloyd-Jones, *Blood for the Ghosts* (1982) 169 n.8.

5. The German term was *Stammeskultur.* See Burkert (1980) 162–168 and the provocative study of Bernal (1987), who is sharply critical of this anti-oriental stance; see for discussion of his position: "The Challenge of 'Black Athena,'" *Arethusa* special issue 1989. K. O. Müller had challenged the Semitic etymology of the name Kadmos: *Orchomenos und die Minyer* (1820) 113–122 and (1844²) 107–116.

6. See L. Poliakov, *Le mythe arien* (1971), *The Aryan Myth* (1974). A basic contrast between Greeks and Semites is stated, e.g., by F. G. Welcker, *Griechische Götterlehre* I (1857) 116–118—a scholar who was anything but narrow-minded.

7. See, e.g., K. Lehrs, *Populäre Aufsätze aus dem Alterthum* (1856) viii; cf. (1875²) vi: "dass ich unter Griechen dasjenige Volk verstehe, welches in Griechenland wohnte und Griechen hiess, durchaus keine Nation am Ganges oder Himalaya." See also idem, *Kleine Schriften* (1902) 388 f. Karl Lehrs was born a Jew, but assimilated to German-Christian culture.

8. See also the arguments of E. Zeller against the supposed oriental "origin" of Greek philosophy in his *Die griechische Philosophie in ihrer geschichtlichen Entwicklung* I² (1856) 18–34 and I⁶(1919) 21–52; H. Diels uses a sharper tone in his review of Gruppe (1887), *AGPh* 2 (1889) 88–93; idem, "Thales ein Semite?" ibid. 165–170.

9. U. von Wilamowitz-Moellendorff, *Homerische Untersuchungen* (1884) 215: "die seit jahrhunderten faulenden völker und staaten der Semiten und Aegypter, die den Hellenen trotz ihrer alten cultur nichts hatten abgeben können als ein paar handfertigkeiten und techniken, abgeschmackte trachten und geräte, zopfige ornamente, widerliche fetische für noch widerlichere götzen"; idem, *Hellenistische Dichtung* I (1924) 2: "aus dem Orient und ist dem echten Hellenentum todfeind"; see also idem, *Aus Kydathen* (1880) 40; he also wrote that Poseidonios is "doch schon orientalisch infiziert" (*Die Kultur der Gegenwart* [1910³] 145), although "eine Naturwissenschaft wie die des Poseidonios hat kein Semit im Altertum auch nur von fern begriffen" (*Der Glaube der Hellenen* II [1932] 403). Yet he acknowledges the parallel of Hesiod and Amos, *Antigonos von Karystos* (1881) 314 f., and provides more balanced judgments on the orientalizing period in *Der Glaube der Hellenen* I (1931) 76, II

(1932) 7. Wilamowitz had learned Hebrew at Schulpforta—see his *Inwieweit befriedigen die Schlüsse der erhaltenen griechischen Trauerspiele?* ed. W. M. Calder (1974) 116 f.—but he did not let this show in his later publications.

10. As a young man Wilamowitz ridiculed Schliemann; see his *Erinnerungen* (1928) 148. The interrelations of Mycenaean civilization and Homer drew attention esp. in English scholarship; an influential synthesis was given by M. P. Nilsson, *Homer and Mycenae* (1933); see esp. 19–30 on the history of scholarship.

11. A. Jeremias, *Izdubar-Nimrod, eine altbabylonische Heldensage* (1891) and *RML* (1890/94) II 773–823, repudiating the reading "Gilgamesh," 774; "Izdubar" also in H. Usener, *Die Sintfluthsagen* (1899) 4 ff., who tries to prove the independence of the Greek myth of the flood from the Semites. In *RE* I A 1405 (Tkac, 1920) one finds "Gis-dubarru, auch Gibil-gamis und Namrudu genannt." On the forms of spelling Gilgamesh in cuneiform see H. Zimmern in Oberhuber (1977) 23.

12. See Wilamowitz, *Die Heimkehr des Odysseus* (1927) vi, about "die Anfänge der Assyriologie, die ich miterlebt habe": "auf dem Nachbargebiet wartet man besser ab." The slogan "Babel und Bibel" was launched by two lectures given in the presence of the emperor by F. Delitzsch, published in Berlin in 1903; the designation "Panbabylonismus" was used by A. Jeremias in his preface to *Das Alte Testament im Lichte des alten Orients* (1906², 1930⁴); see also A. Jeremias, *Die Panbabylonisten* (1907); *Handbuch der altorientalischen Geisteskultur* (1913, 1929²); H. Winckler, *Die babylonische Geisteskultur* (1907, 1912²); P. Jensen, *Das Gilgamesch-Epos in der Weltliteratur* I/II (1906/28); see also Jensen (1912/13) and (1924).

13. Wirth (1921); see Chapter 3. As to the history of religion, only Farnell (1911) undertook methodical discussion; see Chapter 2, "Purification."

14. E. Meyer, *Geschichte des Altertums* I (1884), I³ (1913); oriental history and classical history were also combined in the work of C. F. Lehmann-Haupt; W. Otto changed the title of *Handbuch der klassischen Altertumswissenschaft* to *Handbuch der Altertumswissenschaft* in 1920. Much earlier A. Boeckh and F. Hultsch had proved remarkable connections between Greek and oriental civilization in metrology, the system of measures and weights.

15. J. Beloch, "Die Phoeniker am aegaeischen Meer," *RhM* 49

(1894) 111–132; idem, *Griechische Geschichte* I (1893) 75 f., 167 f. and I 2² (1913) 65–76. On Julius Beloch see A. Momigliano, *Terzo contributo alla storia degli studi classici e del mondo antico* (1966) 239–269; K. Christ, *Von Gibbon zu Rostovtzeff* (1979) 248–285. In fact even F. C. Movers, *Die Phönizier* (1841/56), Lewy (1895), and Brown (1898) had remained outsiders, as did Bérard (1902/03 and many later publications). For corrections of Beloch's picture of the Phoenicians see Niemeyer (1982), esp. the article by Coldstream.

16. Hogarth (1909) had concentrated on Ionia. Poulsen (1912) also dealt with Homer (168–183). See also Müller (1929), Barnett (1956), Akurgal (1968), and Strøm (1971); cf. Chapter 1, "Oriental Products in Greece."

17. See Schefold (1967) 19: "Es ist also eine nicht sehr glückliche Gewohnheit, die Kunst des 7. Jahrhunderts 'orientalisierend' zu nennen." The term *the orientalizing revolution* is from Boardman (1990).

18. See his review of *CAH* in *Gnomon* 7 (1931) 65–74.

19. F. Boll and K. Bezold, *Reflexe astrologischer Keilinschriften bei griechischen Schriftstellern*, Sitzungsber. Heidelberg 1911.7; idem, *Zenit- und Aequatorialgestirne am babylonischen Fixsternhimmel*, ibid. 1913.11; idem, "Eine neue babylonisch-griechische Parallele," in *Aufsätze zur Kultur- und Sprachgeschichte E. Kuhn gewidmet* (1916) 226–235; idem, *Sternglaube und Sterndeutung* (1918, 1931⁴); F. Boll, "Zur babylonischen Planetenordnung," *ZA* 25 (1911) 372–377; idem, "Neues zur babylonischen Planetenordnung," ibid. 28 (1914) 340–351; idem, *Antike Beobachtungen farbiger Sterne*, Abh. München 30 (1916). Boll's obituary of Carl Bezold is in F. Boll, *Kleine Schriften zur Sternkunde des Altertums* (1950) 397–405; cf. ibid. xxiii f.; O. Neugebauer, "Zur Geschichte des Pythagoräischen Lehrsatzes," *NGG math.-ph. Kl.* (1928) 45–48; cf. Burkert (1972) 429.

20. Dornseiff (1933) 25–27, following E. Honigmann, *RE* IV A (1932) 1577 s.v. Syria; and W. Porzig, "Illuyankas und Typhon," in *Kleinasiatische Forschungen* I 3 (1930) 379–386. See further Dornseiff (1934) and (1937).

21. H. G. Güterbock, *Kumarbi, Mythen vom churritischen Kronos* (1946) and *The Song of Ullikummi* (1952); Lesky (1950), (1954), (1955); Dirlmeier (1955); Heubeck (1955); Steiner (1959); Walcot (1966); West (1966); see already Dornseiff (1937) = (1959) 55.

22. Lesky (1955); Dirlmeier (1955); Gordon (1955) with the review of Lesky *Gnomon* 29 (1957) 321–325; Webster (1956) and (1958); H. Haag, *Homer, Ugarit und das Alte Testament* (1962); going too far was Astour (1965), criticized by J. Boardman, *CR* 16 (1966) 86–88.

23. Eissfeldt (1939), (1952); Heubeck (1955); see now Baumgarten (1981).

24. See Gordon (1955), Webster (1958), Astour (1965) with his characteristic subtitle, Harmatta (1968), Laroche (1973), Stella (1978), Duchemin (1980a) 848 f.; J. Bouzek, *The Aegean, Anatolia and Europe: Cultural Interrelations in the 2nd Millennium B.C.* (1985); J. L. Crowley, *The Aegean and the East* (1989); C. Lambrou-Philippson, *Hellenorientalia: The Near Eastern Presence in the Bronze Age Aegean, ca. 3000–1100 B.C.* (1990).

25. A. Rehm, *Handbuch der Archäologie* I (1939) 197 f.; cf. 194 f.: "lieber ins X. als ins IX. Jahrhundert"; hence G. Klaffenbach, *Griechische Epigraphik* (1957) 35, more cautious (1966²) 36; see also W. Schadewaldt, *Von Homers Welt und Werk* (1951²) 26 and 94 n.4; Heubeck (1955) 521 n.56: "Auf alle Fälle kommen wir beträchtlich vor die Epoche der 'orientalisierenden' Kunst." The early date for Greek writing was refuted by Jeffery (1961); see Chapter 1, "Writing and Literature in the Eighth Century."

26. See Chapter 1.

27. See also Jeffery (1976), Murray (1980).

28. It was Heubeck (1955) who argued for post-Mycenaean transmission of eastern, esp. Hittite mythology; see also F. Schachermeyr, *Die griechische Rückerinnerung im Lichte neuer Forschungen,* Sitzungsber. Wien 404 (1983) 23.

29. *Od.* 17.383–385. See Contents.

30. See esp. Walcot (1966) and West (1966), (1978b). An important new parallel to the adornment of Pandora is W. R. Mayer (1987).

31. The *locus classicus* for this thesis is already [Plat.] *Epin.* 987d; cf. Orig. *Cels.* 1.2.

32. The author is a Hellenist, not an orientalist, but he has made some effort to study the Semitic texts in the original.

33. Special fields are drifting apart: The extremely useful article "Griechen" by W. Röllig in *RlA* III (1971) 643–647 ignores the presence of Greeks in Syria and Cilicia during the eighth century,

hence judges the oldest cuneiform text about Greeks (see Chapter 1, "Historical Background," note 15) to be "quite uncertain" (643), and states that there can be no question of any direct influence on Homer ("dass etwa von einem direkten Einfluss auf Homer . . . keine Rede sein kann," 646).

1. "Who Are Public Workers"
HISTORICAL BACKGROUND

1. For a historical survey see *CAH* III 3, including Braun (1982a), (1982b); Klengel (1980); Murray (1980). A keen and interesting study by Mazzarino (1947) is now outdated in some respects; see also A. Momigliano, *Quarto contributo alla storia degli studi classici e del mondo antico* (1969) 581–588. The names of Assyrian and Babylonian kings usually appear in four variants in our tradition, depending on the Hebrew Bible, the Greek Bible (Septuagint), the Latin Bible, and technical transcription of Akkadian, respectively. Here the (questionable) praxis of *CAH²* is followed.

2. See *Sendschirli* I–V (the Turkish name of this site has been spelled Zincirli since the introduction of the Latin alphabet in Turkey); Landsberger (1948); more recent special studies are Winter (1973), Genge (1979), and a survey in van Loon (1991) 1–15.

3. A bronze bowl with a Phoenician inscription was found in a tomb at Knossos, dated about 900 B.C.: *Arch.Rep.* 1976/77, 11–14; M. Sznycer, *Kadmos* 18 (1979) 89–93; Coldstream (1982) 263, 271, pl. 27. See also Stucky (1981), Blome (1982).

4. See Oppenheim (1967/69), Wäfler (1982), Röllig (1982) 26.

5. See Chapter 1, "Writing and Literature in the Eighth Century."

6. See V. Karageorghis, *Kition, Mycenaean and Phoenician* (1976); idem, *Excavations at Kition* III (1977) 7–10; N. Coldstream, *JHS* 102 (1982) 288 f., in his review of V. Karageorghis and J. Des Gagniers, *La céramique chypriote de style figuré* (1974/79); Coldstream, *Archaeology in Cyprus* (1985) 58. Cf. in general S. Frankenstein, "The Phoenicians in the Far West: A Function of Neo-Assyrian Imperialism," in *Power and Propaganda,* ed. M. Trolle Larsen (1979) 263–294.

7. See Woolley (1953); Murray (1980) 91–93; Boardman (1980) 35–54 and (1990); Braun (1982a) 7–11; Coldstream (1982) 262; Riis (1982).

8. Boardman (1965) and (1980) 45 f.

9. Riis (1970), and (1982); P. Courbin, "Fragments d'amphores protogéometriques grecques à Bassit," in *Resurrecting the Past,* ed. P. Matthiae, M. van Loon, and H. Weiss (1990) 49–64.

10. Popham, Sackett, and Themelis (1980); cf. *Arch.Rep.* 1984/ 85 (relations to Athens and to the Orient) and 1988/89, 117–129; the Heroon of the tenth century: M. R. Popham, "The Hero of Lefkandi," *Antiquity* 51 (1982) 169–176. Euboea has made its impact on Homeric studies: West (1978a), (1978b) 29 f., (1988) 165–169; P. Wathelet, "La langue homérique et le rayonnement littéraire de l'Eubée," *AC* 50 (1981) 819–833; Blome (1984). West thinks (oral communication) that "farther than Euboea" in the mouth of imaginary Phaeacians (*Od.* 7.321) means that, *e contrario,* Euboea is the center in the real world.

11. The finds, mainly due to Giorgio Buchner, have never been fully published; the greatest sensation was created by the "cup of Nestor" in 1955. See G. Buchner in Ridgway and Ridgway (1979) 129–144 and (1982); Boardman (1980) 165–169; Kopcke (1990) 101–110; on Egyptian objects Hölbl (1979); on the documents for writing see Chapter 1, "Writing and Literature in the Eighth Century."

12. See Chapter 1, "Writing and Literature in the Eighth Century."

13. On *solos* see Chapter 1, "The Problem of Loan-Words," note 29. For "Chalkis" see M. Meier, *-id-. Zur Geschichte eines griechischen Nominalsuffixes* (1975) 52 f.; *Taršiš,* foundry (Assyrian *rašašu*): W. F. Albright, *BASOR* 81 (1941) 14 f.; it is controversial whether *Taršiš* refers to Tarsos or to some place in Spain: M. Koch, *Tarschisch* (1984).

14. *Od.* 1.184; the place-name mentioned in this verse was controversial already in antiquity: Τεμέσην is the reading of the manuscripts and should refer to a place in southern Italy, but Steph.Byz. s.v. *Tamasos* attests Τάμασον, i.e., a city in Cyprus; cf. Braun (1982a) 13; K. Hadjiioannou, *AA* 81 (1966) 205–210, suggested ἔς τ' Ἀλασιν, Alasia being the Bronze Age name either of Cyprus or of the most important city of Cyprus (Enkomi).

15. H. W. Saggs, *Iraq* 25 (1963) 76–78; Braun (1982a) 15. The bronze plaques of King Hazael, piously dedicated to Hera of Samos and Apollo of Eretria in consequence (see Chapter 1, "Oriental

Products in Greece," note 14), may well have been looted at such an occasion. Eph'al and Naveh (1989) conclude from the inscription "What Hadad has given to Lord Hazael from Umqi . . ." that Hazael himself had taken the pieces as booty, but they do not see such a chance for Greeks (200).

16. Beloch (1913) I 2² 67 f.; L. W. King, *JHS* 30 (1910) 327–335; Luckenbill (1933); Mazzarino (1947) 112–130; Braun (1982a) 1–5. "Jawan" appears among the progeny of Noah in the "table of nations" in Genesis 10:2–4; his "sons" seem to refer to Cyprus, Tarsos, and Rhodes; see West (1985) 14 f.

17. An inscription of Essarhaddon has both names, *Iadnana* and *Iawan,* and keeps them distinct; see Hirschberg (1932) 68; Borger (1956) 86 § 57 line 10; cf. Luckenbill (1933), Braun (1982a) 3, 20; against Beloch and Mazzarino, who identified both names. All the evidence about *Iadnana* and *Iamani* is in S. Parpola, *Neo-Assyrian Toponyms* (1970) 183, 186 f.

18. *Il.* 13.685. U. von Wilamowitz-Moellendorff, *Die Ilias und Homer* (1916) 227 n.1, wrote: "Die Ionier sind mit den Athenern identisch"—for him, this is a "late" interpolation; he was unaware of the importance of Euboea and Athens in the eighth century. The problem about Ἰάϝονες is that especially in the Attic/Ionian dialect ϝ had disappeared early and contraction occurred, resulting in Ἴωνες. It has been suggested that Ἰάϝονες is much older than the eighth century; see J. Chadwick in *Greece and the Eastern Mediterranean in Ancient History and Prehistory, Studies Presented to F. Schachermeyr* (1977) 106–109: "A group of the Mycenaean inhabitants of Greece called themselves Ἰάϝονες" (109). Yet it is a fact that the uncontracted form remained in current use, and this is hardly a result of the epic tradition: It must have been used by non-Ionians, i.e., Dorians and Cyprians; Tarsos, Cyprus, and Rhodes were prominent in the view from the East (see note 16 above); people from these places will have referred to Euboeans and Athenians as *Iawones.* For Persians speaking of *Iaones,* see Aesch. *Persae,* Aristoph. *Ach.* 104. Even the "Ionians" of Sicily do not stem from Asia Minor, but from eighth-century Naxos. The "Ionian" sea seems to mark the Euboean-Naxian route to Italy and Sicily (although the development from *Ἰαόνιος to Ἰόνιος is not without difficulty either).

19. Stele of Kition: Luckenbill (1927) II §§ 179–189; cf. §§ 70,

99; Elayi and Cavigneau (1979). Iamani: Luckenbill (1927) II §§ 30, 62–63, 79–80, 294–295; *ANET* 285 f.; hailed by H. Bengtson, *Griechische Geschichte* (1950) 21 and 69, (1977⁵) 24 and 77, as the first contact of Greeks and Assyrians. H. Tadmor, *JCS* 12 (1958) 80 n.219; Elayi and Cavigneau (1979) plead to understand *Iamani* as a personal name of local type, not meaning "the Greek."

20. See Laminger-Pascher (1989) 16–25.

21. Berossos; *FGrHist* 680 F 7 p. 386; Abydenos: *FGrHist* 685 F 5 § 6; Streck (1916) cccxci–iii. The more authentic tradition is to be found with Abydenos; see Momigliano (1934); cf. Mazzarino (1947) 125 f., Boardman (1965).

22. Borger (1956) 60; Luckenbill (1927) II § 690.

23. First mentioned by Hdt. 2.150.3 and Hellanikos, *FGrHist* 4 F 63, i.e., before the histories of Ktesias. See Streck (1916) I ccclxxxvi–cdv; an important document is Streck II 140 f., the prism of Ashurbanipal containing a list of kings of Cyprus; cf. C. Baurain, *BCH* 105 (1981) 366–370.

24. Hence G. Scheibner, *Wissenschaftliche Zeitschrift der Friedrich-Schiller-Universität Jena, gesellsch. u. sprachwiss.,* Reihe 15 (1965) 93–96, thinks this is a *terminus ante quem* for the Homeric poems which acknowledge the riches of Sidon; cf. Burkert, *WSt* 89 (1976) 20.

25. For the various consecutive versions of the contacts with Lydia in Ashurbanipal's *Annals* see Cogan and Tadmor (1977); the final version is in Streck (1916) II 20–23; cf. Luckenbill (1927) II §§ 849, 909 f.

26. Herodotus 5.49–53 describes the "Royal Road" which still goes via Gordion in Phrygia; i.e., it presupposes the route Phrygia–Cilicia–Assyria, whereas Xenophon in the service of Cyrus took the shorter route via Kelainai–Ikonion. See R. W. Macan, *Herodotus Books IV V VI* (1895) II 289–303; Hanfmann (1948). Before the discoveries at Euboea and Al Mina, scholars, following Hogarth (1909), had overestimated the importance of "Ionia" in Asia Minor as to oriental contacts for the early period. Barnett (1956) had assumed another route from Urartu to Trapezunt at the Black Sea; *contra,* Carter (1972) 41 with n. 86. For a reassessment of the development of Ionia see R. M. Cook, "Ionia and Greece in the Eighth and Seventh Centuries B.C.," *JHS* 66 (1946) 67–98.

ORIENTAL PRODUCTS IN GREECE

1. See Poulsen (1912), Dunbabin (1957), Akurgal (1968), Herrmann (1975), Helck, (1979), Boardman (1980), Braun (1982a), Kopcke (1990); cf. also Introduction at note 16.

2. Barnett (1948), (1956); Greifenhagen (1965); B. Freyer-Schauenburg, *Elfenbeine aus dem samischen Heraion* (1966); E.-L. Marangou, *Lakonische Elfenbein- und Beinschnitzereien* (1969); I. Winter, *Iraq* 38 (1976) 1–26; G. Herrmann, *Iraq* 51 (1989) 85–109; see also Helck (1979) 175 n.28; Boardman (1980) 62 f., who also illustrates the remarkable ivory statuettes from a tomb at Athens, third quarter of the eighth century.

3. E. Diehl, *AA* 1965, 827–850; R. A. Stucky, *Engraved Tridacna Shells* (1974); Boardman (1980) 71 f.; S. Boessneck and A. von den Driesch, *MDAI* (Athens) 98 (1983) 22–24.

4. *Il.* 14.183; see C. Kardara, *AJA* 65 (1961) 62–64; cf. E. L. Smithson, *Hesperia* 37 (1968) 77–116 with pl. 33: a necklace from a tomb at the Areopagus, Athens, mid-ninth century; Popham, Sackett, and Themelis (1980) 221 pl. 231d; cf. *BSA* 77 (1982) pl. 30b: import and local imitation; see further Helck (1979) 203 f.; Boardman (1980) 76; Coldstream (1982) 266.

5. J. Boardman, *Island Gems* (1963) and *Archaic Greek Gems* (1968); Boardman and Vollenweider (1978); Boardman (1980) 71; and *AA* 1990, 1–17; a deposit at the temple of Apollo, Eretria: *BCH* 103 (1979) 597–599 and 104 (1980) 657 f. fig. 156; *Arch.Rep.* 1980/ 81, 8 fig. 8.

6. Boardman and Buchner (1966); cf. P. Zazoff, *Die antiken Gemmen* (1983) 59.

7. Popham, Sackett, and Themelis (1980) pls. 233e, 235c–e; Coldstream (1982) 264 f.; C. Bérard, *Eretria* III: *L'Héroon à la Porte de l'Ouest* (1970) 14–16; Murray (1980) 79.

8. A. Furtwängler, "Die Bronzen und die übrigen kleineren Funde von Olympia," in *Olympia* IV (1890) 187; E. Diehl, *AA* 1965, 823–827 (Samos); H. Gallet de Santerre and J. Tréheux, *BCH* 71/72 (1947/48) 240–243 fig. 39 (Delos).

9. *Il.* 23.741–745; *Od.*4. 615–619; for the shield of Achilles, *Il.* 18, see Fittschen (1973). The bronze and silver bowls have been comprehensively treated by Markoe (1985); earlier studies include K. Kübler, *Kerameikos* V 1 (1954) 201–205; Canciani (1970); Carter

(1972); Imai (1977); Borell (1978) 74–92. See, in general, Curtis (1988), esp. G. Falsone, "Phoenicia as a Bronzeworking Centre in the Iron Age," 227–250.

10. Olympia: Furtwängler (see above, note 8) 141 pl. 52; *CIS* II 112 (not in *KAI*). Bowl from Pontecagnano near Salerno, in the Tyskiewicz Collection, Paris: B. D'Agostino, *Stud.Etr.* 45 (1977) 51–58; G. Garbini, ibid. 58–62. Praeneste, Tomba Bernardini: *CIS* I 164; Guzzo Amadasi (1967) 157 f. Falerii: M. Cristofani and P. Fronzardi, *Stud.Etr.* 39 (1971) 313–331. See also above, "Historical Background," note 40, on the Phoenician bowl from Knossos. Cf. Borell (1978) 80–82.

11. To be published by B. Seidel-Borell; cf. E. Kunze, *Arch.Delt.* 17 B (1961/62) 115 f. pls. 129-130 and 19 B (1964) pl. 181 b–c; A. Mallwitz and H. V. Herrmann, *Die Funde aus Olympia* (1980) 53 f. pls. 23–24. For a Late Hittite lion protome found at Olympia (from a votive shield?), see *Illustrated London News,* 25 July 1964, 121; H. V. Herrmann, *10. Bericht über die Ausgrabungen in Olympia* (1981) 72–82.

12. H. V. Herrmann, *Die Kessel der orientalisierenden Zeit I/II* (Olympische Forschungen 6 and 11) (1966, 1979); cf. idem, *JdI* 81 (1966) 79–141; Herrmann (1975) 306 f.; Boardman (1980) 64–67.

13. Kunze (1931); Canciani (1970); Herrmann, *Olympische Forschungen* 6 (1966) 179–185 and (1975) 308, thinks they are imports; Helck (1979) 191 f.; Boardman (1980) 58–60; H. Verbruggen, *Le Zeus crétois* (1981) 71–99; Blome (1982) 15–23; Kopcke (1990) 111 thinks of a cult by "Semites"; see also at n.38. For recent excavations in the Idaean cave see J. A. Sakellarakis in Hägg, Marinatos, and Nordquist (1988) 173–193, esp. n.6.

14. Herrmann (1975) 308 f.; Helck (1979) 187–190; Burkert (1979) 114–118; Boardman (1980) 69 f.; H. Philipp, *10. Bericht über die Ausgrabungen in Olympia* (1981) 91–108. Hazael's bronze plates: Charbonnet (1986); Kyrieleis and Röllig (1988); Bron and Lemaire (1989); D. Parayre, *Rev. d'Ass.* 83 (1989) 45–51; Eph'al and Naveh (1989); possibly looted first by Hazael, then by Greeks (see "Historical Background," note 15).

15. Coldstream (1969), (1982) 268 f.; on Beloch, see Introduction at note 15 and below, note 37. There are Greek testimonies as to Phoenicians at Rhodes (Ath. 360 f. = Ergias, *FGrHist* 513 F 1; Polyzelos, *FGrHist* 521 F 6), and Zeus Atabyrios at Rhodes seems

to be the Baal from Tabor/Atabyrion; A. B. Cook, *Zeus* II 2 (1925) 922–925; O. Eissfeldt, *Kleine Schriften* II (1963) 29–54; Helck (1979) 160.

16. G. M. Hanfmann, *Bibl.Or.* 30 (1973) 199; and H. V. Herrmann, *Gnomon* 47 (1975) 401, in their reviews of Jantzen (1972); cf. Börker-Klähn (1973); Hazael's bronze plate, note 14, above.

17. See notes 4, 5, and 7 as to Eretria and Athens, notes 11–12 as to Olympia; C. Rolley, "Bronzes géométriques et orientaux à Délos," *BCH* suppl. 1 (1973) 523 f.

18. W. L. Brown (1960); Strøm (1971); A. Rathje in Ridgway and Ridgway (1979) 145–183; Verzár (1980); E. Richardson, *Etruscan Votive Bronzes* (1983).

19. *Not.Scav.* 1876, 282–295; C. D. Curtis, "The Bernardini Tomb," *Memoirs of the American Academy in Rome* 3 (1919) 9–90; G. Proietti and M. Pallottino, *Il Museo Nazionale Etrusco di Villa Giulia* (1980) nos. 363–379; *Civiltà del Lazio primitivo* (1976) 213–249; A. Bedini, *PP* 32 (1977) 274–309.

20. See notes 2, 12, and 40.

21. See Ahlberg (1967), (1971); Borell (1978); Helck (1979) 192; Boardman (1980) 77–82; Stucky (1982).

22. On the "mistress/master of animals" see Blome (1982) 65–76; B. Johnson, *Lady of the Beasts* (1988). The pattern is found at Mycenae as well as on one of the Cassite seals which came from Mesopotamia to Bronze Age Thebes (P. Amiet, *Orientalia* 34 [1976] 28 fig. 13; K. Demakopoulou and D. Konsola, *Archaeological Museum of Thebes* [1981] 52 f.), but it also appears again and again on objects imported during the orientalizing period. Boardman (1980) 78 finds it "virtually impossible to demonstrate the transmission" in such cases. For one line of tradition which goes from Syria to Boeotia see Coldstream (1977) 13; cf. Helck (1971) 223–229, (1979) 210.

23. For some time a geometric representation from Athens, mid-eighth century, was held to be the first example (Schefold [1964] pl. 5a), until a ninth-century picture appeared at Knossos; H. Sackett, *BSA* 71 (1976) 123 f.; Boardman (1980) 78. See in general W. L. Brown (1960); Gabelmann (1965); Carter (1972); Blome (1982) 93–97 and *AA* 1988, 559–565; G. E. Markoe, *ClAnt* 8 (1989) 86–115. On the etymology of the word *lion* see Chapter 1, "The Problem of Loan-Words," note 30.

24. Helck (1979) 194–197; Boardman (1980) 78 f. On the sphinx, see Vermeule (1977) and H. Demisch, *Die Sphinx* (1977) 77–82. On griffins, see A. Dierichs, *Das Bild des Greifen in der früh-griechischen Flächenkunst* (1981) 275–294.

25. "Chimaera" of Carchemish: E. Akurgal, *Die Kunst der Hethiter* (1976²) pl. 110; of Zincirli: *Sendschirli* III (1902) pl. 43; cf. Helck (1979) 212 f.; Boardman (1980) 79.

26. On fishmen, called *kulilu* in Akkadian (*AHw* 501), see E. Unger, *RlA* III 70 f.; Rittig (1977) 94–96; Helck (1979) 219; R. Stucky, ed., *Trésors du musée de Bagdad* (1977) no. 141. See also K. Shepart, *The Fish-tailed Monster* (1940); H. P. Isler, *Acheloos* (1970) 92–95.

27. A remarkable "tree of life" appears on the "Cesnola *krater*"; P. P. Kahane, *AK* 16 (1973) 114–138; see further C. P. Kardara, "Oriental Influences on Rhodian Vases," in *Les céramiques de la Grèce de l'est et leur diffusion en occident,* Coll. internat. du centre J. Bérard (1976/78) 66–70; Boardman (1980) 81 f.

28. For *prothesis* see K. A. Sheedy, *MDAI* (Athens) 105 (1990) 117–151; for symposium scenes H. Kyrieleis, *Thronen und Klinen* (1965); B. Fehr, *Orientalische und griechische Gelage* (1971); J. M. Dentzer, *Le motif du banquet couché et le monde grec du VIIe au IVe siècle avant J.-C.* (1982) 143–153. A well-known picture of reclining Herakles by the Andokides painter, *LIMC* Herakles no. 1487 (cf. 1486), is iconographically a direct descendant of "Ashurbanipal's garden party," Meissner (1920/25) I fig. 46.

29. E. Kunze, *A&A* 2 (1946) 95–115; D. Collon, "The Smiting God," *Levant* 4 (1972) 111–134; Burkert (1975); Helck (1979) 179–182; H. Seeden, *The Standing Armed Figurines in the Levant* (1980); H. Gallet de Santerre, "Les statuettes de bronze mycéniennes au type dit du 'dieu Rechef' dans leur contexte égéen," *BCH* 111 (1987) 7–29; Blome (1990) nos. 12 and 16.

30. P. Jacobsthal, *Der Blitz in der orientalischen und griechischen Kunst* (1906); additions and corrections in G. Furlani, *Stud.Etr.* 5 (1931) 203–231; see also H. L. Lorimer, *BSA* 37 (1936–37), on the god with two lightnings, Zeus Dipaltos.

31. See P. J. Riis, *Berytus* 9 (1949) 69–90 and (1960) 193–198; Helck (1971) 233 f. and (1979) 173–177; Boardman (1980) 76 f.; U. Winter (1983); comprehensive treatment now in Boehm (1990).

32. For an Assyrian image of a goddess with high hat (*polos*)

at Samos, dated to the reign of Sargon II, see Jantzen (1972) B 165 pl. 69; Herrmann, *Gnomon* 47 (1975) 398; Helck (1979) 184–186; see also Kranz (1972).

33. See A. L. Oppenheim, "The Golden Garments of the Gods," *JNES* 8 (1949) 172–193; Fleischer (1973) 96 and (on the fillet, "Rückentaenie") 50 f.; Börker and Klähn (1973) 45. Ishtar is said to "hold *keppê*" (e.g., "Descent of Ishtar" 27, *ANET* 107); according to B. Landsberger, *WZKM* 56 (1960) 121–124 and 57 (1961) 23, this is a jump rope, "Springseil" (*AHw* 467); Landsberger refers to representations of the goddess on seals such as W. H. Ward (1910) nos. 912–923; in these the "rope" in the hands of the goddess, though, is meant to be the seam of her garment lifted up by her; cf. Helck (1971) 112 f. Still the similarity to the ribbons the goddess is holding at Ephesos and Samos (Fleischer 102–111) is highly suggestive.

34. Samos: H. Walter, *Das griechische Heiligtum. Heraion von Samos* (1965) 28. Sparta: R. M. Dawkins, "The Sanctuary of Artemis Orthia," *JHS* suppl. 5 (1929) 163–186 pls. 47–62; Boardman (1980) 77; J. B. Carter, "The Masks of Ortheia," *AJA* 91 (1987) 355–383; her further suggestion (in Hägg, Marinatos, and Nordquist [1988] 89–98) that the masks were used in a sacred marriage ritual in the context of Alkman's Partheneion will hardly find consent. On Mesopotamian and Syro-Phoenician masks, found in tombs, see R. D. Barnett in *Eléments* (1960) 147 f.; A. Parrot, *Ugaritica* VI (1969) 409–418; S. Moscati in *Near Eastern Studies in Honour of W. F. Albright* (1971) 356 f., 362 f.; H. Kühne, *Bagdader Mitt.* 7 (1974) 101–110; E. Stern, *Palestine Exploration Quart.* 108 (1976) 109–118; S. Moscati, ed., *The Phoenicians* (1988) 354–369; for three Punic protomes at Brauron, see M. Bell, *Morgantina* I (1981) 87; see also Chapter 2, "Hepatoscopy," note 23, Humbaba mask from Gortyn.

35. H. Luschey, *Die Phiale* (1939); cf. Herrmann (1975) 309; Boardman (1980) 68. On the use of frankincense see K. Nielsen, *Incense in Ancient Israel* (1986); D. Martinetz, K. Lohs, and J. Janzen, *Weihrauch und Myrrhe* (1989); W. Zwickel, *Räucherkult und Räuchergeräte* (1990); cf. Chapter 1, "The Problem of Loan-Words," at note 8.

36. See J. W. Shaw, *Hesperia* 51 (1982) 185–191 and *AJA* 93 (1989) 165–183; cf. Boardman (1990) 184; Blome (1991) 54f.

37. On Phoenicians see Dunbabin (1957) 35–43; W. A. Ward (1968); esp. Coldstream (1969), (1982); Muhly (1970); Edwards (1979); Bunnens (1979); Niemeyer (1982); Bammer (1985); Gubel and Lipinski (1985); Gehrig and Niemeyer (1990), esp. J. Latacz, "Die Phönizier bei Homer," 11–20. The direct but late evidence on Phoenicians in Greece is collected by F. Vattioni, "Fenici, Siri e Arabi emigrati in area greca," *AION* 9/10 (1987/88) 91–124. See also above, note 15; "Historical Background," notes 3, 6; for Beloch, see Introduction at note 15.

38. Boardman (1961) 150 f.; (1967) esp. 63–67; (1970) 14–25; (1980) 56–62; see also Barnett (1948) 6; P. Jacobsthal, *JHS* 71 (1951) 91–93; Dunbabin (1957) 40 f.; Greifenhagen (1965) 127, 136; Coldstream (1968) 348 f.; van Loon (1974); Murray (1980) 71.

39. Greifenhagen (1965); Boardman (1980) 71; Coldstream (1982) 266.

40. Van Loon (1974) 23; cf. Boardman (1980) 57 with n.73: "Techniques such as these cannot be learned by observation."

41. Dunbabin (1957) 37, 59 n.5; Riis (1960) 197; Rizza and Santa Maria Scrinari (1968) 212–245; Boardman (1980) 76 f.; Blome (1982) 28–36; Boehm (1990) 73–86.

42. Herrmann prefers to think the tympanon found in the Idaean cave (see note 13 above) was imported from the East; (1975) 304; *contra,* Blome (1982) 16.

43. Helck (1979) 55, 226–228; cf. I. Winter (1973) 477–482; Grottanelli (1982b) 664.

44. Plut. *Sol.* 24.4: μετοικίζεσθαι ἐπὶ τέχνηι. See in general F. Coarelli, *Artisti e artigiani in Grecia* (1980); L. Neesen, *Demiurgoi und Artifices. Studien zur Stellung freier Handwerker in antiken Städten* (1989).

45. Corinth: Hdt. 2.167.2; Athens: Diod. 11.43.3.

46. See J. Boardman, "Amasis: The Implications of His Name," in *Papers on the Amasis Painter and His World* (Malibu 1987), 141–152.

47. Arist. *Polit.* 1278a7: δοῦλον τὸ βάναυσον ἢ ξενικόν, διόπερ οἱ πολλοὶ τοιοῦτοι καὶ νῦν. Slave women were "taken" and traded as weavers: *Il.* 6.290 f., 23.263; *Od.* 15.418; cf. Helck (1979) 226 on Egypt. On the "craftsmen's tax" (χειρωνάξιον, Arist. *Oik.* 1345b7) and its Persian background see M. Wörrle, *Chiron* 9 (1979) 91 f.

48. οἱ μεταπορευόμενοι τεχνῖται: M. Wörrle, *Chiron* 9 (1979) 83.

49. Sirac. 38.30, following the Syrian text; see E. Kautzsch, *Die Apokryphen und Pseudepigraphen des Alten Testaments* I (1900) 422.

50. S. Kroll in D. Ahrens, ed., *Archäologie entdeckt Geschichte: Urartu* (1979) 53.

51. Strabo 5 p. 220: εὐπορία δημιουργῶν τῶν συνακολουθησάντων οἴκοθεν; Plin. *N.H.* 35.152; cf. 12.5: *Helico ex Helvetiis ob . . . fabrilem artem Romae commoratus.*

52. I Kings 5:32, 15-25; cf. 5:20; Röllig (1982) 22.

53. *Ahiqar* 16.3: F. Nau, *Histoire et sagesse d'Ahikar l'Assyrien* (1909) 204; F. C. Conybeare, J. Rendell Harris, and A. Smith Lewis, *The Story of Ahikar from the Aramaic, Syriac, Arabic, Armenian, Ethiopic, Old Turkish, Greek and Slavonic Versions²* (1913) 115.

54. Luckenbill (1927) II §§ 100, 105.

55. Sasson (1968) 47.

56. *Atrahasis* p. 128 f.; *Gilgamesh* XI 85.

57. J. Friedrich, *Staatsverträge des Hatti-Reiches* (1930) 77 § 18 lines 65, 67 (restored); Sasson (1968) 51.

58. Sasson (1968) 48 f.

59. Hdt. 3.125-137.

60. E. F. Weidner in *Mélanges Syriens offerts à R. Dussaud* (1939) II 932 f.; *ANET* 308b; Boardman (1980) 52.

61. G. M. A. Richter, *AJA* 50 (1946) 15-30; C. Nylander, *Ionians at Pasargadae* (1970); Boardman (1980) 102-105 and *JHS* 100 (1980) 204-206.

62. On the inscription on the Tyskiewicz bowl, see note 10, above. Cf. Chapter 2, "Craftsmen of the Sacred," note 29.

63. Hdt. 2.152.

64. Alcaeus fr. 350; cf. 48—the first mention of Babylon and Askalon in Greek literature; Sappho fr. 202 = Hdt. 2.135. See also *A Selection of Greek Historical Inscriptions,* ed. R. Meiggs and D. Lewis (1969), no. 7.

65. II Sam. 8:18, 15:18, 20:7, 23; I Kings 1:38.

66. II Kings 11:4; on Carians in Egypt see Hdt. 2.152; O. Masson and J. Yoyotte, *Objects pharaoniques à inscription carienne* (1956); O. Masson, *Carian Inscriptions from North Saqqara and Buhen* (1978).

67. See "Historical Background," note 20, above.

68. On Assyrian and Urartaean prototypes of the Greek hoplite shield see A. Snodgrass, *Early Greek Armour and Weapons* (1964) 66 f.; Gorgon shield from Carchemish: L. Woolley, *Carchemish* II (1921) 128; H. L. Lorimer, *Homer and the Monuments* (1950) 191 A 6; Boardman (1980) 51; Gorgon shield from Olympia: E. Kunze, 5. *Bericht über die Ausgrabungen in Olympia* (1956) 46–49 pls. 12–14; from Delphi: L. Lerat, *BCH* 104 (1980) 103–114. On the shields from the Idaean cave see note 13, above.

WRITING AND LITERATURE IN THE EIGHTH CENTURY

1. The basic book from the Greek side is Jeffery (1961, 1990²); see also Guarducci (1967); U. Hausmann, ed., "Die Schrift und die Schriftzeugnisse," in *Handbuch der Archäologie* I (1969) 207–393; a series of articles with the collective title "Dal sillabario miceneo all'alfabeto greco," *PP* 31 (1976) 1–102; Immerwahr (1990); Powell (1991); *PHOINIKEIA GRAMMATA. Lire et écrire en Méditerranée,* ed. C. Baurain, C. Bonnet, and V. Krings (1991); an excellent account given by Heubeck (1979) is already outdated in some details. He did not yet know the sensational alphabet from Izbet Sartah, twelfth-century Palestine: M. Kochavi, *Tel Aviv* 4 (1977) 1–13; A. Demsky, ibid. 14–27 and in ʿIzbet Sartah, "An Early Iron Site near Rosh Haʿayin," *Israel* (1986) 186–197; J. Naveh, *Bibl. Archaeologist* 43 (1980) 22–25 and (1982) 36 f.; K. Seybold in J. von Ungern-Sternberg and H. Reinau, eds., *Vergangenheit in mündlicher Überlieferung* (1988) 142; nor about the Phoenician alphabet from the eighth century: A. Lemaire, *Semitica* 28 (1978) 7–10; nor about the eighth-century alphabet from the Athenian agora: Johnston in Jeffery (1990) 431 no. 2a; Immerwahr (1990) 8 fig. 2. Cf. also M. Lejeune, *RPh* 57 (1983) 7–12.

2. See M. P. Nilsson, *Opuscula Selecta* II (1952) 1029–56 (originally published 1918); Jeffery (1961) 22; Helck (1979) 165–167. It must still be stressed that the use of *aleph, jod, waw* to indicate *a, i, u* is common in Aramaic from early times; in form, Greek Y is almost identical with Semitic waw; F is a variant of it.

3. For the dependence of the Phrygian script on the Greek, see Heubeck (1979) 78 against R. S. Young, *Proc. Am. Philos. Soc.* 107 (1963) 362–364. Phrygian script seems to be in evidence since about 725 B.C., although a later dating was advocated by A. M. Snodgrass, *The Dark Age of Greece* (1971) 349 f.; more likely it arrived

on the route from Cilicia to Gordion rather than from either the Troad or Ionia; see "Historical Background," note 26, above.

4. Hdt. 5.58; ποινικαστάς was the designation for a "writer," a secretary in archaic Crete; L. H. Jeffery and A. Morpurgo Davies, *Kadmos* 9 (1970) 118–154 and *SEG* 27, no. 631.

5. Pride of place remains for the Dipylon jug at Athens, which for a long time was by far the earliest document, dated ca. 735–725; *IG* I² 919; Jeffery (1990) 68, 76 no. 1; Heubeck (1979) 116–118; Boardman (1980) 83; *SEG* 30 no. 46, 38 no. 34; Y. Duhoux, *Kadmos* 30 (1991) 153–169. But an inscription from Ischia is now considered to be older: Buchner (1978) 135–137 (ca. 750–730); cf. Johnston (1983) and in Jeffery (1990) 453 with pl. 76. A geometric sherd from Naxos with a graffito has been dated to 770 by the excavator: B. Lambrinoudakis, *BCH* 106 (1982) 605, 604 fig. 132; *SEG* 33, 677; Johnston in Jeffery (1990) 466 A with pl. 78; cf. graffiti from Andros (750–720), Johnston in Jeffery (1990) 466, 52a. For Lefkandi, see Jeffery in Popham, Sackett, and Themelis (1980) 89–92; for Eretria, Johnston in Jeffery (1990) 434 with pl. 73; in general, Powell (1991) 123–180. Some material from Euboea is still unpublished. Of special importance is the "cup of Nestor" from Ischia, dated to 730–720: Jeffery (1961) 235 no. 1; Heubeck (1979) 109–116. It evidently reflects a practice of writing books; cf. Immerwahr (1990) 18 f.

6. A two-letter graffito from Ischia with sidelong A, P. K. McCarter, *AJA* 79 (1975) 140 f., is taken to be Greek by Guarducci (1967) 225 and Heubeck (1979) 123, but as Aramaic by Garbini (1978) and Coldstream (1982) 271; cf. Johnston in Jeffery (1990) 454 f. A Greek and an Aramaic graffito occur on the same sherd; Johnston (1983) 64 fig. 2. Graffito from Al Mina, Oxford: J. Boardman, *Oxford Journal of Archaeology* 1 (1982) 365–367; *CAH*² III: *Plates* (1984) 291 f. no. 316e; Johnston in Jeffery (1990) 476 D.

7. See the recent discussions of B. B. Powell, "The Origin of the Puzzling Supplements φ χ ψ," *TAPA* 117 (1987) 1–20; and R. Wachter, "Zur Vorgeschichte des griechischen Alphabets," *Kadmos* 28 (1989) 19–78; the "colors" to characterize Greek alphabets were introduced by A. Kirchhoff, *Studien zur Geschichte des griechischen Alphabets* (1863; 1887⁴).

8. V. Karageorghis, *CRAI* 1980, 122–136; E. and O. Masson in V. Karageorghis, *Ausgrabungen in Alt-Paphos auf Cypern* III (1983)

411–415; for the role of Cyprus see also Heubeck (1979) 85–87; cf. 64–70; Johnston (1983).

9. See Lipiński (1988) 242. For the varying direction of writing in Cypriote linear script see O. Masson, *Les inscriptions chypriotes syllabiques* (1983²) 78.

10. Jeffery (1961) 310–313; Boardman (1970) 18–23 and (1980) 60; for the Phoenician bowl, see "Historical Background," note 3, above, and, in general, Chapter 1, "Oriental Products in Greece." The earliest Greek writing on Crete so far is an owner's inscription on a geometric pithos from Phaistos (ca. 700?); *Kret. Chron.* 21 (1969) 153–170; Heubeck (1979) 125; Johnston in Jeffery (1990) 468 no. 8a.

11. Jeffery (1961) 13–16.

12. Esp. J. Naveh, *AJA* 77 (1973) 1–8, (1982), and *Kadmos* 30 (1991) 143–152. He is contradicted not only by specialists for Greek—see McCarter (1975); B. S. Isserlin, *Kadmos* 22 (1983) 151–163; Johnston in Jeffery (1990) 426 f.—but also by some Semitists: A. Demsky, *Tel Aviv* 4 (1977) 22 f.; Lipiński (1988); Sass (1991). Lipiński and Sass still think the ninth century would be the latest possible date.

13. An important new document from the mid-eighth century was published in 1982: A. Abou-Assaf et al., *La statue de Tell Fekherye et son inscription bilingue assyro-araméenne* (1982); it has some surprisingly "archaic" letter forms; see Lipiński (1988) 242. The relations between Greek and Aramaic script were stressed by S. Segert, *Klio* 41 (1963) 38–57; for a balanced judgment, see Lipiński (1988) 243 f.; cf. also Coldstream (1982) 271; Johnston in Jeffery (1990) 425. The role of cursive forms was discussed by Johnstone (1978).

14. Ugaritic alphabets: *KTU* 5.6; for earliest "Phoenician" alphabets see note 1, above.

15. Lemaire (1981).

16. Ios. *c.Ap.* 1.28.

17. Σάν: Pindar fr. 70 b 3; cf. E. Schwyzer, *Griechische Grammatik* I (1939) 140 f.; R. Wachter, *Kadmos* 30 (1991) 49–80.

18. Galling (1971); *KTU* 5.7; in Hebrew: *Lachish I: The Lachish Letters* (1938) 79 f.; *KAI* no. 194; A. Lemaire, *Inscriptions Hébraïques* I: *Les ostraca* (1977) 110 f.; *KAI* 43.12; cf. Masson (1967) 64. The Akkadian word for writing tablet is different, *le'u,* Hebrew

*lu*ᵃ*h,* Aramaic *luḫa.* For *malthe* see M. Stol, *Phoenix* 24 (1978) 11–14; *HAL* 558.

19. For the wreck, see G. Bass, *National Geographic* 172 (1987) 633–733, esp. 731; idem et al., *AJA* 93 (1989) 1–29, esp. 10; for the Nimrud tablets, D. J. Wiseman, "Assyrian Writing-Boards," *Iraq* 17 (1955) 1–13; M. Howard, "Technical Description of the Ivory Writing-Boards from Nimrud," ibid. 14–20; H. T. Bossert, "Sie schrieben auf Holz," in *Minoica, Festschr. J. Sundwall* (1958) 67–79; H. Hunger, *Babylonische und Assyrische Kolophone* (1968) 7 f.; Heubeck (1979) 143 f.

20. *Il.* 6.119–211; Burkert (1983c) 51–53. The "fatal letter" motif is now attested not only in the story of Uriah (II Sam. 11:1–27) but already in the Sumerian legend of Sargon: B. Lewis, *The Sargon Legend* (1980); B. Alster, "A Note on the Uriah Letter in the Sumerian Sargon Legend," *ZA* 77 (1987) 169–173.

21. Aesch. *Eum.* 275, fr. 281a 21 Radt, *Prom.* 789 (overlooked by Masson [1967] 62); δέλτοι χαλκαῖ: Pollux 8.128; cf. R. Stroud, *Hesperia* 32 (1963) 138–143.

22. O. Masson, *Les inscriptions chypriotes syllabiques* (1983²) no. 217.26, cf. Masson (1967) 61–65.

23. Wendel (1949). For a new Akkadian-Aramaic document from Syria see note 13, above. The Akkadian term for scroll scribe, *sepiru,* is a loan-word from Aramaic; cf. Hebrew *sefer,* book; *AHw* 1036b. Aramaic leather scrolls from Egypt: G. R. Driver, *Aramaic Documents of the Fifth Century B.C.* (1954).

24. R. A. Bowman, *Aramaic Ritual Texts from Persepolis* (1970) 17–19; cf. Ktesias in Diod. 2.32.4.

25. Archilochus fr. 185 West; the meaning "letter" is contested by S. West, *CQ* 38 (1988) 42–49.

26. Hdt. 5.58; *diphtherion:* J. G. Vinogradov, *"Olbia." Xenia, Konstanzer althistorische Beiträge und Forschungen* 1 (1981) 19; *molibdion: SEG* 26 no. 845 rev.; cf. *SEG* 38 no. 13. The use of diminutives seems characteristic for writing materials, as also in *deltion* and *biblion.*

27. Eur. fr. 627; there is a proverb "older than the leather [scroll]," ἀρχαιότερα τῆς διφθέρας, Diogen. 3.2 (*Paroemiogr.Gr.* I 214); cf. Zenob. 4.11; Porphyry in Schol. B *Il.* 1.175; Hsch. δ 1992 attests the term διφθεραλοιφός for Cyprus (see note 8, above), which sounds archaic and may refer to the use of leather scrolls.

28. See D. van Berchem, *MH* 48 (1991) 129–145, esp. 140 f.; for Guzana, see J. Friedrich, G. R. Meyer, A. Ungnad, and E. Weidner, *Die Inschriften vom Tell Halaf* (1940) 47 (nos. 101–106) and 70–78 (nos. 1–5); on Tarsos see Chapter 2, "Hepatoscopy," note 7 and "Purification," note 6; O. R. Gurney, J. J. Finkelstein, and P. Hulin, *The Sultantepe Tablets* (1957–1964); cf. M. Hutter, *Altorientalische Vorstellungen von der Unterwelt* (1985) 18–20; the tablets are dated between 718 and 619 B.C.

29. Wendel (1949).

30. F. C. Conybeare, J. Rendell Harris, and A. Smith Lewis, *The Story of Ahiḳar from the Aramaic, Syriac, Arabic, Armenian, Ethiopic, Old Turkish, Greek and Slavonic Versions* (1913²; the first edition, 1898, did not yet have the Aramaic text); F. Nau, *Histoire et sagesse d'Ahikar l'Assyrien* (1909); for the text from Elephantine, see E. Sachau, *Aramäische Papyrus und Ostraka aus einer jüdischen Militär-Kolonie zu Elephantine* (1911) 147–182 pls. 40–50; A. Ungnad, *Aramäische Papyrus aus Elephantine* (1912); E. Meyer, *Der Papyrusfund von Elephantine und seine Bedeutung* (1912) 102–128; T. Nöldeke, *Untersuchungen zum Achiqar-Roman*, Abh. Göttingen N.F. 14.4 (1913); A. Hausrath, *Achiquar und Aesop*, Sitzungsber. Heidelberg 1918.2; B. E. Perry, *Aesopica* (1952) 1–10; P. Grelot, *Documents araméens d'Egypte* (1972) 427–452; F. M. Fales, "La tradizione Assira ad Elefantina d'Egitto," *Dialoghi di Archeologia* III 5 (1987) 63–70; see also Lipinski (1976) on Akkadian religious tradition among Aramaeans. Ahiqar is mentioned in the book Tobith 14.10.

31. *Rev. Bibl.* 52 (1985) 60–81; cf. Fales (note 30) 70.

32. *GLGMS:* J. T. Milik, *The Books of Enoch* (1976) 313; *Gilgamos:* Ael. *Nat.An.* 12.21.

33. Rodriguez Adrados (1979) 290–293, 674 f., 680–687; idem, *QUCC* 30 (1979) 93–112. But Ἀκίχαρος was known to Theophrastus; Diog.Laert. 5.50; still Democritus B 299 = Clem. *Str.* 1.69.4 is apocryphal; the reading of Poseidonios fr. 133 Theiler = Strab. 16 p. 762 is uncertain: Ἀχαίχαρος (?) παρὰ βοσπορηνοῖς.

34. J. Goody and J. Watt in J. Goody, ed., *Literacy in Traditional Societies* (1968) 42; see Chapter 3.

35. For the "Bileam" text from Deir ʿAlla see J. Hoftijzer and G. van der Kooij, *Aramaic Texts from Deir ʿAlla* (1976); J. A. Hackett, *The Balaam Text from Deir ʿAlla* (1984); *Der Königsweg* (1988)

no. 157 with bibliography; Burkert in D. Hellholm, ed., *Apocalypticism in the Mediterranean World and the Near East* (1983) 246; for Mopsos and Karatepe see Chapter 2, "Hepatoscopy," note 31.

THE PROBLEM OF LOAN-WORDS

1. See, e.g., Vermeule (1971) 185 f.: "If eastern influence had been comparatively recent, one might expect the seams to show, or names and terms to have been merely transliterated from another language."

2. See Introduction at note 15. A local substrate is readily assumed for characteristic Mediterranean flora such as "wine" (Greek *woinos,* Aramaic *wajn,* Hebrew *jain;* see J. P. Brown [1969] 147–151) and "rose" (Arabic *ward,* Aramaic *werad,* Greek *(w)rhodon;* J. P. Brown [1980] 11, 19 n.1).

3. *RhM* 49 (1894) 130, accepted by Hiller von Gärtringen, *RE* II 1887; see above, Chapter 1, "Oriental Products in Greece," note 15.

4. O. Hoffmann and A. Debrunner, *Geschichte der griechischen Sprache* I (1953³) 18: "ganz verschwindend gering"; A. Meillet, *Aperçu d'une histoire de la langue grecque* (1935⁴) 56 = (1965⁷) 59: "n'atteint sans dout pas la dizaine."

5. Masson (1967) has also a survey of older studies; see also Hemmerdinger (1970); Krause (1970)—without original contributions; J. P. Brown (1965), (1968), (1969); Salonen (1974); Szemerényi (1974); idem, *Gnomon* 53 (1981) 113–116; idem, *o-o-pe-ro-si: Festschr. E. Risch* (1986) 425–450.

6. Cf. L. Deroy, *L'emprunt linguistique* (1965); R. Schmitt, *Probleme der Eingliederung fremden Sprachguts in das grammatische System einer Sprache,* Innsbrucker Beiträge zur Sprachwissenschaft 11 (1973); Öttinger (1981). As an example for the manifold levels and problems of cultural borrowings see H. Kahane and R. Kahane, "Byzantium's Impact on the West: The Linguistic Evidence," *Illinois Classical Studies* 6 (1981) 389–415.

7. E.g., E. Boisacq, *Dictionnaire étymologique de la langue grecque* (1916) VII: "l'influence sémitique . . . bornée à l'adoption . . . de quelques termes commerciaux"; A. Meillet, *Aperçu* (see note 4 above) 55; Masson (1967) 114; she treats *kanna,* reed, p. 47 f. but forgets *kanon,* measuring rod.

8. This is following Masson (1967), although the words treated in nn. 9–11, 16, 19, 21–26, 31–33, and 36 are missing in her collection.

9. Akkadian *lipû,* accusative *lipâ,* fat, employed especially in magic; see *AHw* 555. It is true there are Indo-European comparative materials for Greek *lipa;* Chantraine (1968/80) 642.

10. Through Latin *simila* it even reached German, *Semmel;* see Szemerényi (1974) 156; Chantraine (1968/80) 996.

11. Salonen (1974) 143.

12. Cf. J. Tischler, *Glotta* 56 (1978) 60 f.; Chantraine (1968/80) 1026; for Mycenaean *pa-ra-ku* see E. Risch, *Cahiers Ferdinand de Saussure* 41 (1987) 167.

13. The Semitic word, however, is not documented but has been inferred; G. Garbini, *Riv. di Studi Fenici* 3 (1975) 15 f.

14. Chantraine (1968/80) 594; already attested in Mycenaean.

15. Ibid. 212.

16. Ibid. 660.

17. Masson (1967) 32–34; Niemeyer (1984) 69. The standard weight was the mina of Carchemish; Oppenheim (1967/69) 239 n. 8. The word *mana* is also attested in Hieroglyphic Luwian; G. Neumann, *ZVS* 98 (1985) 306; see also H. Büsing, "Metrologische Beiträge," *JdI* 97 (1982) 1–45. On *talanton* see Chantraine (1968/80) 1089.

18. *Sendschirli* V 119 ff. with pl. 58; specialists are still discussing to what extent this should be considered as a precursor or an early form of minted money; see M. S. Balmuth, *AJA* 67 (1963) 208 and in D. G. Mitten et al., eds., *Studies Presented to G. M. A. Hanfmann* (1971) 1–7; N. F. Parise, *Dialoghi di Archeologia* 7 (1973) 382–391.

19. The Semitic parallel is mentioned in *LSJ,* not in Masson (1967); "hypothèse . . . en tout cas aberrante": Chantraine (1968/80) 1247. Semitic *ḥeṭ* is H in the Greek alphabet, but Akkadian *ḥuraṣu* corresponds to Greek χρυσός; the name Ham is Χαμ in the Septuagint; Mount Hazzi is rendered Κάσιον ὄρος (cf. Hemberg [1950] 129, 320)—there are no phonetic rules in loan-words. *Haraṣu* is used in the sense of "writing," *Gilgamesh* I 1.8.

20. *AHw* 48a; on distributive *ana* in Greek see T. Horovitz, *Vom Logos zur Analogie* (1978) 137–144.

21. *AHw* 898; cf. 650. H. Kronasser, *Kratylos* 7 (1962) 163, maintains that *qanû* was borrowed indirectly, "höchstwahrschein-lich durch mehrere anatolische Sprachen."

22. Akkadian *ṭidu:* see *AHw* 1391.1: "zum Bauen und Ver-putzen"; Hebrew *ṭiṭ;* the Semitic parallels are not mentioned in the etymological lexicons of Boisacq, Frisk, and Chantraine, nor in Masson (1967). On a possible association with "Titans" see Chap-ter 3, "From *Atrahasis* to the 'Deception of Zeus,'" notes 28–29.

23. Akkadian *gaṣṣu: AHw* 282; Salonen (1974) 139.

24. *AHw* 522; J. P. Brown (1968) 182; Szemerényi (1974) 149. The mirage of an "Aegean" suffix *-inthos* created by the adaptation to Greek is no argument against this derivation; see note 11 above on *lekane*.

25. *AHw* 332; Hemmerdinger (1970) 45; the axe (*haṣṣinnu*) is now attested as the symbol of the weather god carried in procession at Bronze Age Emar: Arnaud (1985/87) no. 369 line 45. Salonen (1974) also compares Greek *sphen*, wedge, with Akkadian *suppinu;* but according to *AHw* 1060 the meaning of this word is unclear.

26. *AHw* 627: tent, also in Aramaic; Szemerényi, *Gnomon* 53 (1981) 114; cf. Hebrew *miškan*, abode.

27. See Chapter 2, "Craftsmen of the Sacred," notes 28–30, 36; cf. above, "Oriental Products in Greece," note 62.

28. Szemerényi, *Gnomon* 43 (1971) 647 and (1974) 156, referred to Akkadian *bel qati*, "Lord of Hand," which, however, means "guarantor"; *AHw* 120; but in Hittite the same expression (always with Sumerian-Akkadian spelling, *EN qati*) means "craftsman"; J. Friedrich, *Hethitisches Wörterbuch* (1952) 271. The Hittite word may well have been the model for *cheironax*, either directly or indirectly.

29. Laroche (1973); for *Soloi* as place-name see above, "Ori-ental Products in Greece," note 13.

30. Masson (1967) 86; *lis* occurs a few times in Homer; the normal Greek word, *leon*, seems to come from Egypt; see J. C. Billigmeier, *Talanta* 6 (1975) 1–6.

31. Aramaic *tawr(u)*, Hebrew *šor; HAL* 1346–48; J. P. Brown (1969) 159–164. In spite of this close similarity Chantraine (1968/80) states: "Il n'y a pas lieu . . . d'évoquer les formes sémitiques."

32. Hebrew *ḫäräb;* J. P. Brown (1968) 178–182; the *harpe* is specially used by orientalizing Perseus; see Jameson (1990) 218. But

there is a satisfactory Indo-European etymology too: Chantraine (1968/80) 114.

33. For σκῦλον see Szemerényi, *Gnomon* 53 (1981) 115; for συλᾶν Akkadian *šalalu*, to loot, *AHw* 1142, with imperative *šulla!* (cf. Zeus Syllanios and Athana Syllania in the Spartan Rhetra, Plut. *Lyc.* 6?).

34. There is no Indo-European etymology for *machomai*, and "la structure de μαχέσσασθαι reste obscure"; Chantraine (1968/80) 674. For *mahaṣ/maha* see *HAL* 541; 537.

35. See *AHw* 34 s.v. *alalu*, "a cry used at work." Of course exclamations can originate spontaneously (Chantraine [1968/80] 530), but "Hurrah!" has both its (Germanic) etymology and its diffusion in European warfare.

36. See above, "Oriental Products in Greece," note 67.

37. Astour (1965) went furthest in this sport. There remains the old equation of Iapetos, father of Prometheus, with Japhet, son of Noah (see West [1966] 202 f.); but also Nereus, god of waters, father of the Nereids, is remarkably similar to the Semitic word for river, Akkadian *nâru*, Hebrew *nahar*. See for Asgelatas Chapter 2, "Asclepius and Asgelatas," note 8; for Tethys, Chapter 3, "From *Atrahasis* to the 'Deception of Zeus,'" note 15; for Lamia, Chapter 2, "Lamashtu, Lamia, and Gorgo," note 10; for Titans, Chapter 3, "From *Atrahasis* to the 'Deception of Zeus,'" notes 28–29.

38. See for *haruspex* Chapter 2, "Hepatoscopy," note 24; for *kathairo, lyma, ara,* Chapter 2, "Purification," notes 46–48; for Embaros, Chapter 2, "Substitute Sacrifice," note 8.

39. *HAL* 878—not a Semitic word in origin; cf. J. P. Brown (1968) 166–169; Chantraine (1968/80), without presenting the Semitic words, declares: "L'hypothèse d'un emprunt sémitique . . . n'est acceptée par personne."

2. *"A Seer or a Healer"*
"CRAFTSMEN OF THE SACRED"

1. The expression is used in Plat. *Phdr.* 248d. For a modern investigation into the interrelation of magic and scientific medicine see G. E. R. Lloyd, *Magic, Reason and Experience* (1979); on "craftsmen of the sacred" see Burkert (1982a) and (1987a) 31.

2. Papyrus of Derveni in *ZPE* 47 (1982) col. XVI 3 f.: ὁ τέχνημ

ποιούμενος τὰ ἱερά. Strab. 10.3.23 p. 474: τὸ φιλότεχνον . . . τὸ περὶ τὰς Διονυσιακὰς τέχνας καὶ τὰς Ὀρφικάς. Hippocr. *Morb.Sacr.* 18, VI 396 Littré: βαναυσίη.

3. West (1971) 239-242 has stressed the importance of migrant *magi* for Iranian-Greek contacts in the sixth century B.C.

4. Numbers 22:5, 24. For the surprising evidence about Bileam/Baʿalam in the Deir ʿAlla inscription see Chapter 1, "Writing and Literature in the Eighth Century," note 35.

5. Helck (1979) 226 f.; E. Edel, *Ägyptische Ärzte und ägyptische Medizin am hethitischen Königshof* (1976); see Knudtzon (1915) no. 49.22 for Ugarit, no. 35.26 for Alasia.

6. Meissner (1920/25) II 198 (*KBo* I 10 Rs.42 ff.).

7. See Grottanelli (1982b) esp. 651, 655 f., 664 f.

8. Hdt. 9.33-36; on the Melampodidae see I. Löffler, *Die Melampodie* (1963); Kett (1966) 94-96.

9. Plat. *Rep.* 364b-e; cf. *Leg.* 909b.

10. *FGrHist* 475, esp. T 4b; Burkert (1972) 15 f.

11. Plut. *De sera* 560e-f and fr. 126; *Phigalia* is a conjecture (Mittelhaus) instead of the transmitted names *Italia* or *Thettalia*. See *RE* XIX 2084; Burkert, *RhM* 105 (1962) 48 f.

12. Plut. *Mus.* 42.1146b-c = Pratinas *TGrF* 4 F 9, Philodem. *Mus.* 4 = Diogenes of Babylon *SVF* II 232; Plut. *Mus.* 9 f., 1134b-e following Glaukos of Rhegion. The date is established by the connection with the founding of the festival Gymnopaidia in Sparta; Plut. *Mus.* 1134c; cf. Euseb. *Chron. a.Abr.* 1348 = Olympiad 27 = 672-668 B.C.

13. ἐπιδημοῦντα κατὰ τέχνην μαντικήν: Arist. *Polit.* 1274a25-28. On the practice and concept of *epidemia* see H. Diller, *Wanderarzt und Aitiologe* (1934).

14. Plat. *Symp.* 201d-e.

15. Empedocles B 115.13; cf. B 112, where he introduces himself arriving at Akragas as a seer and a healer.

16. See note 8, above.

17. Pind. *Ol.* 6; Hepding, *RE* IX 685-689 s.v. *Iamos;* Kett (1966) 84-89. Telmissos: Arr. *Anab.* 2.3.3 f.

18. See K. Clinton, *The Sacred Officials of the Eleusinian Mysteries* (1974); Burkert (1987a) 36 f.

19. Plut. *Is.* 28.362a; Tac. *Hist.* 4.83 f.; A. Alföldi, *Chiron* 9 (1979) 554 f.; Burkert (1987a) 37.

20. Isocr. 19.5 f., 45; Kett (1966) 49 f., 66 f.—who does not realize that the activities of Polemainetos as a seer must be dated about fifty years before the trial. On the legal issue underlying the speech see H. J. Wolff, Sitzungsber. Heidelberg 1979.5, 15–34.

21. Demosth. 19.249; 18.120; 259 f.; H. Wankel, *Demosthenes, Rede für Ktesiphon über den Kranz* (1976) 710–712, 1132–49; a family of seers: *SEG* 16 no. 193, with an epigram alluding to Amphiaraos (*Thebais* fr. 7 Davies = Pind. *Ol.* 6.13).

22. W. Schubart, *Amtliche Berichte aus den Kgl. Preussischen Kunstsammlungen* 38 (1916/17) 189 f.; see G. Zuntz, *Opuscula Selecta* (1972) 88–101; P. M. Fraser, *Ptolemaic Alexandria* II (1972) 345 f.; Burkert (1987a) 33. Cf. II Timothy 3:14 (and 2:1): "know from whom you have learnt . . ."

23. O. Kern, *Die Inschriften von Magnesia* (1900) no. 215 a; cf. A. Henrichs, *HSCP* 82 (1978) 123–137.

24. M. Berthelot, *Collection des anciens alchimistes grecs* (1888) II 30.7: ἐφορκίσας . . . μηδενὶ μεταδιδόναι εἰ μὴ μόνον τέκνωι καὶ φίλωι γνησίωι. *PGM* 4.475: μόνωι δὲ τέκνωι παραδοτά; cf. 1.193.

25. The real existence of "Asclepiads" in the classical period, which had been contested by E. J. and L. Edelstein, *Asclepius* II (1945) 52–63, was proved by an inscription from Delphi; see J. Bousquet, "Delphes et les Asclépiades," *BCH* 80 (1956) 579–593; *SEG* 16 no. 326; M. Gamberale, "Ricerche sul GENOS degli Asclepiadi," *RAL* 33 (1978) 83–95; S. M. Sherwin-White, *Ancient Cos* (1978) 257–263. Asclepiads are mentioned by Plato *Prot.* 311b, *Rep.* 408b, *Phdr.* 270c; the physician Eryximachos in *Symp.* 186e refers to Asclepius as "our ancestor"; "they were trained at their parents' from childhood": Galen *Anat.Admin.* 2.1, II 280 f. Kühn; Soran. *Vit.Hippocr.* 1 f.

26. L. Edelstein, *The Hippocratic Oath* (1943), reedited in L. Edelstein, *Ancient Medicine* (1967) 3–63, esp. 40–44; he was thinking of a special Pythagorean provision, because he failed to see the craftsmen's tradition.

27. *Lex* 5, IV 642 Littré.

28. Codex Hammurapi § 188; Borger (1979) 37; *ANET* 174 f.

29. *bn nsk;* see Chapter 1, "Oriental Products in Greece," note 10 and at note 62.

30. *Mudû, mâr ummani:* Schrank (1908) 16; cf. *mâr barê,* "son

of the seer," Zimmern (1901) no. 1.1 p. 97 f.; Zimmern p. 87 on the "guild" of seers. Cf. Amos 7:14: "I am not a prophet, nor the son of a prophet."

31. M. Weinfeld, *The Organizational Pattern and the Penal Code of the Qumran Sect* (1986) 61; cf. Ebeling (1931) 37, 47, 111.

32. Zimmern (1901) 118 f., no. 24.19–22.

33. Diod. 2.29.4—his source cannot be identified; probably not Poseidonios; cf. *FGrHist* II C p. 157.

34. See Thulin (1905/09) III 131–149; Pfiffig (1975) 36–41, 115–127. J. Heurgon, "Tarquitius Priscus et l'organisation de l'ordre des haruspices sous l'empereur Claude," *Latomus* 12 (1953) 402–417.

35. Tac. *Ann.* 11.15: *Primores Etruriae . . . retinuisse scientiam et in familias propagasse;* Cic. *Div.* 1.92: *ut de principum filiis X ex singulis Etruriae populis in disciplinam traderentur; ad Fam.* 6.6.3 (to A. Caecina): *Tuscae disciplinae, quam a patre . . . acceperas.*

36. Dion.Hal. *Ant.* 3.70; see below, "Hepatoscopy," note 9.

37. Diod. 1.73.5; J. Bidez and F. Cumont, *Les mages hellénisés* II (1938) 8 f., 119. Siberian shamanism too is transmitted from father to son; see M. Eliade, *Schamanismus und archaische Ekstasetechnik* (1957) 22, 24 f., 28 f., 30–32.

38. Noted as a case of linguistic borrowing by Szemerényi (1974) 157; Fehling (1980) 15 f.

39. Plat. *Rep.* 408b, *Leg.* 769b. For oriental examples see notes 28–30, above.

40. υἷες Ἀχαιῶν belongs to the Homeric formulas; oriental influence is by no means excluded even in this case (see Chapter 3, "From *Atrahasis* to the 'Deception of Zeus'"). Λυδῶν παῖδες: Hdt. 1.27.4. "Sons of Hatti" (= Hittites), "sons of Mittanni" (*marê Hatti, marê Mittanni*) in a treaty between Hittites and Hurrites: E. F. Weidner, *Politische Dokumente aus Kleinasien* (1923) 20.68, etc.

41. "Sons of men" equivalent to "men," Gospel of Thomas 28; see A. Guillaumont in *Studies in Gnosticism and Hellenistic Religions Presented to G. Quispel* (1981) 191.

HEPATOSCOPY

1. A Babylonian hepatoscopy text was first published by Lenormant in 1873; cf. Bezold in Blecher (1905) 247. For general references to the Babylonian provenience of Greek hepatoscopy see

Bouché-Leclercq (1879/82) I 170; Farnell (1911) 248 f. On the Mesopotamian-Etruscan relations see Boissier (1905); Blecher (1905), esp. n. 5; Thulin (1905/09) II; R. Pettazzoni, *Stud. Etr.* 1 (1927) 195–199; Nougayrol (1955b) and (1966); M. Pallottino, *Etruscologia* (1963⁵) 247 f.; Pfiffig (1975) 115–127. For Mesopotamia see H. Dillon, *Assyro-Babylonian Liver-Divination* (1932); A. Boissier, *Mantique babylonienne et mantique hittite* (1935); G. Contenau, *La divination chez les Assyriens et les Mésopotamiens* (1940); *La divination en Mésopotamie ancienne,* 14ᵉ Recontre Assyriologique International (1966); Nougayrol (1968); Jeyes (1980); Starr (1983); Meyer (1987).

2. See *HKL* III 96. A first foundation was laid by Boissier (1905); a rich selection in German translation is to be found in Jastrow (1905/12) II 213–415. See R. Labat, *Commentaires assyro-babyloniennes sur les présages* (1933); B. Meissner, Omina zur Erkenntnis der Eingeweide des Opfertiers," *AOF* 9 (1933) 118–122; J. Nougayrol, "Textes hépatoscopiques d'époque ancienne conservés au Musée du Louvre," *RA* 38 (1941) 67–88; A. Goetze, "Reports on Acts of Extispicy from Old Babylonian and Kassite Times," *JCS* 11 (1973) 89 ff.; Starr (1983).

3. Found in 1877; see W. Deecke, "Das Templum von Piacenza," *Etruskische Forschungen* 4 (1880); Blecher (1905) 201; Thulin (1905/09) II 20 f., 37–39, pls. I, II; idem, *Die Götter des Martianus Capella und die Bronzeleber von Piacenza* (1906); Pfiffig (1975) 121–127; L. B. van der Meer, *The Bronze Liver of Piacenza: Analysis of a Polytheistic Structure* (1987). Another liver model, made of clay, from Falerii: Nougayrol (1955b) 513, 515–517; Pfiffig (1975) 116 f. fig. 45.

4. BM Bu 89-4-26, 238, published by T. G. Pinches, *CT* 6 (1898) pls. 1–3; A. Boissier, *Note sur un monument babylonien se rapportant à l'extispicine* (1899); Thulin (1905/09) II pl. II; Meissner (1920/25) II fig. 40; Nougayrol, *RA* 38 (1941) 77–79. Another exemplar, BM Rm 620, in Thulin pl. III and Boissier (1905) 76–78; a third in Nougayrol (1966).

5. Blecher (1905) 199–203, 241–245.

6. Thulin (1905/09) II 30.

7. See now Meyer (1987). Hittites: *KUB* IV 71–75, XXXVII 68–72 nos. 216–230; A. Goetze, *Kulturgeschichte Kleinasiens* (1957²) pls. 11, 21. Mari: M. Rutten, *RA* 35 (1938) 36–70. Alalakh: L. Woolley, *Alalakh* (1955) 250–257 pl. 59. Tell el Hajj: R. A. Stucky,

AK 16 (1973) 84 pl. 15.2; Ugarit: *Ugaritica* VI (1969) 91–119; cf. 165–179; O. Loretz, *Leberschau Sündenbock Azazel in Ugarit und Israel* (1985). Hazor: B. Landsberger and H. Tadmor, *Israel Explor. J.* 14 (1964) 201–218. Meggido: H. T. Bossert, *Altsyrien* (1951) no. 1193. Cyprus: *BCH* 95 (1971) 384 with fig. 93a; *Kadmos* 11 (1972) 185 f. A text from Tarsos: Goetze (1939) 12–16.

8. Pfiffig (1975) 117. Meyer (1985), by contrast, suggests the Etruscans brought hepatoscopy with them when they immigrated from the East in the age of the Sea Peoples.

9. In the enumeration of Etruscan *saecula,* Varro in *Cens.* 17, the first four of these are given round numbers, 100 each, but then specific numbers are presented, according to celebrations actually held. This indicates that from about 600 B.C. Etruscans had detailed—written—documentation, in contrast to vague "reconstructions" about the earlier period; cf. Thulin (1905/09) III 66; see also above, "Craftsmen of the Sacred," note 36.

10. See Chapter 1, "Oriental Products in Greece," note 18.

11. *Il.* 1.69; cf. Bouché-Leclercq (1879/82) I 168 f.

12. *Il.* 24.221; *Od.* 21.145, 22.318–323.

13. Dion.Hal. *Ant.* 1.30; cf. Lydos *Mag. prooem.*

14. Van der Meer (1979); J. L. Durand and F. Lissarague, *Hephaistos* 1 (1979) 92–108; R. Bloch, *BCH* suppl. 14 (1986) 77–83; the so-called Diotima statue from Mantinea: *BCH* 12 (1888) 376–380; Blecher (1905) pl. 3.3; H. Möbius, *JdI* 49 (1934) 45–60.

15. Plat. *Phdr.* 244c: τελεώτερον καὶ ἐντιμότερον μαντικὴ οἰωνιστικῆς.

16. Tac. *Hist.* 2.3.1: *scientiam artemque haruspicum accitam et Cilicem Tamiram intulisse . . . ipsa, quam intulerant, scientia hospites cessere: tantum Cinyrades sacerdos consulitur.* Bouché-Leclercq (1879/82) I 170 combines this with the cult of Zeus Splanchnotomos, "cutting the entrails" (Hegesandros in Ath. 174 a) and the alleged invention of sacrifice on Cyprus (cf. Burkert [1975] 76 f.). Herodotus 2.58 asserts that sacrificial divination came from Egypt; there is nothing to substantiate this claim.

17. Hsch. s.v. *pylai* = Aristoph. fr. 554 Kassel-Austin; Cic. *Div.* 1.91; cf. above, "Oriental Products in Greece," note 65.

18. One example, from the British Museum (116624), is often illustrated, e.g., *Eléments* (1960) pl. IIa; Caquot and Leibovici

(1968) opposite p. 32; T. Jacobsen, *The Treasures of Darkness* (1976) 194; it is dated to 700–500 B.C. See S. Smith, "The Face of Humbaba," *Annals of Archaeology and Anthropology* 11 (1924) 107–114 and *JRAS* (1926) 440–442.

19. Rizza and Santa Maria Scrinari (1968) 206 pl. 32 no. 215; cf. below, "Foundation Deposits," note 10. For Ortheia see above, "Oriental Products in Greece," note 34.

20. The "place" (*mazzazu*), the "path" (*padanu*), the "strength" (*dananu*), the "gate of the palace" (*bab ekalli*), the *šulmu* (unclear), the "gall" (*martu*), the "left path of the gall" (*padan šumel marti*), the "finger" (*ubanu*), the "yoke" (*niru*), the "appendix" (processus papillaris) (*ṣibtu*); see Jeyes (1978).

21. See Thulin (1905/09) II 50–54; the most detailed Greek text is Rufus *Onom.* 158.5 f. ed. Daremberg-Ruelle (πύλαι, τράπεζα, μάχαιρα, ὄνυξ). "Gate": Eur. *El.* 828, Aristoph. fr. 554 Kassel-Austin, Plat. *Tim.* 71c, Arist. *Hist.an.* 496b32. "Head": see note 23, below; cf. Thulin 30–34. "Head of the liver" (*reš amutim*): *AHw* 46b. "Head of the finger" (*reš ubanim*): *AHw* 975a. "River": Hsch. s.v. *potamos.* "River of the liver" (*nar amutim*): *AHw* 46b, Thulin 54. "Path": Hsch. s.v. *akeleutha.* A "weapon" in the liver: *AHw* 46b; cf. μάχαιρα in Rufus. See also Nougayrol (1955) 512; Starr (1983) 77–91.

22. Thulin (1905/09) II 34 f., following Boissier (1905) 220–234; Starr (1983) 15–24.

23. Missing "head": Plut. *Kim.* 18.5, *Marc.* 29; Liv. 41.14 f. Two "heads": Sen. *Oed.* 353–365; Lucan *Bell.civ.* 1.618–629; too-direct lines are drawn by W. G. Schileico, "Ein Omentext Sargons von Akkad und sein Nachklang bei römischen Dichtern," *AOF* 5 (1928/29) 214–218.

24. A. Boissier, *Mémoires de la Société linguistique* 11 (1901) cxxxix, 330; Thulin (1905/09) II 3 n.1; A. Ernout and A. Meillet, *Dictionnaire étymologique de la langue latine* (1959⁴) 290, with question mark.

25. *AHw* 46.

26. M. Pallottino, *Etruscologia* (1963⁵) 247 f.

27. *AHw* 1350 f.; cf. Zimmern (1901) 88 f.

28. Cic. *Div.* 2.28: *nec esse unam omnium scientiam;* cf. Blecher (1905) 202.

29. The main texts are collected in Prinz (1979) 382–384, who thinks all of it is pure invention; see also I. Löffler, *Die Melampodie* (1963) 47–51.

30. The so-called Maduwattas text, A. Goetze, *Maduwattas*, Mitteilungen der Vorderasiatisch-ägyptischen Gesellschaft 32 (1928) 37; on the date of this text, see H. Otten, *Sprachliche Stellung und Datierung des Maduwatta-Textes* (1969); J. D. Muhly, *Historia* 23 (1974) 139–145; R. D. Barnett, *CAH* II 2³ (1975) 363–366.

31. *KAI* no. 26, I 16, II 11, III 12; see F. Bron, *Recherches sur les inscriptions de Karatepe* (1979) 172–176; Barnett, *CAH* II 2³ (1975) 363–366; A. Strobel, *Der spätbronzezeitliche Seevölkersturm* (1976) 31–38.

32. Xanthos the Lydian, *FGrHist* 765 F 17. A name *mo-qo-so* also appears in Linear B, KN De 1381 B; PY Sa 774.

33. For Mallos see *RE* XIV 916 f.; fourth-century coins have a winged figure reminiscent of the winged sun disk of Syrian-Persian iconography; one type of these coins has a bilingual, Aramaic-Greek inscription; see C. M. Kraay, *Archaic and Classical Greek Coins* (1978) 285.

34. "If a woman gives birth to a lion" occurs in an Akkadian text, as in Hdt. 1.84; cf. Cic. *Div.* 1.53; see G. Bunnens, *Hommages Renard* II (1968) 130–132.

35. For birds, see Hunger (1909) 23–25; Jastrow (1905/12) II 798–812; E. Reiner, *JNES* 19 (1960) 28. For lecanomancy, see Zimmern (1901) 85, 89; J. Hunger, *Becherwahrsagung bei den Babyloniern nach zwei Keilschrifttexten aus der Hammurabi-Zeit* (1903); Jastrow (1905/12) II 749–775; see also Ganszyniec, *RE* XII 1879–88 s.v. *Lekanomanteia*.

36. Aesh. *Ag.* 322; Farnell (1911) 301; cf. J. Nougayrol, "Aleuromancie babylonienne," *Orientalia*, n.s. 31 (1963) 381–386.

FOUNDATION DEPOSITS

1. See E. D. van Buren, *Foundation Figurines and Offerings* (1931); Ellis (1968); *RlA* III (1971) 655–661 s.v. *Gründungsbeigaben*. Magical figurines deposited in clay capsules are to be distinguished from these; see Rittig (1977); see also J. M. Weinstein, *Foundation Deposits in Ancient Egypt* (1973).

2. *ANET* 356 f.

3. East room of the sanctuary at Archanes, pebbles: I. Sakel-

larakis, *Praktika* 1979, 381. Miniature vessels, animal bones, one seal under a rock placed in the room at Knossos where evidence for cannibalistic feasts seems to come from: P. Warren in R. Hägg and N. Marinatos, eds., *Sanctuaries and Cults in the Aegean Bronze Age* (1981) 166. Three pairs of *kylikes* under a cult room at Tiryns: K. Kilian, ibid. 53.

4. V. Karageorghis, *BCH* 99 (1975) 831–835.

5. Boardman (1967) 57–67 and (1980) 57; cf. Chapter 1, "Oriental Products in Greece," note 38. See now in general for this and the following finds Wells (1988), who draws attention especially to foundation deposits of clay vessels under fortification walls of Asine, 720–700 B.C.

6. H. Gallet de Santerre and J. Tréheux, *BCH* 71/72 (1947/48) 148–254; H. Gallet de Santerre, *Délos primitive et archaïque* (1958) 129; V. R. d'A. Desborough, *The Last Mycenaeans and Their Successors* (1964) 45 f., thinks that the Mycenaean objects had been accidentally discovered and reinterred during the building process. One may compare the fact that the Assyrians intentionally sought for the "ancient *temennu*" when rebuilding temples: Ellis (1968) 147–150.

7. A. Bammer, "Neue Grabungen an der Zentralbasis des Artemision von Ephesos," *JOEAI* 58 (1988) *Beiblatt* 1–32. For the older discussion, see P. Jacobsthal, *JHS* 71 (1951) 85–95; L. Weidauer, *Probleme der frühen Elektronprägung* (1975) 72–80; Boardman (1980) 101; A. Heubeck, *Kadmos* 22 (1983) 62; D. Kagan, *AJA* 86 (1982) 343–360. For Priene, Perachora, Isthmia, see Sinn (1985) 136 f. n.23 with further bibliography.

8. Rizza and Santa Maria Scrinari (1968) 24 f.

9. Cf. the inscription from Kallipolis commanding the erection of a statue of Apollo in order to get rid of a plague; K. Buresch, *Klaros* (1889) 81–86; J. Krauss, *Die Inschriften von Sestos* (1980) no. 11. On boundary stones, see *Die Schriften der römischen Feldmesser,* ed. K. Lachmann I (1848) 141.

10. Sinn (1985).

11. Ellis (1968) 42 f.

12. See ibid. 138–140, 167 f. with the vague formulation: "to enhance the value of the building and the validity of the ceremonies connected with its construction" (140).

13. Ibid. 16, 31, 34; the formula *ina šipir ašiputi* in D. D. Luck-

enbill, *The Annals of Sennacherib* (1924) 137.31 (= Luckenbill [1926/27] II § 437) and in S. Langdon, *Die neubabylonischen Königsinschriften* (1912) 62, 40-43 (Nabopolassar).

PURIFICATION

1. Prokl. *Chrestom.* p. 106 f. Allen = p. 47 Davies; Schol. T *Il.* 11.690a (III 261 Erbse): παρ' Ὁμήρωι οὐκ οἴδαμεν φονέα καθαιρόμενον; but cf. *Il.* 24.480 with schol.

2. Nilsson (1967) I 91 f., 632-637; idem, *Greek Piety* (1948) 41-47; Dodds (1951) 28-63; L. Moulinier, *Le pur et l'impur dans la pensée et la sensibilité des grecs* (1952); but Parker (1983) 15 f., 66-70, 115 f., 130-143 warns against simplistic ideas of "development."

3. K. Meuli, "Skythica," *Hermes* 70 (1935) 121-176 = *Gesammelte Schriften* II (1975) 817-879; cf. Dodds (1951) 135-178.

4. Farnell (1911) 289; Farnell's book seems to be the only unprejudiced and careful discussion of the problem to date, even though he seems not to have studied the eastern languages. Cf. above, "Hepatoscopy," note 36.

5. Survey in *HKL* III 85-93; see also Meissner (1920/25) II 198-241; E. Reiner, *La magie babylonienne* (1966); G. R. Castellino, "La letteratura magica," in *Storia delle letterature d'oriente,* ed. O. Botto, I (1969) 227-238. Earlier editions include Zimmern (1901), Fossey (1902), Thompson (1903/04), Thureau-Dangin (1921), Ebeling (1931); there are good editions of *Maqlû* (G. Meier 1937) and *Shurpu* (E. Reiner 1958).

6. Goetze (1939) 11 ff. (an amulet?).

7. See Zimmern (1901) 82-93; Meissner (1920/25) II 64-66.

8. Heraclitus B 5; φόνωι φόνον as a formula in Soph. *O.T.* 100; Eur. *Herc.* 40, *I.T.* 1213, *Or.* 510, 816.

9. Aesch. *Eum.* 441, frs. 89-93 Radt; written ΗΙΞΙΩΝ on a vase painting, i.e., associated with ἱκέτης, suppliant; E. Simon, *Würzburger Jahrb.* I (1975) 177-185. Hdt. 1.35.2 says that the Lydians had the same method of purification as the Greeks. Myth has even Apollo undergo purification after killing, be it with Karmanor in Crete (Paus. 2.30.3, 10.7.2; Schol. Pind. *Pyth.* hypothesis c), at Tempe (*Hymn of Aristonoos at Delphi* I 17, p. 163 Powell; Ael. *V.H.* 3.1), or through exile with Admetus (Eur. *Alk.* 5-7).

10. Aesch. *Eum.* 281: μίασμα ἔκπλυτον; 283: καθαρμοῖς ἡλάθη χοιροκτόνοις; cf. 448-452. The most detailed description

of purification from murder in later literature is in Apollonius Rhodius 4.662–717; see Parker (1983) 370–374. There is now an extensive "sacred law" from Selinus, fifth century B.C., in the J. Paul Getty Museum, part of which contains detailed prescriptions for purification; it will be published by M. Jameson, D. Jordan, and Roy Kotansky.

11. *Il.* 1.314: "They threw the *lymata* into the sea."

12. Louvre K 710: A. D. Trendall and A. Cambitoglou, *The Red-Figured Vases of Apulia* I (1978) no. 4/229; G. Schneider-Hermann, *AK* 13 (1970) 59 pl. 30.1; A. Kossatz-Deissmann, *Dramen des Aischylos auf westgriechischen Vasen* (1978) 107–111; cf. R. R. Dyer, "The Evidence for Apollo Purification Rituals at Delphi and Athens," *JHS* 89 (1969) 38–56, with additional illustrations from vases.

13. Farnell (1911) 129 f. For Mesopotamian blood rituals see L. Cagni in F. Vattioni ed., *Sangue e antropologia biblica* (1981) 74–76; R. Gellio, ibid. 438–445. There are important blood rituals in Hittite and Hurrite ritual texts, too.

14. E. Langlotz and M. Hirmer, *Die Kunst der Westgriechen* (1963) 24; A. D. Trendall, *The Red-Figured Vases of Lucania, Campania and Sicily* (1967) 602 no. 103; G. Schneider-Herrmann, *AK* 13 (1970) 59 f. pl. 30.2; a similar representation is found on a cameo from the Collection Fouad, *RML* II 2574. For the myth of the Proetids see Burkert (1983a) 168–173.

15. Cf. Soph. *Tr.* 1235: "he might be sick on account of avenging demons," ἐξ ἀλαστόρων νοσοῖ.

16. Thompson (1903/04) II 16–21 (with slight adjustments of the translation); Meissner (1920/25) II 222.

17. See the comic description of the purification of the Proetids in Diphilos fr. 125 Kassel-Austin, Melampus operating "with one torch, one squill . . . with sulphur, asphalt, and loud-roaring sea."

18. Ov. *Fast.* 6.158–162. There is an equally close parallel in a Hittite incantation text; see H. Kronasser, *Die Sprache* 7 (1961) 140–167; V. Haas, *Orientalia* 40 (1971) 410–430; H. S. Versnel, *ZPE* 58 (1985) 267.

19. *Od.* 5.396: στυγερὸς δέ οἱ ἔχραε δαίμων. For the doglike Erinyes see Aesch. *Cho.* 1054, *Eum.* 264–267; see also below, "Substitute Sacrifice," note 2.

20. *arrat šaggašte* in *Shurpu* 5.48 f. Closer to the Greek is the

Old Testament: the spilled blood "cries" from the earth, Gen. 4:10, just as in Aesch. *Cho.* 400–404.

21. See above, "Craftsmen of the Sacred," note 10; cf. Parker (1983) 125 f.

22. For the figurines, see Rittig (1977) 188–194. Expulsion of "ravenous hunger" (*bulimos*) at Chaironeia: Plut. *Q.Conv.* 693 f.: ἔξω βούλιμον· ἔσω δὲ πλοῦτον καὶ ὑγίειαν.

23. Unclean hands, etc.: Thompson (1903/04) II 138–141; cf. Leviticus 5:2 f.; "Lord of guilt" (*bel arni*): *Shurpu* III 134–137; ἀβλαβὴς συνουσία: Aesch. *Eum.* 285. "No speaking": ibid. 448 and in the aetiology of the Anthesteria ritual, Burkert (1983a) 221 f.

24. *Ludlul bel nemeqi* III 23–28. Lambert (1960) 48 f.; cf. *ANET* 436, Castellino (1977) 487. Branchos: Apollodorus of Kerkyra in Clem. *Strom.* 5.48.4; Callim. fr. 194.26–31.

25. For the identification of this figure—often but wrongly called Oannes after Berossos, *FGrHist* 680 F 1 § 4—see Kolbe (1981) 14–30; cf. *AHw* 58 s.v. *apkallu(m);* represented, e.g., beside the bed of the sick on the Lamashtu tablet (see below, "Lamashtu, Lamia, and Gorgo," note 15); representation from Terqa, northern Syria: Genge (1979) 44 referring to *Annales archéologiques de Syrie* 2 (1952) 179 pl. 2.

26. Demosth. 18.259; Harpokr. s.v. ἀπομάττων; Soph. fr. 34 Radt: στρατοῦ καθαρτὴς κἀπομαγμάτων ἴδρις. A real case of "purifying" an army: Xenoph. *Anab.* 5.7.35; cf. W. K. Pritchett, *The Greek State at War* III (1979) 200 f.

27. *AHw* 442 f.; Zimmern (1901) 92; Schrank (1908) 81–88.

28. *AHw* 509; Sophron fr. 5 Kaibel; for Melampus see note 17, above.

29. *Shurpu* 1.13, 18, rev. 9', 5.60–72; Kratinos fr. 250 Kassel-Austin; Diphilos fr. 125.3 (see note 17, above); Theophr. *Char.* 16.14; σκίλλη Ἐπιμενίδειος: Theophr. *H.Plant.* 7.2.1.

30. *Shurpu* 8.89 f.; *Maqlû* 7.81.

31. Ebeling (1931) 80–82 no. 21.1–38; 138 no. 30 C 9.

32. Hsch.: φαρμάκη· ἡ χύτρα ἣν ἑτοίμαζον τοῖς καθαίρουσιν τὰς πόλεις. In the Latin comedy *Querolus* (p. 38.10–15 Ranstrand) the would-be magician asks for a little coffer, *arcula inanis . . . in qua lustrum illud exportetur foras*. In the Hittite Telepinu text, "Telepinus' rage, anger, malice [and] fury" are enclosed in subterranean bronze caldrons; *ANET* 128.

33. Ebeling (1931) 138 no. 30 C 11; 82 no. 21.38; *Shurpu* 7.64 ff.; cf. Ebeling (1918/19) I 33 = Castellino (1977) 633.

34. Hippocr. VI 362 Littré.

35. Thompson (1903/04) II 138 f. Petronius 134.1: *quod purgamentum in nocte calcasti in trivio aut cadaver;* Liv. 8.10.12: *ubi illud signum defossum erit, eo magistratum Romanum escendere fas non esse.*

36. Arist. fr. 496 Rose = Paus. *Att.* φ 5 Erbse; Leviticus 14:4–7; 49–53.

37. Diog.Laert. 1.114 = Epimenides, *FGrHist* 457 T 1.

38. Ebeling (1931) 150 no. 30 F 35 f.

39. *Historia Alexandri Magni* 2.31.3 Kroll; *Testamentum Alexandri,* R. Merkelbach, *Die Quellen des griechischen Alexanderromans* (1977²) 254; cf. Paus. 8.18.6: The water of Styx can be kept only in a horse's hoof.

40. Diog.Laert. 8.3. Epimenides mentioned the Idaean cave in the context of the myth of Zeus, *FGrHist* 457 F 18. The name of Epimenides' mother, Balte, has been associated with Semitic *Baʿalat;* Grottanelli (1982b) 659; T. Poliakov, *RhM* 130 (1987) 411 f.

41. See Chapter 1, "Oriental Products in Greece," note 13.

42. See above, "Craftsmen of the Sacred," note 12.

43. See note 9, above.

44. Apollo and *numenia:* Hdt. 6.57.2; Philochoros, *FGrHist* 328 F 88, *numeniastai* of Apollo Delphinios: F. Graf, *MH* 31 (1974) 214; cf. *RE* XVII 1293. For the celebration of the new moon in Israel see, e.g., I Samuel 20:3, II Kings 4:23, Ezra 3:1. Apollo and "Seven": ἑβδομαγέτας, Aesch. *Sept.* 800 f.; cf. Hdt. 6.57.2; Ἑβδόμειος: *IG* II/III² 4974; Ἑβδομαίων: *Inschriften von Erythrai* (1972/73) 207.87; a festival Ἑβδομαῖα of the *Molpoi* of Miletos, *LSAM* 50.6; 21, etc. See also Burkert (1975).

45. See notes 9 and 25, above. Rhakios is the husband of Manto, mother of Mopsos. Akkadian *raḫu* is a sort of magician; *AHw* 944a.

46. S. Levin, *SMEA* 13 (1971) 31–50 commenting on *nektar;* Burkert (1975) 77; cf. *AHw* 907 (*qataru*), 930 f. (*qutrenum,* sacrifice of incense); *HAL* 1022–24; on II Kings 23:5, e.g., the form is *jeqatter(u),* "they burnt incense," which, transcribed, would produce something like ἐκάθηραν. For the mirage of a Greek-sounding suffix in καθαρός (G. Neumann, *ZVS* 98 [1985] 305 f.); cf. λεκάνη,

Chapter 1, "The Problem of Loan-Words," note 11. It is even more tempting to assume that the name of Aphrodite the goddess of incense, Κυθέρεια, is from the same Semitic root; cf., e.g., Hebrew *mequtteret*, "filled with fragrance" (in spite of Greek popular etymology connecting the name with the island Κύθηρα; the change η–ε is linguistically impossible; cf. G. Morgan, "Aphrodite Cytherea," *TAPA* 108 [1978] 115–120 for another etymology). "He cleaned/fumigated with sulphur," ἐκάθηρε θεείωι: *Il.* 16.228; cf. *Od.* 22.481 f.

47. *AHw* 565; the root is used as adjective and verb, the noun is *lutu;* for its use in purification ceremonies, see, e.g., *Maqlû* 1.102; 1.105; 3.113. On the problems of word formation as to λῦμα/λύθρον see Chantraine (1968/80) 650 f.; for a detailed investigation into the meaning of these words see E. Tagliaferro in *Sangue e Antropologia Biblica* I (1980) 182 n.36, 186–189. For *lustrum* see note 32, above.

48. On *araru* see *AHw* 65, *HAL* 88; used as a loan-word in Hurrite; E. Laroche, *RHA* 28 (1970) 61. Bileam: Numbers 22:6; cf. above, "Craftsmen of the Sacred," note 4; on ἀρά see Chantraine (1968/80) 100 f.

SPIRITS OF THE DEAD AND BLACK MAGIC

1. Cf. above, "Purification," note 19.

2. *AHw* 263 f.

3. See Rohde (1898), esp. I 259–277, "Elemente des Seelencultes in der Blutrache und Mordsühne."

4. See below, Chapter 3, "From *Atrahasis* to the 'Deception of Zeus,'" note 1.

5. Ebeling (1931) 68 f. no. 15.23–25 (burial in the context of a ritual of substitution; cf. Chapter 2, "Substitute Sacrifice").

6. Aesch. *Pers.* 611–618; cf. Eur. *I.T.* 159–166: water, milk, wine, honey.

7. Spirits lacking the "pourings of water" (*naq mê*) become unruly; Thompson (1903/04) I 40. Ashurbanipal reinstated food offerings and "pourings of water" for the earlier kings; Streck (1916) II 250 f.; cf. Ebeling (1931) 131 no. 30 A 38; Farber (1977) 150 f., text A II a 158. On offerings of water in the Greek cult of the dead see Burkert (1985) 73, 194.

8. Noticed by T. Wiegand, *Sechster vorläufiger Bericht über die in*

Milet und Didyma vorgenommenen Ausgrabungen, Abh. Berlin (1908) 27; hence Nilsson (1967) 177 n.1; *RE* Suppl. VIII 136.

9. *CAD* II (A) 324 s.v. *arutu* (this word is interpreted differently by Ebeling [1931] 132 and *AHw* 72b).

10. Aristoph. fr. 322 Kassel-Austin; see T. Gelzer, *ZPE* 4 (1967) 123–133.

11. Esp. in Ebeling (1931) no. 30 A–F; no. 31.

12. Ibid. 84 no. 21.1; 138 no. 30 C 1; 142 no. 30 D 1.

13. Ibid. 141 no. 30 C verso 10 f. = *SAHG* 341.

14. Ebeling (1931) 84 no. 21 verso 23; cf. Castellino (1977) 647.

15. Thompson (1903/04) I 38 f., from the series *utukki lemnuti; Gilgamesh* XII 151 f.; cf. Ebeling (1931) 145 no. 30 C 22–29.

16. Ebeling (1931) 145 no. 30 E 22.

17. *Il.* 22.358, *Od.* 11.73.

18. Plat. *Phdr.* 244d, *Leg.* 854b; cf. *Trag.Adesp.* F 637.16 Snell; Eur. *Phoen.* 934: in both these passages there is a *mantis* to deal with the *menima.* Cf. I. M. Linforth, "Telestic Madness in Plato," *UCPCP* 13 (1946) 163–172; Burkert (1987a) 19, 24.

19. Arist. *Rhet.* 1418a24–26 = Epimenides, *FGrHist* 457 F 1.

20. J. Trumpf, "Fluchtafel und Rachepuppe," *MDAI* (Athens) 73 (1958) 94–102; cf. Burkert (1985) 75; Faraone (1991) and *ClAnt* 10 (1991) 164–203; Faraone and Obbink (1991) index s.v. *voodoo dolls. Maqlû* 4.27–47; cf. 1.1; Ebeling (1918/19) II 38.26 = Castellino (1977) 675.27; Farber (1977) 211–213, text A III 10; Ebeling (1931) 133 no. 30 A *subscriptio.*

21. *Maqlû* 1.131 ff. = Castellino (1977) 618, Biggs (1967) 28.

22. Theocr. 2.53.

23. Biggs (1967), esp. 28.22–24: figurines made of wax, fat, bitumen, gypsum; cf. Ebeling (1925).

24. Theocr. 2.162.

25. Plat. *Leg.* 933b.

26. Ebeling (1931) 71 no. 17.2.

27. The second tale in A. Erman, "Papyrus Westcar," in *Die Literatur der Ägypter* (1923) 66; E. Brunner-Traut, *Alt-Ägyptische Märchen* (1965²) 12 f. Cf. the magical destruction of Apopi in G. Roeder, *Der Ausklang der ägyptischen Religion mit Reformation, Zauberei und Jenseitsglauben* (1961) 150 f.; P. Derchain, *Le papyrus Salt 825* (1965) 161 f.; E. Hornung, *Altägyptische Höllenvorstellungen,*

Abh. Leipzig 59.3 (1968) 27; M. J. Raven, "Wax in Egyptian Magic and Symbolism," *OMRO* 54 (1983) 7–47. Figurines of wax and fat in Hittite magic: Gurney (1954) 162.

28. Text of Sfire: *ANET* 660, *KAI* 222, Fitzmyer (1967) 14 f., 16 f. (I 35, 42); Lemaire and Durand (1984). Esarhaddon: D. J. Wiseman, *Iraq* 20 (1958) 75 f.; *ANET* 540.608–610; S. Parpola and K. Watanabe, *State Archives of Assyria II: Neo-Assyrian Treaties and Loyalty Oaths* (1988). Hittite: J. Friedrich, "Der hethitische Soldateneid," *ZA* 35 (1924) 161–192; *ANET* 353; N. Oettinger, *Die militärischen Eide der Hethiter* (1976) 6–17; see D. J. McCarthy, *Treaty and Covenant* (1963, 1978²); M. Weinfeld, *JAOS* 93 (1973) 190–199. Burning of effigies is common in *Maqlû*.

29. S. Ferri, *Abh. Berlin* 5 (1925) 19–24; *SEG* 9 no. 3; R. Meiggs and D. Lewis, *A Selection of Greek Historical Inscriptions* (1969) no. 5.44; κηρίνος πλάσσαντες κολοσὸς κατέκαιον. On this text see A. D. Nock, *ARW* 24 (1926) 172 f.; A. J. Graham, *JHS* 80 (1960) 95–111; Murray (1980) 113–119. According to S. Dusanic, *Chiron* 8 (1978) 55–76, it is a forgery (or "reconstruction") from the fourth century B.C.

30. *PGM* 2.34; 4.339, 1419, 2485, 2750, 2912; 5.340, 425; 7.317, 985; 13.923; 70; etc.; it occurs also in defixions and on magical gems; see Drexler, *RML* II 1584–87.

31. S. Ferri, *Notiziario Archeologico* 4 (1927) 91–145; *SEG* 9 no. 72; U. von Wilamowitz-Moellendorff, "Heilige Gesetze. Eine Urkunde aus Kyrene," *Sitzungsberichte Berlin* (1927) 155–176; G. I. Luzzato, *La Lex Cathartica di Cirene* (1936); H. Jeanmaire, *REG* 58 (1945) 66–89; J. Servais, *BCH* 84 (1960) 112–147; *LSS* 115; Parker (1983) 332–351. It must now be compared with the unpublished *lex sacra* about purification from Selinus; see above, "Purification," note 10.

32. J. Gould, "Hiketeia," *JHS* 93 (1973) 74–103.

33. *LSS* 115 B 35–39: κολοσὸς ποιήσαντα ἔρσενα καὶ θήλεια[ν] ἢ καλίνος ἢ γαίνος ὑποδεξάμενον παρτιθ[έ]μεν τὸ μέρος πάντων· ἐπεὶ δέ κα ποιῆσες τὰ νομιζόμενα, φέροντα ἐς ὕλαν ἀεργὸν ἐρε[ῖ]σαι τὰς κολοσὸς καὶ τὰ μέρη. For conjuring a spirit "either male or female" cf. *Maqlû* 1.73–86 = Castellino (1977) *Maqlû* II 38–49 = Castellino 620; *Maqlû* II 108–110 = Castellino 622 f.; *Maqlû* II 131 = Castellino 623; cf. 632.28–30.

34. Ebeling (1931) 80–82 no. 21 recto lines 1–39, cf. ibid. 82

f., 84 f. verso lines 23–32. For the pot see above, "Purification," notes 31–32.

35. Plat. *Rep.* 364c: ἐπαγωγαῖς τισι καὶ καταδέσμοις; Eur. *Hipp.* 318: ἐξ ἐπακτοῦ πημονῆς; cf. Theophr. *Char.* 16.7; Hippocr. *Morb.Sacr.* 1, VI 358 Littré; *Vict.* 4.89, VI 652 Littré; Parker (1983) 348.

36. This interpretation was first advanced by H. J. Stukey, *CP* 32 (1937) 32–43, followed by Parker (1983) 348 f.

37. This was Stukey's opinion too, but Parker (1983) 348 thinks the second and third sections deal with a *hikesios* who is "palpably human."

38. "To do rites on," according to K. Dowden, *RHR* 197 (1980) 415 f.

39. Thus *LSJ* s.v. *prophero* and *telisko;* cf. Sokolowski on *LSS* 115.40–49.

40. Hdt. 5.66.1. The new *lex sacra* from Selinus (note 31, above) speaks about establishing a cult to an *elasteros* (opposite to *hikesios?*).

41. *LSJ* Suppl. has "dub. sense" for *autophonos,* but "to supplicate" for *aphiketeuein. autophonos* occurs a few times in poetry; it refers to suicide in Opp. *Cyn.* 2.480.

42. ἴσσαντα line 52 in opposition to ἰσσάμενος line 40 f. must be transitive. Is it the corpse of the suicide which "is seated"?

43. τριφυλίαν is preceded by . . .]πολιαν; ἀλλο]πολίαν is a possible supplement. [μέχρι ὄρω]ν ([ἐπὶ ἰαρῶ]ν is the supplement at line 55 by Oliverio printed in *LSS.* Cf. Plat. *Leg.* 873d: A suicide is to be interred "at the borders of the twelve sections."

44. Cf. Epicharm. fr. 165 Kaibel; Hsch. s.v. *kreittones;* Schol. Aristoph. *Av.* 1490.

45. There seems to be a certain parallel to the Skira procession in Athens, an *apopompe* where a ram's fleece is of some importance; see Burkert (1985) 230.

46. Paus. 2.18.2; ἐρινῦς καὶ ποινὰς καὶ προστροπαίους τῶν δι' ἐκεῖνον ἠτυχηκότων: Polyb. 23.10.2.

47. Antiph. 2.3.10; 4.1.4; 4.2.8 (the passages are parallel, but *LSJ* translates "suppliant for vengeance" at 2.3.10 and "avenger" at 4.2.8); Aesch. *Ch.* 286 f.: τὸ γὰρ σκοτεινὸν τῶν ἐνερτέρων βέλος ἐκ προστροπαίων ἐν γένει πεπτωκότων, "the dark missile of those below, from *prostropaioi* killed within the family." The ancient com-

mentator explains: "from Agamemnon, who supplicates the gods to obtain avenge"; this has misled *LSJ* astray to translate "suppliant for vengeance" instead of avenging spirit who "attaches himself" to the culprit. Rohde (1898) I 264 n.2. had it right, notwithstanding his animistic interpretation: "Die zürnende Seele wird zum προστρόπαιος." See also Aeschin. 2.158 with Harpokr. s.v. προστρόπαιον· μίασμα. Cf. H. J. Stukey, *CP* 32 (1937) 40; Parker (1983) 108, 349.

SUBSTITUTE SACRIFICE

1. See Burkert (1979) 70–72 and (1981b) 115 f.
2. See Furlani (1940) 285–305, esp. 290 f.; cf. Chapter 2, "Purification," at note 19.
3. Paus.Att. ε 35 ed. Erbse; Zenob. Ath. 1.8 p. 350 Miller; the common source is Didymos; cf. Rupprecht, *RE* XVIII 4, 1754 f.; cf. W. Sale, *RhM* 118 (1975) 265–284. Menand. *Phasma* 80 Sandbach and fr. 368 Koerte.
4. Lex XII Tab. VIII 24a, explained by Festus 347, 351 M = 470, 476 L.
5. Ebeling (1931) 65–69 no. 15; cf. Furlani (1940) 294 f. and *RA* 38 (1941) 60. A similar but shorter text in Ebeling 69 f. no. 16; for Ereshkigal see above, "Purification," note 30; for libations see above, "Spirits of the Dead and Black Magic," note 5.
6. *Gell.* 5.12.12.
7. Ael. *Nat.An.* 12.34; cf. Burkert (1983a) 183.
8. *AHw* 109 f.

ASCLEPIUS AND ASGELATAS

1. Kyrieleis (1979); cf. A. Furtwängler, *AK* 21 (1978) 113 f.
2. Fuhr (1977) 136.
3. Paus. 2.27.2, confirmed by coins; cf. Fuhr (1977) 140 fig. 10. The relief from Epidaurus, Athens NM 1426: U. Hausmann, *Kunst und Heiltum* (1948) fig. 10; K. Kerényi, *Der göttliche Arzt* (1948) fig. 15; cf. Nilsson (1906) 409 n.7.
4. Apollod., *FGrHist* 244 F 138.
5. *IG* II/III² 4962 = *LSCG* 21.9 f.: κυσὶν πόπανα τρία· κυνηγέταις πόπανα τρία.
6. Plato, *Phaon* fr. 188.16 Kassel-Austin. The beginning of the verse is corrupt; see Kassel-Austin for suggested emendations.

7. K. L. Tallqvist, *Akkadische Götterepitheta* (1938) 5; Fuhr (1977); *AHw* 92b; in Aramaic–Syrian *asja,* physician, is a current word, too.

8. Asgelatas: *IG* XII 3.248 = *LSCG* 129 = *SIG* 977.8, 27 (end of second century B.C.); Asgelaia: *IG* XII 3.249; cf. Nilsson (1906) 175 f.

9. See U. von Wilamowitz-Moellendorff, *Isyllos von Epidauros* (1886) 93. A Hittite etymology for Asclepius is advanced by Szemerényi (1974) 155.

10. Esp. at the Black Sea; W. M. Calder, *AJA* 75 (1971) 325–329; *SEG* 30 no. 880; Aristoph. *Av.* 584, *Plut.* 11, etc.

11. Paus. 8.41.7–9; even if the name Epikurios originally designated the god of mercenaries, the interpretation "the Helper" as given by Pausanias shows what Greeks would normally expect.

12. *IG* XII 3 412 (Thera, fifth century B.C.); XII 3 259, 260 (Anaphe); Apoll.Rhod. 4.1716; Callim. fr. 7.23; Aiglatas as a personal name: Jeffery (1990) 199 no. 22.

13. κάρος is not found in Chantraine (1968/80). For *kâru* and *karû* see *AHw* 452a. For symposium couches see Chapter 1, "Oriental Products in Greece," note 28.

ECSTATIC DIVINATION

1. Heraclitus B 92; Aesch. *Ag.* 1072–1263; cf. H. L. Jansen, "Die Kassandragestalt in Aischylos' Agamemnon," *Temenos* 5 (1969) 107–119; Hdt. 8.135; cf. also Pindar *Pyth.* 4.10 f. on Medea prophesying: ζαμενὴς . . . ἀπέπνευσε. Already in the *Odyssey* Theoklymenos the seer is said to be "out of his mind," ἀφραίνει (*Od.* 20.360); cf. S. Scheinberg, *HSCP* 83 (1979) 16.

2. Plat. *Phdr.* 244a; the ecstasy of the Pythia was contested by P. Amandry, *La mantique apollinienne à Delphes* (1950); and by J. Fontenrose, *The Delphic Oracle* (1978) 204–212, who would allow "enthusiasm but not uncontrolled and irrational frenzy" for the Pythia—as if divination were not irrational in any case. See Dodds (1951) 70–74.

3. Esp. *Def.Or.* 51.438a–d; interesting details also in Lucan *Phars.* 5.69–236, though overlaid with reminiscences of Virgil *Aeneid* VI.

4. Farnell (1911) 303.

5. F. Ellermeier, *Prophetie in Mari und Israel* (1968); E. Noort,

Untersuchungen zum Gottesbescheid in Mari (1977); Wen-Amon: *ANET* 26; cf. Grottanelli (1982b) 666–668; on *mahhu, mahhutu* see *AHw* 852 f.

6. Jastrow (1905/12) II 158–165; Luckenbill (1926/27) II 238–241; *ANET* 449 f.; cf. A. K. Grayson and W. G. Lambert, *JCS* 18 (1964) 7–30; W. W. Hall, *Israel Explor. J.* 16 (1966) 231–242.

7. See Rzach, *RE* II A 2073–2183 s.v. *Sibyllen.*

8. The fame of the Sibyl of Erythrae seems to date from her rediscovery by a prophetess at the time of Alexander; Kallisthenes, *FGrHist* 124 F 14; cf. Apollodorus, *FGrHist* 422; *Die Inschriften von Erythrai und Klazomenai* II (1973) 224–228; Graf (1985) 335–350.

9. The origin and date of the *libri Sibyllini* in Rome will remain controversial; see R. Bloch in *Neue Beiträge zur Geschichte der Alten Welt* II (1965) 281–292; R. M. Ogilvie, *A Commentary on Livy I* (1965) 654 f.

10. Cf. A. Peretti, *La sibilla babilonese nella propaganda ellenistica* (1943); further Semitic etymologies for Sibylla in O. Gruppe, *Griechische Mythologie und Religionsgeschichte* II (1906) 927; H. Lewy, *Philologus* 57 (1898) 350 f.; F. Ellermeier, *Sibyllen, Musikanten, Haremsfrauen* (1970) 7–9; R. B. Coote, *Journal of North West Semitic Languages* 5 (1977) 3–8.

11. Schol. Plat. *Phdr.* 244b = Nikanor, *FGrHist* 146; Berossos, *FGrHist* 680 F 7; cf. Höfer, *RML* IV 264–269.

12. M. P. Nilsson, "Die älteste griechische Zeitrechnung, Apollon und der Orient," *ARW* 14 (1911) 423–448 = *Opuscula Selecta* I (1951) 36–61; idem, *Die Entstehung und religiöse Bedeutung des griechischen Kalenders* (1918, 1962²); Nilsson's ideas are outdated insofar as Linear B has proved that there was already a Mycenaean system of month names, but this does not invalidate the whole of his theory. See also Auffahrt (1991) 417–420 on the nineteen-year period. Cf. B. C. Dietrich, "Reflections on the Origins of the Oracular Apollo," *BICS* 25 (1978) 1–18. M. L. West thinks it possible that the Hurrian-Hittite myths reached Hesiod via Delphi: *JHS* 105 (1985) 175.

13. See A. Mallwitz and H. M. Lee in *The Archaeology of the Olympics,* ed. W. J. Raschke (1988) 79–109 and 110–18.

14. Plut. *Def.Or.* 435c, 437b—"sprinkling an ox with water to observe its reaction": Reiner (1960a), 25, 28.

15. See also K. Latte, "The Coming of the Pythia," *HThR* 33 (1940) 9–18.

16. *Apollo* from Akkadian *abullu*, Aramaic *abul*, city gate: E. Simon, *Die Götter der Griechen* (1967) 132; from Akkadian *aplu*, son: H. Lewy, *Wochenschrift für Klassische Philologie* 10 (1893) 860; L. R. Palmer in A. Heubeck and G. Neumann, eds., *Res Mycenaeae* (1983) 362.

LAMASHTU, LAMIA, AND GORGO

1. See Reiner (1960b), esp. 154.

2. F. Thureau-Dangin, *RA* 18 (1921) 192–198; Frank (1941) 15–23; H. W. Saggs, "Pazuzu," *AOF* 19 (1959/60) 123–127; *ANEP* 857; from Zincirli: *Sendschirli* V (1943) 31 figs. 24–25 and pl. 12a–d.

3. In cuneiform, the signs *maš* and *bar* (no. 74 Borger) have become identical; the earlier reading had been *Labartu*. The reading *Lamaštu* was established by a text published in 1934; see Frank (1941) 4 n.1. Earlier studies include D. W. Myhrman, "Die Labartu-Texte," *ZA* 16 (1902) 141–200; reliefs: K. Frank, *Babylonische Beschwörungsreliefs*, Leipziger Semitistische Studien 3.3 (1908); F. Thureau-Dangin, "Rituels et amulettes contre Labartu," *RA* 18 (1921) 161–198; Frank (1941); F. Koecher, *Beschwörungen gegen die Dämonin Lamaštu*, Diss. Berlin (1949); L. J. Krusina-Cerny, "Three New Amulets of Lamashtu," *Arch. Orientalni* 18.3 (1950) 297–303; H. Klengel, "Neue Lamaštu-Amulette aus den Vorderasiatischen Museen zu Berlin," *Mitt. d. Inst. f. Orientforsch.* 7 (1960) 334–355; cf. 8 (1963) 25–29; W. von Soden, *AOF* 20 (1963) 148; Leibovici (1971) 92, 95 f.; E. Lichty, "Demons and Population Control," *Expedition* 13.2 (1971) 22–26; M. V. Tonietti, "Un incantesimo sumerico contra la Lamaštu," *Orientalia* 48 (1978) 301–323; G. Wilhelm, *ZA* 69 (1979) 34–40; Patzek (1988); see also *RML* III 269; Meissner (1920/25) II figs. 33–34; *ANEP* 857. A comprehensive survey is given by W. Farber, *RlA* VI (1983) 439–446; he mentions sixty-three reliefs (441–443).

4. Patzek (1988); for Humbaba and dog-leaders see above, "Hepatoscopy," note 19; and "Asclepius and Asgelatas," note 1.

5. Sappho 178 A Voigt; Maas, *RE* VII 1005 f. with reference to modern Greek beliefs about Γυλλώ, cf. R. Reitzenstein, *Poiman-*

dres (1904) 299 and *ZA* 23 (1909) 157–163; J. C. Lawson, *Modern Greek Folktale and Ancient Greek Religion* (1910) 176–179.

6. C. Frank, *ZA* 24 (1910) 161–165; Meissner (1920/25) II 200; cf. *AHw* 275; *contra,* W. Eilers, Sitzungsber. München 1979.7, 58 f.

7. See Chapter 1, "Writing and Literature in the Eighth Century," at note 18; and above, "Asclepius and Asgelatas," note 8.

8. Stesichorus 220 *PMG*/Davies; Duris, *FGrHist* 76 F 17; Diod. 20.41.3; equated with Gello in Schol. Theocr. 16.38/39c; allusions in Aristoph. *Vesp.* 1035 and 1177, *Pax* 758, fr. 724 Kassel-Austin; cf. Schwenn, *RE* XII 544–546; J. Fontenrose, *Python* (1959) 100–104; on the problem of Greek pictorial representations see Vermeule (1977).

9. Stoll, *RML* II 1820 f.; Schwenn, *RE* XII 545 f.; Lawson (note 5, above) 173–176.

10. See note 3, above.

11. Ugarit: J. Nougayrol, *Ugaritica* VI (1969) 393–408; Boghazköy: ibid. 405; Carchemish: Goldman (1961) pl. 4.1; Zincirli: ibid. pl. 4.2; Klengel (note 3, above) nos. 46–47; cf. *RlA* VI 442.

12. C. Clermont-Ganneau, *Etudes d'archéologie orientale* 1 (1895) 85–90; cf. W. Culican, "Phoenician Demons," *JNES* 35 (1976) 21–24. Patzek (1988): amulet from Poggio Civitate, 675–650 B.C. Patzek also suggests that Homer's calling Artemis "lioness for women" (*Il.* 21.483) is dependent on the image and function of Lamashtu.

13. H. Gollancz, "A Selection of Charms from Syriac Manuscripts," *Actes du XI Congrès International des Orientalistes* (1897) IV 77–97, esp.80, 85.

14. Schol. Aristoph. *Pax* 758.

15. For some representations see note 3, above; the standard illustration is the big amulet in the Louvre, Collection de Clercq, *RML* III 269, *RlA* VI 442; the "Mistress of Animals" schema is especially clear in Meissner (1920/25) II pl. 34, which also has a horse next to Lamashtu.

16. On the iconography of the Gorgon see T. G. Karayorga, Γοργείη Κεφαλή (1970); J. Floren, *Studien zur Typologie des Gorgoneion* (1977); the oriental connections are discussed in C. Hopkins, "Assyrian Elements in the Perseus-Gorgon Story," *AJA* 38 (1934) 341–358; M. E. Will, *Rev. Arch.* VI 27 (1942) 60–76; Barnett (1960)

145–158; Hopkins (1961); Goldman (1961); Kantor (1962); Akurgal (1968) 187; W. Culican, "Phoenician Demons," *JNES* 35 (1976) 21–24; Helck (1979) 214 f.; for details borrowed from Pazuzu heads see Boardman (1980) 79.

17. For Corfu see, e.g., G. Richter, *A Handbook of Greek Art* (1959) 63; Schefold (1964) 49. For the horse besides Lamashtu see note 15, above; Gorgon holding two snakes: gold pendant from Delphi, Hopkins (1961) pl. 15.2. See also Burkert (1987b) 26–32.

18. Strab. 16 p. 759; Konon, *FGrHist* 26 F 1.40; Ios. *Bell.Iud.* 3.420; Plin. *N.H.* 5.69; 128; Paus. 4.35.9.

19. Coins of Tarsos: Burkert (1983a) 210 n.26.

20. Burkert (1987b) 28 nn.79–80 with fig. 2.7, esp. "Williams cylinder"; Ward (1910) 201 no. 578; P. Amiet, *Syria* 42 (1965) 245; also in West (1971) pl. IIa.

21. The so-called Polyphema type: E. Unger, *DLZ* 85 (1964) 694; M. Knox, *JHS* 99 (1979) 164 f.

22. Berlin VA 2145; M. Ohnefalsch-Richter, *Kypros, the Bible, and Homer* (1893) pl. 31.16; cf. p. 208; A. de Ridder, *BCH* 22 (1898) 452 fig. 4; Ward (1910) 212 no. 643c; A. Moortgat, *Vorderasiatische Rollsiegel* (1940) no. 781; C. Hopkins, *AJA* 38 (1934) 351 fig. 5 and (1961) pl. 15.3; Amiet (1976) 26 f.; B. Brentjes, *Alte Siegelkunst des Vorderen Orients* (1983) 165, 203, with the information that it was bought at Baghdad, whereas Ohnefalsch-Richter had made people think of Cyprus; Burkert (1987a) 276 f. fig. 2.3.

23. E. Kuhnert, *RML* III 2032; also in Goldman (1961) 21 f.

24. Amiet (1976) 26, preceded by Hopkins (1961) 31.

25. An old and impressive instance: steatite vessel from Khafajah, dated about 2700 B.C., BM 128887, Strommenger (1962) pl. 38 f.; cf. a circular amulet from Luristan in Geneva, Goldman (1961) pl. 1b.

26. Pind. *Nem.* 1.43–47, fr. 52u 7–18 Snell-Maehler; Eur. *Herc.* 1266–68; Theocr. 24; for pictures see *LIMC* Herakles nos. 1598–1664; for some other eastern elements in the myth and iconography of Herakles see Burkert (1979) 80–83 and (1987b).

27. Egyptian Bes amulets were reinterpreted to represent Herakles the "Daktylos"; see C. Grottanelli, "Eracle dattilo dell'Ida, Aspetti 'Orientali,'" *Oriens Antiquus* 11 (1972) 201–208; that the iconography of Herakles is dependent on that of Bes had been

shown already by A. Furtwängler, *RML* I 2143–45 and *ARW* 10 (1907) 325 = *Kleine Schriften* II (1924) 420; see also A. M. Biri, "Da Bes a Herakles," *Riv. Stud. Fen.* 8 (1980) 15–42.

28. J. Boardman, *Pre-Classical: From Crete to Archaic Greece* (1967) 106, wrote: "In the art of the 'orientalizing' period we look in vain for anything which we might call religious art"; this statement overlooks the Ida tympanon (Chapter 1, "Oriental Products in Greece," note 13; see Figure 1), and of course there were votive offerings and also divine images; but it captures a characteristic of the epoch.

29. See Faraone (1987) on *Od.* 7.91–94.

3. "Or Also a Godly Singer"
FROM *ATRAHASIS* TO THE "DECEPTION OF ZEUS"

1. "The Gilgamesh Epic . . . may well be called the Odyssey of the Babylonians"; A. Heidel, *The Gilgamesh Epic and Old Testament Parallels* (1949²) 1. A catalogue of parallels in Auffahrt (1991) 136–139; see also Gresseth (1975); Wilson (1986); Burkert (1991). Jensen (1902), (1912/13), (1924) and Ungnad (1923) called attention esp. to Kalypso and Siduri the ale wife, Alkinoos, and Utnapishtim. Utnapishtim's ferryman quits his service after the transport of Gilgamesh (XI 234–236), just as the transport of Odysseus is the last ever done by the Phaeacians (*Od.* 13.125–187). See also G. Crane, "Circe and the Near East," in *Calypso. Backgrounds and Conventions of the Odyssey* (1988) 61–85. Fries (1910) reached an extreme position; more solid is Wirth (1921). Most specific is Enkidu coming up from the dead to meet his friend (*Gilgamesh* XII), just as Patroklos' soul meets Achilles (*Il.* 23.65–107): "The comparison . . . is, indeed, almost irresistible"; G. S. Kirk, *Myth* (1970) 108; cf. idem, *The Nature of Greek Myths* (1974) 260 f.; see also Chapter 2, "Spirits of the Dead and Black Magic," at note 4. There are also connections with *Od.* 11, the *Nekyia;* cf. C. F. Lehmann-Haupt, *RE* XI 433; G. Germain, *Genèse de l'Odyssée* (1954) 342–346; Dirlmeier (1955) 30–35; "A faintly possible model": G. S. Kirk, *The Songs of Homer* (1962) 107. For the beginning of the *Odyssey* and of *Gilgamesh* see Chapter 3, "Common Style and Stance in Oriental and Greek Epic," at note 17.

2. *Atrahasis* ed. Lambert and Millard (1969), with von Soden (1978); Bottéro and Kramer (1989); Dalley (1989).

3. See *Atrahasis* ed. Lambert and Millard (1969) 11–13.

4. *Atrahasis* I 7–10 = *Gilgamesh* XI 15–18 (the word translated "sheriff" in line 10 by Lambert and Millard is problematic; see their note p. 147; "contre-maître": Bottéro and Kramer 530: "canal-controller": Dalley 9); *Atrahasis* I 11–17; the translation by Lambert and Millard has been modified here, following von Soden and Dalley.

5. II v 16–19, 30–3', pp. 80–83; tablet X rev. I 4–7; II 2.5, pp. 116–119; cf. the commentary by Lambert and Millard p. 166.

6. *Il.* 15.187–193. The three divine brothers are illustrated on a black-figure vase by the Xenokles painter (ca. 540–530 B.C.), BM B 425, *ABV* 184; A. B. Cook, *Zeus* II (1925) 745. The drawing of lots (*klêroi*) was said to have happened at the site of Apollo's sanctuary at Klaros, Schol. Apoll.Rhod. 1.308. Further from Homer and *Atrahasis* is a Hittite text: "When they had created heaven and earth, they divided. The upper gods took heaven, the lower gods took earth and the lower countries for themselves"; H. Otten and J. Siegelová, *AfO* 23 (1970) 32 f. This lacks the tripartite structure and the drawing of lots.

7. Hes. *Theog.* 883.

8. Heaven-earth-underworld: the oath: *Il.* 15.36 f.; cf. 3.277–279; *Od.* 5.184 f. Earth-heaven-sea: *Il.* 18.483 (description of the shield of Achilles); *Od.* 1.52 f.; Hes. *Theog.* 847; *Hymn. Dem.* 33 f. Heaven-underworld-earth-sea: Hes. *Theog.* 736 f. Cf. already Wirth (1921) 132; E. G. Schmidt, "Himmel-Erde-Meer im frühgriechischen Epos und im alten Orient," *Philologus* 125 (1981) 1–24 (still without knowledge of *Atrahasis*).

9. Cf. already Gruppe (1887) 612–618; U. von Wilamowitz-Moellendorff, *Kleine Schriften* V 2 (1937) 167 and *Der Glaube der Hellenen* I (1931) 341: "die fremde Genealogie"; W. Theiler, *Untersuchungen zur antiken Literatur* (1970) 24–26; A. Dihle, *Homer-Probleme* (1970) 83–92. For the function of the scene in the *Iliad* see H. Erbse, *A&A* 16 (1970) 93–112. See now R. Janko, *The Iliad: A Commentary* IV (1992) 168–207.

10. Plat. *Krat.* 402ab; *Tht.* 152e, 180c–d; cf. *Tim.* 40e; Arist. *Met.* 983b27; *Aet.* 1.3.2; Plut. *Is.* 364c–d referred to Egypt for comparison. Cf. J. Mansfeld, *Mnemosyne* 38 (1985) 123–129.

11. Ὠκεανόν τε θεῶν γένεσιν καὶ μητέρα Τηθύν: *Il.* 14.201 = 302; Ὠκεανοῦ, ὅς περ γένεσις πάντεσσι τέτυκται: 246.

Oceanus and Tethys also appear in Hes. *Theog.* 133–136 and in the genealogy of Phoroneus Apollod. *Bib.* 2.1; both are represented on the *dinos* of Sophilos (about 570 B.C.), BM 1971.11–1.1; cf. A. Birchall, *Brit. Mus. Quart.* 36 (1971/72) pl. 37; G. Bakir, *Sophilos* (1981) 64 fig. 3; D. Williams in *Greek Vases in the J. Paul Getty Museum* I (1983) 9–34; Tethys is spelt ΘΕΘΥΣ by Sophilos.

12. U. Hölscher, "Anaximander und der Anfang der Philosophie," *Hermes* 81 (1953) 257–277, 385–418, revised in *Anfängliches Fragen* (1968) 9–89, esp. 40–43; cf. G. S. Kirk, J. E. Raven, and M. Schofield, *The Presocratic Philosophers* (1983²) 10–17; W. K. C. Guthrie, *A History of Greek Philosophy* I (1962) 58–61; Walcot (1966) 34; West (1966) 204. The relevance of *Enuma Elish* for Hesiod was established by F. M. Cornford, "A Ritual Basis for Hesiod's *Theogony,*" in *The Unwritten Philosophy* (1950) 95–116.

13. *Enuma Elish* I 1–5.

14. *AHw* 1353 f.; *ta-à-wa-ti* (genitive): *Enuma Elish* IV 65 p. 23 Lambert and Parker; *ti-à-wa-ti:* II 81, p. 12 Lambert and Parker; *ta-ma-tu:* I 33, p. 2 Lambert and Parker. The sign *wa* can also be read *aw.* For the change *m/w* see W. von Soden, *Grundriss der Akkadischen Grammatik* (1952) §§ 21d, 31a. The first to see the connection between *Enuma Elish* and Homer, Tiamat and Tethys was W. E. Gladstone, *Landmarks of Homeric Study* (1890), appendix; then F. Lukas, *Die Grundbegriffe in den Kosmogonien der alten Völker* (1893) 154 n.; cf. also Duchemin (1980a) 851, 858 f., 864, 868; Szemerényi (1974) 150.

15. For Sophilos see note 11, above; Eudemos fr. 150 Wehrli = Damask. *Princ.* I 322.1 f.; for *theta* reproducing Semitic *taw* see also E. Schwyzer, *Griechische Grammatik* I (1939) 154.

16. R. Gusmani in *Studies in Greek, Italian and Indoeuropean Linguistics Presented to L. R. Palmer* (1976) 77–82, against E. Laroche, *Mélanges P. Chantraine* (1972) 83–91.

17. On the date of *Enuma Elish* see Walcot (1966) 33; Reiner (1978) 175; Dalley (1989) 229 f.; "neo-oriental": West (1971) 205.

18. On the *kestos Il.* 14.214 see C. Bonner, *AJP* 70 (1949) 1–6; F. E. Brenk, *Class. Bull.* 54 (1977) 17–19; C. A. Faraone, *Phoenix* 44 (1990) 219–243. Zeus's catalogue, *Il.* 14.315–328; cf. *Gilgamesh* VI 42–78, but also Kalypso's catalogue of goddesses who have loved mortals, *Od.* 5.118–128. For the oriental background of Aphrodite see Chapter 3, "Complaint in Heaven."

19. *Il.* 15.36–38 = *Od.* 5.184–186. Inscriptions from Sfire (see above, Chapter 2, "Spirits of the Dead and Black Magic," note 28): I A 11 f., *ANET* 659, Fitzmyer (1967) 12 f. "Oath of Heaven and Earth" also in the Sumerian *Descent of Ishtar* 241; Bottéro and Kramer (1989) 285; in *Tukulti Ninurta* III (IV) 40, *Annals of Archaeology and Anthropology* 20 (1933) 121, 126; even Jahwe takes his oath "by heaven and earth," Deut. 4:26—but also Mongols and Manchus in A.D. 1628, R. Merkelbach, *Mithras* (1984) 5 f. n.7. The oriental background of state treaties was already stressed by Schwahn RE IV A 1107 f.; see now M. Weinfeld, "The Common Heritage of Covenantal Traditions in the Ancient World," in *I trattati nel mondo antico,* ed. L. Canfora, M. Liverani, and C. Zaccagnini (1990) 175–191.

20. Cf. E. D. van Buren, "The Rain-Goddess as Represented in Early Mesopotamia," *Analecta Biblica* 12 (1959) 343–355, esp. 350 f., pl. XXVI 9 (Syria, second millennium); R. M. Boemer, *Die Entwicklung der Glyptik während der Akkad-Zeit* (1965) 62–64 with figs. 333, 364, 367, 368, 371, 373, etc. (third millennium); U. Winter (1983) 276 with fig. 273. *Lugal-e* 26: "Anu fecundated earth"; *Erra* I 28 f.: "Anu, king of the gods, mated with earth: seven gods she bore to him"; incantation text Ebeling (1918/19) II 45: "As heaven mated with earth, and plants grew abundant . . ."

21. Niemeyer (1984) 68 f.; the statuette also in Schefold (1964) pl. 39; *LIMC* Hera no. 202.

22. *Il.* 14.274, 279; 15.225; 8.478 f.; 5.848 (οὐρανίωνες); cf. West (1966) 200 f.; Burkert (1985) 174; F. Solmsen, "The Two Near Eastern Sources of Hesiod," *Hermes* 117 (1989) 413–422.

23. On *karuiles siunes* see H. Otten, *ZA* 54 (1961) 135–141, 157; E. Reiner and H. G. Güterbock, *JCS* 21 (1967) 265 f.; V. Haas and G. Wilhelm, *Hurritische und luwische Riten aus Kizzuwatna* (1974) 50–53; Gurney (1977) 15; V. Haas, *Hethitische Berggötter und Hurritische Steindämonen* (1982) 32–34, 133.

24. Ebeling (1931) 38 no. 8.5 (the "seven gods" who have been vanquished/bound by Anu the god of heaven); *Enuma Elish* 4.127; cf. 7.27. *AHw* 433 translates *kamû* 'to bind,' but *CAD* VII (K) 127 f. insists on the meaning "to vanquish." Cf. B. Landsberger and J. V. Kinnier Wilson, *JNES* 20 (1961) 178 f.; J. S. Cooper, *Analecta Orientalia* 52 (1978) 141–154; Van Dijk (1983) 10 f.; Haas (1986) 45 f., 91–93.

25. Orph. fr. 114.

26. See above, Chapter 1, "The Problem of Loan-Words," note 22; and Chapter 3, "Common Style and Stance in Oriental and Greek Epic."

27. Eustath. 332.24–28; A. Dieterich, *RhM* 48 (1893) 280 = *Kleine Schriften* (1911) 121; J. E. Harrison, *Prolegomena to the Study of Greek Religion* (1922³) 491–493; L. R. Farnell, *The Cults of the Greek States* V (1909) 172.

28. Cf. already E. Assmann, "Titaia, Titanen und der Tartaros," *Babyloniaca* 6 (1912) 236–239; Astour (1965) 196 n.3. But for striking assonances note also that the mythical ancestor of the kings of Ugarit, in the assembly of the netherworld, is *Ditanu;* O. Loretz, *Ugarit und die Bibel* (1990) 69.

29. Ebeling (1931) 76 no. 20.4; 138 no. 30 C 4; E. D. Van Buren, *Orientalia* 10 (1942) 69 f.; *ṭiṭu* in particular is the material from which man has been created: Zimmern (1901) 158 f. no. 48.1; *Atrahasis* I 203.

30. Reiner (1978) 157.

31. See Chapter 1, "Writing and Literature in the Eighth Century."

32. Cf. West (1988) 169. There will not easily be agreement on the process of composition and the date of our text of the *Iliad*. Suffice it to refer to A. Lesky, *RE* Suppl. XI 687–846 s.v. *Homeros* (1968); A. Heubeck, *Die Homerische Frage* (1988²); J. Latacz, *Homer* (1989²). I, for one, am inclined to think that our text is a well-planned composition from beginning to end, to be dated in the first half of the seventh century, though relying on generations of earlier oral singers (cf. *WSt* 89 [1976] 5–21).

COMPLAINT IN HEAVEN

1. See, e.g., P. Von der Mühll, *Kritisches Hypomnema zur Ilias* (1952), who assigns practically all the divine scenes to his "Bearbeiter B"; cf. 96 f. on *Il.* 5.353–431.

2. Esp. L. A. Stella, *Il poema di Ulisse* (1955) 188–205; Stella (1978) 73–123.

3. *Gilgamesh* VI 1–91; *ANET* 83 f., modified according to von Soden.

4. *Il.* 5.330–431.

5. This was noticed by Gresseth (1975) 14, who also compares

the threat of Ishtar to release the dead from the underworld, if Anu does not grant her wish (*Gilgamesh* VI 96–100), with the reverse threat of Helios in the *Odyssey* to go down to the underworld, if Zeus does not grant his wish (12.382 f.). See also Burkert in *Eranos Jahrbuch* (1982) 335–367.

6. *Il.* 21.505–513.

7. Cf. Burkert (1985) 152–156; for Anchises and Aphrodite see L. H. Lentz, *Der Homerische Aphroditehymnus und die Aristie des Aineias in der Ilias* (1975), esp. 104–107, 144–152. Helck (1979) 243–249 holds that practically the whole Homeric pantheon reproduces North Syrian/Late Hittite gods.

8. Dione is mentioned Hes. *Theog.* 17 in a catalogue which is close to Homer (cf. West [1968] 156) and in *Theog.* 353 among the daughters of Oceanus; for Dodona, see Strab. 7 p. 392, who says that Dione has been secondarily introduced there; cf. Escher, *RE* V 878–880. G. Murray, *Five Stages of Greek Religion* (1925) 77, argued that Dione had preceded Hera as Zeus's wife; this is refuted by Linear B, where Hera is the wife of Zeus. For *Diwija* see M. Gérard-Rousseau, *Les mentions religieuses dans les tablettes mycéniennes* (1968) 67–70. The suffix -ώνη remained productive in the Greek language, so that female names could always be formed with it; cf. Danae Akrisione, *Il.* 14.319; Helena Argeione, Hes. fr. 23a20.

9. Callim. *Hymn.* 5, esp. 5.35 with schol.; see W. Burkert, *Zeitschrift für Religions- und Geistesgeschichte* 22 (1970) 361 f.; see also the Catalogue of Ships, *Il.* 2.559–568; Ø. Andersen, "Die Diomedesgestalt in der Ilias," *Symb. Oslo.* suppl. 25 (1978). Note that Diomedes is immortal (*Thebais* fr. 5 Davies).

10. Porph. *Abst.* 2.54 f.; this section is not taken from Theophrastus, but no further details can be made out; neither "King Diphilos of Cyprus" nor "Seleukos the theologian" mentioned in the text is known elsewhere. Cf. *RE* I A 1835 s.v. *Salamis.*

11. F. Schwenn, *Die Menschenopfer bei den Griechen und Römern* (1915) 71 f. argues against this thesis.

12. See Chapter 1 "Historical Background," at note 19; and below, "The Overpopulated Earth," note 12.

13. See Burkert (1983a) 60 f.

14. *Gilgamesh* VI 53–57; see above, "From *Atrahasis* to the 'Deception of Zeus,'" note 18.

15. *Od.* 4.759–767.

16. A kind of vegetable offering: L. Deubner, *Kleine Schriften zur klassischen Altertumskunde* (1982) 625; cf. Schol. 761 and Eust. Invented by the poet: S. West in A. Heubeck, S. West, and J. B. Hainsworth, *A Commentary on Homer's Odyssey* I (1988) 240; "ohne jede Analogie" according to K. Meuli, *Ausgewählte Schriften* II (1975) 994 n. 1.

17. *Gilgamesh* III ii 1–21; *ANET* 81; Dalley (1989) 65; supplemented according to von Soden (1982) 38.

18. *Il.* 16.220–253.

19. Cf. Jeremiah 44:17–19 and the Greek Adonia; cf. also the Ugaritic epic of Keret ii 73–80, *ANET* 143.

THE OVERPOPULATED EARTH

1. *Atrahasis* III vii 1–9, p. 102 f. Lambert and Millard. "Birth control" is *aladam pursi,* line 9. Cf. A. D. Kilmer, "The Mesopotamian Concept of Overpopulation and Its Solution as Reflected in the Mythology," *Orientalia* 41 (1972) 160–177. Studies on the motif of overpopulation without knowledge of *Atrahasis* include H. Schwarzbaum, "The Overcrowded Earth," *Numen* 4 (1957) 59–74; G. Dumézil, *Mythe et épopée* I (1974²) 31–257; J. W. de Jong, "The Overburdened Earth in India and Greece," *JAOS* 105 (1985) 397–400.

2. *Atrahasis* I 352–359 = II 1–8.

3. *Kypria* fr. 1 Allen = fr. 1 Davies = Schol. AD *Il.* 1.5.

4. Schol. AD *Il.* 1.5; cf. Schol. Eur. *Or.* 1641; E. Bethe, *Homer* II (1929²) 154 f.; 228. Cf. also *Gilgamesh* XI 182–185: the gods discuss whether mankind should be reduced by flood, man-eating beasts, famine, or plague.

5. Prokl. *Chrestom.* p. 102.13 Allen = p. 31.5 Davies.

6. Hes. fr. 204.96 ff.; cf. M. L. West, *CQ* 11 (1961) 133–136; K. Heilinger, *MH* 40 (1983) 23 f.

7. *Enuma Elish* I 47; *ANET* 61; Dalley (1989) 234; in the transcription of Eudemos (see above, "From *Atrahasis* to the 'Deception of Zeus,'" note 16) Mummu is Μωυμιν.

8. Apollod. *Bibl.* 1.39–44; cf. Burkert (1979) 7–9.

9. W. Kullmann had insisted on the pre-Homeric character of the story; see "Ein vorhomerisches Motiv im Iliasproömium," *Philologus* 99 (1955) 167–192, referring to the *Mahabharata,* as Schwarzbaum, Dumézil, and de Jong (see above, note 1) also did.

And still the parallel with *Atrahasis,* very incompletely known to him, had already been noticed by Wirth (1921) 132.

10. See Rzach, *RE* XI 2379 f.; H. Lloyd-Jones, "Stasinus and the *Cypria,*" in *Stasinos. Syndesmos Hellenon Philologon Kyprou* 4 (1968/72) 115–122, esp. 117 f. A direct link to Kypris = Aphrodite can hardly be accepted—it should result in *Kypridia.

11. Schefold (1964) pl. 29b; *LIMC* Alexandros no. 5 = Aphrodite no. 1423 = Athena no. 405; *Il.* 24.29 f.; cf. K. Reinhardt, *Das Parisurteil* (1938); I. Raab, *Zu den Darstellungen des Parisurteils in der griechischen Kunst* (1972).

12. See V. Karageorghis, "The Age of Exuberance," in *Salamis. Recent Discoveries in Cyprus* (1969); for the "sword with silver nails" see p. 70 pl. 25; for the role of Cyprus see above, "From *Atrahasis* to the 'Deception of Zeus,'" note 19; and "Complaint in Heaven," note 12.

13. H. Bossert, *Altsyrien* (1951) no. 815; Markoe (1985) 278–283, E 2 and E 1; U. Gehring and H. G. Niemeyer, eds., *Die Phönizier im Zeitalter Homers* (1990) 186 f. no. 139 fig. 23.

14. C. Clermont-Ganneau, *L'imagérie Phénicienne et la mythologie iconologique chez les grecs* (1880).

15. I owe this idea to C. Grottanelli and A. Hermary.

16. *Il.* 5.311 f.; cf. 3.373 f., etc.

17. *Atrahasis* I 27–102, pp. 44–49 Lambert and Millard.

18. *Il.* 1.396–406; cf. W. Kullmann, *Das Wirken der Götter in der Ilias* (1956) 14–17; Duchemin (1980a) 864; B. K. Braswell, "Mythological Invention in the Iliad," *CQ* 21 (1971) 18 f.

19. Cf. J. Duchemin, *Prométhée. Histoire du mythe de ses origines orientales à ses incarnations modernes* (1974). On trickster mythology and *Atrahasis* see Burkert (1982b).

SEVEN AGAINST THEBES

1. F. H. Stubbings, *CAH* II 2³ (1975) 168.

2. S. Symeonoglou, *Kadmeia* I (1973) 72–76; F. H. Stubbings, *CAH* II 2³ 168 f.; T. G. Spyropoulos, *Minos* suppl. 4 (1975) 53–55; 58–71. The problem of how to combine the results of excavation with the mythical traditions is discussed in A. Schachter, "The Theban Wars," *Phoenix* 21 (1967) 1–10; Edwards (1979), esp. 104 f.; C. Brillante, "Le leggende Tebane e l'archeologia," *SMEA* 21 (1980) 309–340; "more than one hypothesis will fit": Edwards 189.

Blegen thought the destruction of Thebes (by the Epigoni) and of Troy VII A were about contemporary, ca. 1250. M. I. Finley's denial of the historicity of the Trojan War, *Proc. Brit. Ac.* 60 (1974) 393–412, receives decisive support from the late date for the destruction of Troy VII A, ca. 1140, as established by E. F. Bloedow, *Prähistorische Zeitschrift* 63 (1988) 23–52.

3. *Il.* 2.505 with Schol.B and Strab. 9 p. 412. For the late date of the catalogue see A. Giovannini, *Etude historique sur les origines du catalogue des vaisseaux* (1969); G. S. Kirk, *The Iliad: A Commentary* I (1985) 168–195. Note that the *Iliad* presumes the presence of *Boiotoi* in Boeotia, who, according to local tradition, came there only after the Trojan War.

4. For the history of Boeotia and Thebes in the early archaic period see P. Cloché, *Thèbes de Béotie* (1952); M. Sordi, "Mitologia e propaganda nella Beocia arcaica," *Atene e Roma,* n.s. 11 (1966) 15–24; Jeffery (1976) 77–79; R. J. Buck, *A History of Boeotia* (1979); H. van Effenterre, *Les Béotiens* (1989); bibliography in J. M. Fossey and J. Morin, eds., *Boeotia Antiqua* I (1988).

5. Θήβης ἑπταπύλοιο: *Il.* 4.406; *Od.* 11.263. Fragments of the *Thebais:* pp. 21–26 Davies. The most extensive study of the whole Theban tradition is still C. Robert, *Ödipus* (1915). See also Burkert (1981a) 29–34.

6. Following Keramopoullos, see the map in *RE* V A 1425 f.; cf. T. G. Spyropoulos, *Minos* suppl. 4 (1975) 62; K. Demakopoulou and D. Konsola, *Archaeologisches Museum Theben: Führer* (1981) 22; N. D. Papachatzis, *Pausaniou Periegesis* V (1981) 64 f.; S. Symeonoglou, *The Topography of Thebes from the Bronze Age to Modern Times* (1985) 32–38. The existence of the seven gates was denied by U. von Wilamowitz-Moellendorff, "Die sieben Tore Thebens," *Hermes* 26 (1891) 191–242 = *Kleine Schriften* V 1 (1937) 26–77, esp. 62 f., followed by F. Schober, *RE* V A 1429, who states that only three gates make topographical sense: "drei Tore . . . entsprechen allein der Lage auch der heutigen Stadt, die auch nur drei Ausgänge kennt"; Howald (1939) 3; P. J. Reimer, *Zeven tegen Thebe,* Diss. Amsterdam (1953).

7. The oldest lists are in Aesch. *Sept.* 375–652 and from the Argive dedication at Delphi, Paus. 10.10.4; cf. Apollod. *Bibl.* 3 [63] 6.3; Robert, *Ödipus* (1915) I 237–247.

8. Amphiaraos, originally probably *Amphiares (connected

with Ares; see A. Heubeck, *Die Sprache* 17 [1971] 8–22), called Amphis in Aeschylus fr. 412 Radt, probably had some relation to Amphion, whose tomb was prominent at Thebes. The names Adrastos and Amphios are associated at *Il.* 2.830, somehow reflecting the Thebais(?), cf. B. C. Dietrich, *Historia* 29 (1980) 499. On Diomedes see above, "Complaint in Heaven," notes 9–10.

9. Howald (1939), criticized by A. Lesky, *Die tragische Dichtung der Hellenen* (1972³) 89 with n.25. Sikyon: Hdt. 5.67. On Arion see Burkert (1979) 127.

10. Ed. P. F. Gössmann (1956); Cagni (1969); Labat et al. (1970) 114–137; Bottéro and Kramer (1989) 680–727; Dalley (1989) 285–312; not in *ANET;* cf. Reiner (1978) 166–168. Walcot (1966) 49–54 compares the way the poet introduces himself (*Erra* V 42–61) with the poem of Hesiod. It is strangely reminiscent of Erra the god of war and plague that in Sophocles' *O.T.* Ares the god of war is introduced as the god of plague (190).

11. See Cagni (1969) 44 f.: ninth century at the earliest; Bottéro and Kramer (1989) 720: about 850 B.C.; W. von Soden, *Ugarit-Forschungen* 3 (1971) 255 f.: 765–703 B.C.; cf. Dalley (1989) 282–284.

12. Reiner (1960b); cf. Reiner (1978) 167; Cagni (1969) 45; see above, Chapter 2, "Hepatoscopy," note 7 on Tarsos.

13. See Jastrow (1905/12) I 173 f.; Meissner (1920/25) II 203; D. O. Edzard in H. W. Haussig, ed., *Wörterbuch der Mythologie* I (1965) 124 f.; Gössmann (note 10 above) 70–72. Wirth (1921) 157 already associated the demoniac "Seven" with the "Seven against Thebes."

14. A collection of incantation texts, *Asakki maršuti,* Thompson (1903/04) II 28 f.; for *eṭemmu,* see above, Chapter 2, "Spirits of the Dead and Black Magic," note 2; for *gallu* above, Chapter 2 "Lamashtu, Lamia, and Gorgo," note 6.

15. The collection *utukki lemnuti* XVI, Thompson (1903/04) I 88–103, in the context of the eclipses; cf. Tablet V of the same series, Thompson I 50 f., 74 f.

16. Thompson (1903/04) I 184–201; cf. Meissner (1920/25) II 199 f.

17. Meier (1941/44); earlier treatment by Zimmern (1901) 168 f. n.54; cf. Castellino (1977) 716–725; see now F. A. M. Wiggermann, *Babylonian Prophylactic Figures: The Ritual Texts* (1986) 205–

227. The "divine Seven" and "seven bearers of arms" also appear in a text about the fabrication of magical figurines, Rittig (1977) 154 f., 164 f. (*KAR* 298).

18. Cf. C. L. Woolley, *JRAS* (1926) 689–713; R. Borger, *Bibl. Or.* 30 (1973) 176–183; Rittig (1977); see above, Chapter 2, "Purification," note 31; "Spirits of the Dead and Black Magic," notes 28, 34; and Chapter 3, "From *Atrahasis* to the 'Deception of Zeus,'" note 29.

19. The form used, *mundaḫṣe* (Gt from *maḫaṣu;* cf. Chapter 1, "The Problem of Loan-Words," note 34), basically means "fighting reciprocally" (Meier [1941/44] 151) but is also used in a more general sense for "fighter"; see *AHw* 581, 672.

20. M. von Oppenheim, *Tell Halaf* III: *Die Bildwerke,* ed. A. Moortgat (1955) pl. 35b, A 3, 49, p. 54 states that the sculptor obviously intended to render the figures in mirror symmetry: "Die Absicht des Bildhauers war anscheinend, die Männer spiegelbildgleich zu bilden"; H. T. Bossert, *Altsyrien* (1951) no. 472. See Figure 8. For Etruscan representations see I. Krauskopf, *Der Thebanische Sagenkreis und andere griechische Sagen in der etruskischen Kunst* (1974).

21. II Samuel 2:16; cf. C. Grottanelli, "Horatius, i Curiatii e II Sam. 2, 12–28," *Annali dell'Istituto Orientale di Napoli* 35 (1975) 547–554.

22. Liv. 1.24 f.; see Grottanelli (above, note 21).

23. Pind. frs. 162–163; cf. *Pyth.* 4.88 with Schol.; Diod. 5.50 f.; Apollod. *Bibl.* 1 [53–55] 7.4; Eust. 1687.36. The Aloadae are mentioned in *Il.* 5.385 f., *Od.* 11.305–320; and in Hesiod fr. 19.

24. See R. Hampe, *Frühe griechische Sagenbilder in Böotien* (1936); Schefold (1964) 6a, advocating a date in the eighth century; but see K. Fittschen, *Untersuchungen zum Beginn der Sagendarstellungen bei den Griechen* (1969) 213–221. For the parallels, esp. the seven-headed snake in oriental iconography, see Burkert (1979) 80–83; (1987b) 25–29. Boeotians, *Iawones,* and Locrians are grouped together, *Il.* 13.685; see above, Chapter 1, "Historical Background," note 18.

25. See Chapter 2, "Hepatoscopy" and "Foundation Deposits."

26. J. McK. Camp, "A Drought in the Late Eighth Century B.C.," *Hesperia* 48 (1979) 397–411; *contra,* see I. Morris, *Burial and Ancient Society* (1987) 158–167.

27. I. Krauskopf (see note 20, above) 86, 299, following E. Simon; *LIMC* I 711 s.v. *Amphiaraos*.

28. G. Mylonas, *Praktika* (1953) 81–87, giving a vague date "late geometric"; cf. Paus. 1.39.2; Plut. *Thes.* 29.5; and Eur. *Supplices*.

29. See J. N. Coldstream, "Hero-Cults in the Age of Homer," *JHS* 96 (1976) 8–17.

30. See above, "From *Atrahasis* to the 'Deception of Zeus,'" note 32.

31. For the "Seven Sages" of primordial times (*apkallê*) see *AHw* 58 f.; E. Reiner, *Orientalia,* n.s. 30 (1961) 1–11; R. Borger, *JNES* 33 (1974) 183–196.

32. The *Sibitti* appear in the inscription of Sfire I A 11 (see above, Chapter 2, "Spirits of the Dead and Black Magic," note 28), *ANET* 659, Fitzmyer (1967) 12 f.

COMMON STYLE AND STANCE IN ORIENTAL AND GREEK EPIC

1. Stella (1978) 362–391, with the cautionary statement that direct influence should be excluded: "esclusa naturalmente ogni eventualità di influssi diretti su Omero" (368). Comparisons of Homer with Babylon began with Jensen and Fries and were carried on by Wirth (1921) and Ungnad (1923); for the more recent developments see esp. Bowra (1952), Dirlmeier (1955), Gordon (1955), Walcot (1966), Gresseth (1975), Helck (1979) 249–251. See also Burkert (1991).

2. See M. Parry, *The Making of Homeric Verse* (1971).

3. The bibliography has become abundant. Suffice it to mention R. Finnegan, *Oral Poetry. Its Nature, Significance, and Social Context* (1977); J. M. Foley, *Oral-Formulaic Theory and Research. An Introduction and Annotated Bibliography* (1985).

4. *quradu Enlil* in *Atrahasis* 1.8 = *Gilgamesh* XI 16. See for this and the following also Bowra (1952) 241.

5. *Utnapištim ruqu* in *Gilgamesh* X–XI passim.

6. *qarrad la šanan* in *Erra* passim.

7. *rkb ʿrpt* in *Baal* passim, *btlt ʿnt* in *Baal* and *Aqhat* passim, *dnl rpe* in *Aqhat* passim.

8. *mûdu tuquntu* in *Gilgamesh* IV vi 30.

9. *tabat rigma* in *Gilgamesh* XI 117.

10. *erṣetim rapaštim* in *Gilgamesh* VIII iii–iv 43, 46, 47, p. 49

Thompson; cf. εὐρεῖα χθών. As to "black earth" (γαῖα μέλαινα), Öttinger (1989/90) argues for Hurrite-Hittite provenience.

11. Sumerian prayer to the moon god in *SAHG* 223 = Castellino (1977) 336 line 16. In Hittite Ullikummi is called "father of the gods"; *ANET* 121 f., as El is *ab adm*, father of men, in Ugarit.

12. *pašu ippuš-ma iquabbî, ana . . . (amatam) izakkar* with slight variations; see F. Sonnek, "Die Einführung der direkten Rede in den epischen Texten," *ZA* 46 (1940) 225–235; the formula occurs also in fables, e.g., Lambert (1960) 178.7.

13. *Gilgamesh* X i 11 f.; cf. X iv, 12–14; *Etana* II 99; J. V. Kinnier Wilson, *The Legend of Etana* (1985) 98; in Hittite: J. Siegelova, *Appu-Märchen und Hedammu-Mythus* (1971) 48 f.; in the Old Testament, too, people "speak to their heart": Gen. 27:41 f., I Samuel 1:12 f.; cf. Stella (1978) 365; D. O. Edzard, "Selbstgespräch und Monolog in der akkadischen Literatur," in *Lingering over Words: Studies in Ancient Near Eastern Literature in Honor of W. L. Moran*, ed. T. Abusch, J. Huehnergard, and P. Steinkeller (1990) 149–162.

14. *mimmu šeri ina namari* in *Gilgamesh* XI 48 = 96; cf. Ungnad (1923) 30.

15. *ANET* 124: the weather god sends Tashmeshu as Zeus sends Hermes in *Od.* 5. An important assembly of the gods also takes place in *Gilgamesh* VII 1 3 ff., where the gods decide about the death of Enkidu. The entrance of victorious Ninurta into this assembly, who threatens to rouse panic but is appeased by his mother, in the Sumerian poem *ANGIM* 71 ff. (Bottéro and Kramer [1989] 381 f.), has a marked resemblance to Hom. *Hymn Apoll.* 3–13 (I owe this observation to C. Penglase). For Ugarit, see E. T. Mullen, *The Assembly of the Gods: The Divine Council in Canaanite and Early Hebrew Literature* (1980).

16. See Bowra (1952) 266 f., who includes materials from *Gilgamesh*.

17. See Wirth (1921) 112 f.; A. B. Lord in A. J. B. Wace and F. H. Stubbings, *A Companion to Homer* (1967) 198.

18. *Gilgamesh* III iv 141–148 (in the reconstruction of von Soden), p. 27 Thompson; *ANET* 79; Dalley (1989) 145. *šimatu awilutim* in the Babylonian version X ii 4 p. 53 Thompson. Cf. Gresseth (1975) 14; T. Bauer, *JNES* 16 (1957) 260, who also refers to the expression "to set one's name for people of later times" (*šakin*

šumim ina niši uhhurati) in school texts; on Greek–Indo-European ἄφθιτον κλέος see R. Schmitt, *Dichtung und Dichtersprache in indogermanischer Zeit* (1967) 61–69.

19. *Il.* 12.322–328, imitated by Stesichorus S 11 Page–Davies.

20. *Gilgamesh* VI 162 f., *ANET* 85. Bowra (1952) 63 translates "member" of the bull, which might be misleading. For *imittu*, hind leg, see *AHw* 377.

21. *Il.* 22.20.

22. *Od.* 18.136 f., taken up by Archilochos 131–132 West, then by Heraclitus B 17.

23. *Ludlul bel nemeqi* II 43–45; Lambert (1960) 40 f. translates the text *ki pitê u katami,* "like opening and shutting the legs," which may be the original sense, but the commentary on the passage from the library of Assurbanipal (Lambert 40; cf. 291) paraphrases "day and night"; hence *ANET* 435; so this was the way the passage was understood at the time of Archilochos.

24. See M. Lichtheim, *Ancient Egyptian Literature* II (1976) 57–72 on the various versions, the documents—inscriptions and a papyrus text—and the earlier editions.

25. D. Luckenbill, *The Annals of Sennacherib* (1924) 43–47; transcription in Borger (1979) I 83–85; translation in Luckenbill (1926/27) II §§ 252–254. *Il.* 20.498–501.

26. For mercenaries see Chapter 1, "Oriental Products in Greece," at notes 63–68. Cf. the conclusions drawn from the bowl of Praeneste (Figure 7), Chapter 3, "The Overpopulated Earth," at note 15 (which also has the chariot for the prince).

27. Judges 4.

28. For Ugarit see H. Gese, *Die Religionen Altsyriens* (1970) 54; Dirlmeier (1955) 25 f.; Jeremiah 2:27; *Il.* 22.126; *Od.* 19.163; Hes. *Theog.* 35.

29. *Od.* 19.107–114: ἀρετῶσι δὲ λαοὶ ὑπ' αὐτοῦ (114); Hes. *Erga* 225–247; Assurbanipal in Streck (1916) II 6 f.; cf. Walcot (1966) 92 f.; Jeffery (1976) 39; West (1978b) 213.

30. See above, Chapter 1, "Loan-Words," note 30.

FABLES

1. See in general W. Wienert, *Die Typen der griechisch-römischen Fabel* (1925); K. Meuli, *Wesen und Herkunft der Fabel* (1954) = *Gesammelte Schriften* (1975) 731–756; M. Nøjgaard, *La*

fable antique I (1964); Rodriguez Adrados (1979); T. Karadagli, *Fabel und Ainos* (1981); O. Reverdin, ed., *La fable,* Entretiens sur l'anti-quité classique 30 (1984); for enormous materials on the influence of ancient fables see *Enzyklopädie des Märchens* (1977 ff.) s.v. *Äso-pika, Babrios, Avianus, Fabel,* etc.

2. E. Brunner-Traut, *Altägyptische Tiergeschichte und Fabel* (1970³).

3. E. Ebeling, *Die babylonische Fabel und ihre Bedeutung für die Literaturgeschichte* (1931); see esp. Lambert (1960); *RlA* VII 46.

4. "The king of trees": Judges 9; "The thistle and the cedar tree": II Kings 14:9.

5. H. Diels, "Orientalische Fabeln in griechischem Gewande," *Internationale Wochenschrift* 4 (1910), on Callim. fr. 194 compared with "the palm and the tamarisk," for which see now *ANET* 410 f., Lambert (1960) 151-164. See also A. La Penna, "Letteratura eso-pica e letteratura assiro-babilonese," *RFIC* 92 (1964) 24-39; Rod-riguez Adrados (1979) 301-379.

6. Babrius 2.2 f.: Σύρων παλαιῶν ἐστιν εὕρεμ' ἀνθρώπων, οἳ πρίν ποτ' ἦσαν ἐπὶ Νίνου τε καὶ Βήλου. On the identity of "King Alexandros" mentioned in the dedication of Babrius see B. E. Perry, *Babrius and Phaedrus,* Loeb Classical Library (1965) xlvii–lii; *Inschriften von Ephesus* V: *Die Inschriften Kleinasiens* 15 (1980) no. 1537.

7. On Ahiqar see Chapter 1, "Writing and Literature in the Eighth Century," at note 30; on Lydia, Chapter 1, "Historical Background," notes 25–26. Parallels between Greek and Meso-potamian fables are collected in Rodriguez Adrados (1979) 376–378; Hellenistic parallels in West (1969); Aesop no. 137 Perry, Babrius no. 84. "The fly and the elephant" seemed to be especially close to "the bird and the elephant" (Lambert [1960] 217 f., 339), but the little animal involved in the Akkadian version, *niniqu,* is not identifiable, as Moran (1978) 18 n.7 has stressed.

8. Archilochus fr. 174–181 West; Aesop no. 5 Halm = 1 Perry; cf. Williams (1956); I. Trencsényi-Waldapfel, *Untersuchungen zur Religionsgeschichte* (1966) 186–191; H. Freydank, "Die Tierfabel im Etana-Mythus," *Mitteilungen des Instituts für Orientforschung* 17 (1971) 1–13; Rodriguez Adrados (1979) 319–321. Further Greek ar-chaic fables: Archilochus fr. 187 West = Aesop no. 81 Perry; Se-monides fr. 13 West = Aesop no. 3 Perry.

9. *ANET* 114–118, 517; Labat et al. (1970) 294–305; cf. E. Ebeling, *AOF* 14 (1944) 298–303; W. von Soden, *WZKM* 55 (1959) 59–61; I. Levin, *Fabula* 8 (1966) 1–63.

10. See R. Wittkower, "Eagle and Serpent," *Journal of the Warburg Institute* 2 (1938/39) 293–325; C. Grottanelli, *Riv. Stud. Fen.* 5 (1977) 16–18; B. Garbe, "Vogel und Schlange," *Zeitschrift für Volkskunde* 75 (1979) 52–56; Aesch. *Cho.* 246, etc.

11. Seal cylinders in W. H. Ward (1910) 144 nos. 391–394; *Enciclopedia dell'arte antica* s.v. *Etana*. But there is no direct iconographic link: In Greek art Ganymede and the eagle appear only after the fourth century B.C.; see *LIMC* s.v. *Ganymedes*.

12. Archilochus fr. 196a West = *ZPE* 14 (1974) 97–112; the proverb σπεύδουσα κύων τυφλὰ τίκτει in Aesop 223 Perry, *Paroemiographi Graeci* I 381, II 181 and 491, Schol. Aristoph. *Pax* 1078.

13. See W. H. Moran, *HSCP* 82 (1978) 17–19; J. Bremmer, *ZPE* 39 (1980) 28.

14. See above, Chapter 1, "Writing and Literature in the Eighth Century," note 25.

15. *Gilgamesh* XI 266–289.

16. Ibykos 342 Davies, together with Soph. fr. 362 Radt and other quotations in Ael. *Nat.An.* 6.51; Aesch. fr. 45 Radt; Nik. *Ther.* 343–358; cf. M. Davies, *MH* 44 (1987) 65–75, who speaks of a folktale.

MAGIC AND COSMOGONY

1. See Chapter 2, "Lamashtu, Lamia, and Gorgo."

2. See Chapter 1, "Oriental Products in Greece," note 23; Burkert (1987b).

3. See Chapter 2, "Lamashtu, Lamia, and Gorgo," at note 22.

4. Clay relief from Gortyn, Schefold (1964) pl. 33, *LIMC* s.v. *Agamemnon* no. 91, Burkert (1987b) 28 f., 32.

5. See, e.g., G. van der Leeuw, "Die sogenannte epische Einleitung der Zauberformeln," *Zeitschrift für Religionspsychologie* 6 (1933) 161–180; M. Eliade, "Kosmogonische Mythen und magische Heilungen," *Paideuma* 6 (1954/58) 194–204.

6. The Adapa versions are in *ANET* 102 f.; S. A. Pittioni, *Il poemetto di Adapa* (1981); for *Erra* see Chapter 3, "Purification," at note 16.

7. For *Atrahasis* see Chapter 3, "Craftsmen of the Sacred." The

passage on the creation of man, I 190–217, was understood as "part of an incantation to facilitate childbirth" in *ANET* 99 (corrected in *ANET* 513); an incantation text proper refers to this myth; J. Van Dijk, "Une incantation accompagnant la naissance de l'homme," *Orientalia* 42 (1973) 505. *Atrahasis* and rain charm: *Atrahasis* 27 f.

8. The text is listed *HKL* III 63, "Der Mondgott und die Kuh Amat-Sîn"; see W. G. Lambert, *Iraq* 31 (1969) 31 f.; Labat et al. (1970) 285 f.; connected with the myth of Io by Duchemin (1979), (1980b).

9. "The Worm and the Toothache," *ANET* 100 f., Bottéro and Kramer (1989) 484; B. Landsberger and T. Jacobsen, "An Old Babylonian Charm against *merhu*," *JNES* 14 (1955) 14–21.

10. See C. J. Gadd in S. H. Hooke, *Myth and Ritual* (1933) 47–58; T. H. Gaster, *Thespis* (1961²) 62–64; F. M. Cornford, "A Ritual Basis for Hesiod's *Theogony*," in *The Unwritten Philosophy* (1950) 95–116; Dalley (1989) 231–232.

11. "House of the priest" in Ugarit, containing liver models as well as literary texts: J. C. Courtois, *Ugaritica* 6 (1969) 91–119; for various libraries at Emar see Arnaud (1985/87); a priest's library at Sultantepe: W. G. Lambert, *RA* 53 (1959) 121 f.; cf. Walcot (1966) 47 f.

12. For Orphism, suffice it to refer to Burkert (1982a), West (1983), Burkert (1985) 296–304; see also above, Chapter 2, "Craftsmen of the Sacred," note 2.

13. Cf. above, "Craftsmen of the Sacred," note 9.

14. Olympiodor. *in Phaed.* p. 41 f. Westerink = *Orphicorum Fragmenta* 220; the "four monarchies" enumerated there seem to match with the Derveni text (*ZPE* 47 [1982]) col. X 6: Uranos, Son of Night, the first king; Burkert (1985) 297 f.

15. Eur. fr. 912, in the context of conjuring up the dead.

16. See Chapter 2, "Spirits of the Dead and Black Magic," at note 19.

17. See Chapter 2, "Craftsmen of the Sacred," at note 15.

18. VI 1–34; text from Assur (*KAR* 4) in A. Heidel, *The Babylonian Genesis* (1942) 68–72; Berossos, *FGrHist* 680 F 1 p. 373 Jacoby. See V. Maag, "Sumerische und Babylonische Mythen von der Erschaffung des Menschen," *Asiatische Studien* 8 (1954) 85–106 = V. Maag, *Kultur, Kulturkontakt und Religion* (1980) 38–59; G.

Pettinato, *Das altorientalische Menschenbild und die sumerischen und akkadischen Schöpfungsmythen,* Abh. Heidelberg 1971.1.

19. *Atrahasis* I 213 and 215–217 = 228–230 Lambert and Millard; cf. Bottéro and Kramer (1989) 537; Dalley (1989) 15 with nn. 11–12. Interpretation has remained controversial. W. von Soden, *Symbolae biblicae et mesopotamicae F. M. T. de Liagre Böhl dedicatae* (1973) 349–358 (cf. idem, *ZA* 68 [1978] 80 f.), contested the reading *eṭemmu* and tried to construe a word *edimmu,* wild man; this has not been followed by other specialists. Cf. W. L. Moran, *BASOR* 200 (1970) 48–56; L. Cagni in V. Vattioni, ed., *Sangue e antropologia biblica* (1981) 79–81; J. Tropper, *Ugarit-Forschungen* 19 (1981) 301–308; J. Bottéro in *Societies and Languages of the Ancient Near East. Studies in Honour of I. M. Diakonoff* (1984) 24–31, whom I try to follow.

20. See Chapter 2, "Spirits of the Dead and Black Magic," at note 2.

21. The Derveni text (*ZPE* 47 [1982]) col. IX has Zeus swallowing the phallus of the first cosmic king (this at any rate is what the commentator understood, who was in command of the full text, *pace* West [1983] 85); this introduces the most startling motif of the Kumarbi myth into Orphic literature.

INDEX OF GREEK WORDS

GENERAL INDEX